Ahmad Abdel Tawwab Sharaf Eldin

A Cognitive Linguistic Study of Martin Luther King and Obama Discourse

Ahmad Abdel Tawwab Sharaf Eldin

A Cognitive Linguistic Study of Martin Luther King and Obama Discourse

The Power of Language and Ideology in Persuasion and Cognition

LAP LAMBERT Academic Publishing

Impressum / Imprint
Bibliografische Information der Deutschen Nationalbibliothek: Die Deutsche
Nationalbibliothek verzeichnet diese Publikation in der Deutschen Nationalbibliografie;
detaillierte bibliografische Daten sind im Internet über http://dnb.d-nb.de abrufbar.
Alle in diesem Buch genannten Marken und Produktnamen unterliegen warenzeichen-,
marken- oder patentrechtlichem Schutz bzw. sind Warenzeichen oder eingetragene
Warenzeichen der jeweiligen Inhaber. Die Wiedergabe von Marken, Produktnamen,
Gebrauchsnamen, Handelsnamen, Warenbezeichnungen u.s.w. in diesem Werk berechtigt
auch ohne besondere Kennzeichnung nicht zu der Annahme, dass solche Namen im Sinne
der Warenzeichen- und Markenschutzgesetzgebung als frei zu betrachten wären und
daher von jedermann benutzt werden dürften.

Bibliographic information published by the Deutsche Nationalbibliothek: The Deutsche
Nationalbibliothek lists this publication in the Deutsche Nationalbibliografie; detailed
bibliographic data are available in the Internet at http://dnb.d-nb.de.
Any brand names and product names mentioned in this book are subject to trademark,
brand or patent protection and are trademarks or registered trademarks of their respective
holders. The use of brand names, product names, common names, trade names, product
descriptions etc. even without a particular marking in this works is in no way to be
construed to mean that such names may be regarded as unrestricted in respect of
trademark and brand protection legislation and could thus be used by anyone.

Coverbild / Cover image: www.ingimage.com

Verlag / Publisher:
LAP LAMBERT Academic Publishing
ist ein Imprint der / is a trademark of
OmniScriptum GmbH & Co. KG
Heinrich-Böcking-Str. 6-8, 66121 Saarbrücken, Deutschland / Germany
Email: info@lap-publishing.com

Herstellung: siehe letzte Seite /
Printed at: see last page
ISBN: 978-3-659-42344-4

Copyright © 2013 OmniScriptum GmbH & Co. KG
Alle Rechte vorbehalten. / All rights reserved. Saarbrücken 2013

Dedication

To the soul of my Mom

November 15th, 2013
Virginia- United States

I have a dream that my four little children will one day live in a nation where they will not be judged by the color of their skin, but by the content of their character.
Martin Luther King, Jr.

If you're walking down the right path and you're willing to keep walking, eventually you'll make progress. **Barrack Obama**

TABLE OF CONTENTS:

INTRODUCTION……………………………………………………………………1

CHAPTER 1………………………………………………………………………..14

CHAPTER 2………………………………………………………………………..85

CHAPTER 3……………………………………………..…………………….…127

CHAPTER 4…………………………………………..……………………….…156

CHAPTER 5………………………………………………………………………..186

Summary and Conclusion……………………………………………………….211

Bibliography……………………………………………………………………….216

Introduction

Cognitive linguistics addresses within language the structuring of basic conceptual categories, such as events, entities, processes. It also recognizes that language knowledge resides in the minds of the speakers and when people engage in any language activity, they draw unconsciously on vast cognitive concepts, and create frames to serve their discourses. Cognitive linguistics plays a significant role in critical discourse analysis (CDA) as it organizes the tools that are used to create, process, and convey meanings in various social and political contexts. The concept of meaning in any discourse has a cognitive perspective, so CDA does not only include the concept of verbal features, but it also includes the cognitive representations and strategies involved during the production or comprehension of discourse.

From this perspective, this study attempts to provide a cognitive approach within a critical discourse analysis (CDA) in order to investigate President Obama and Martin Luter i ' political discourses and to trace the linguistic devices in these speeches. In so doing, the study tries to show how language, employed in their speeches, reflects the common conceptual structures and interrelationships they both share. The study is also concerned with uncovering the cognitive operations of ideological disguises and demystifying power relations in discourse within the socio-cognitive context.

0.1 Background of the Study

Cognition is the scientific term for the process of thought. Its usage varies in different ways in accordance with different disciplines. One of the important disciplines that involves cognition is language. That kind of combination of language and cognition is known as cognitive linguistics. Cognitive linguistics, to start with, is the study of language in a way that is compatible with what is known about the human mind, treating language as reflecting and revealing the mind.

Cognitive linguistics focuses on meaning construction or conceptualization, which is a dynamic process whereby linguistic units serve as prompts for an array of conceptual operation and the recruitment of background knowledge. It is noteworthy that discourse and cognition are closely interrelated as discourse involves the process of reproduction and relations of dominance through text and talk. Cognition, on the other hand, involves the shared representations of the social mind of group members.

The relation between Discourse and Cognition

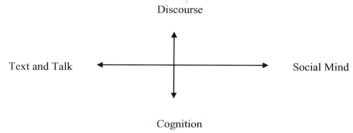

Highlighting the relationship between discourse and cognition, Van Dijk (1993a:110) describes such relationship as social cognition which should be analyzed within the interface of socio-cognition and discourse. It is identified into the following notions:

A) Discourse is produced/interpreted by individuals, and they are able to do so on the basis of society shared beliefs.

B) Discourse can affect social structures through the social-cognitive minds of discourse participants.

Obviously, the relationship between cognition and discourse entails a system of mental strategies and structures shared by group members, and in particular those involved in the understanding, production, or representation of social objects such as situations or interactions. Within the cognitive framework, individuals generally start from their personal mental model of an event or situation. The study of cognitive aspects in discourse focuses on various aspects of information processing. It essentially deals with the acquisition, uses, and structures of mental representations about political situations, events, actors and groups. In other words, typical topics of political discourse from a cognitive approach deal with memory representations and the mental processes involved in political understanding and interaction.

Van Dijk (2002:213) contends that it is essential to encompass cognitive representations that represent beliefs and opinions in CDA. These representations are linked with the notion of ideology which employs a cognitively powerful tool to account precisely for the interface between social belief and discourse. This tool is identified as mental models, which are considered as personal representations of specific events people witness, participate in, or hear/read about. These models are transformed firstly into episodic memory, reflecting the personal interpretations and evaluations of an event, and thus represent what we usually call experiences.

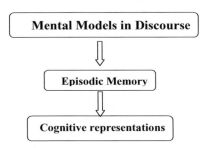

The significance of mental models is that they are used as a cognitive basis for daily discourse production or reception processes. That is why mental models represent an interface between social beliefs and discourse. The second type of cognitive models in understanding discourse is context models which Van Dijk (2002:213) describes as "event models" or "situation models." Van Dijk (2002) contends that in order for addressors to know what information from their models or social representation to include in their discourses, they need to know something about the current communicative situation of their discourse, including the assumed beliefs of their recipients. In other words, what we understand depends basically on some mental elements.

Aspects of Cognitive Discourse

Accessing   Activating   Searching   Comparing   Building

In their classification of these elements, Graesser et al (1997:293) describe the mental process that constructs cognitive representations in five major elements; accessing, activating, searching, composing, and building. They (1997) explain that this process includes accessing words in the mental lexicon, activating concepts in the long term memory, searching for information, comparing structures that are available in working memory, and building structures by adding, deleting, rearranging, or connecting information.

It is noteworthy to mention that the cognitive approach in discourse is well designed to communicate ideas in a social context. Van Dijk (1995:18) links social context with cognition in discourse as "the system of mental representations and processes of group members." Part of the socio-cognitive system is the socio cultural knowledge shared by the members of a specific group in a society. In that direction, ideologies are the basic frameworks for organizing the social cognition shared by groups, organizations or institutions. Therefore, ideologies can be both cognitive and social.

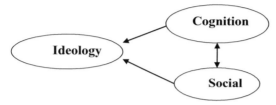

Ideologies are cognitive because they function as representations and processes that underlie discourse and action. Ideologies are as well social as they handle the social position and interests of social groups. Members of groups may share beliefs and opinions organized into social attitudes, sharing concepts of civil rights within the socio-cognitive framework. Ideologies are, then, the overall, abstract mental systems that organize such socially shared attitudes. In her agreement with Van Dijk's concept of mental process, Wodak (2006:180) elaborates that;

> Mental processes must link text production and comprehension to explicit utterances, text and talk as well as to social phenomena. This becomes most apparent while analyzing phenomena such as attitudes towards language as well as stereotypes and prejudices held about specific social groups.

To simplify her view about ideological mental level, Wodak (2006) argues that ideologies are localized between societal structures and the structures of the minds of social members. They allow social actors to translate their social properties (identity, goal, position, etc) into the knowledge and beliefs that make up the concrete models of their everyday life experiences and the mental representations of their actions and discourses in facing social inequality. Through attitudes and knowledge, ideologies control how people plan the structures of text and talk.

It is important to mention that within critical discourse analysis (CDA), the notion of racism is handled as one of the social inequality aspects in a society. The connection between racism and CDA, in Obama's and King's speeches, is discussed in detail in the analysis. Both Obama and King focus on this concept in their speeches, whether directly or indirectly. Racism, according to Van Dijk (1995a) has been classified into two important components:

The Classification of Racism in Discourse

A) Social   **B) Cognitive**

The social aspect of racism is created by social practices of discrimination at the local (micro) level and the relationships of power abuse by dominant groups, organizations and institutions at the global (macro) level of analysis. The second aspect of racism is cognitive. It is cognitive in that the discriminatory practices of members of dominant groups and institutions form the visible and tangible manifestations of everyday racism. Such practices also have a mental basis consisting of a biased model of ethnic events and interactions, which in turn are rooted in racist ideologies.

Cognitive Concept of Racist Ideologies

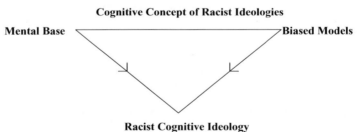

Mental Base   **Biased Models**

Racist Cognitive Ideology

It is obvious that CDA can constitute a resource for struggling with the social power abuse, dominance and inequality, reproduced and resisted by text and talk in the social and cognitive context. Van Dijk (1995) explains that cognitive system is divided into short-term memory in which strategic processes like decoding and interpretation take place. Long term memory, however, serves as a holder of socio-cultural knowledge which consists of knowledge of discourse, communication, groups and events. This study attempts to prove how the cognitive approach can be used within CDA to persuade the addressee of the issues addressed through using facts, logic and past history.

0.2 Statement of the Problem

This study discusses how cognitive linguistic tools are used in the arena of political discourse, or more precisely, how political leaders use them in their discourse. Political speeches are interesting area of research since a speaker must attract the attention of many different minds by employing specific linguistic devices. Trying to gain trust and to persuade their audience of their capability as leaders requires excellence in many fields, where the power to speak with brilliance is an important aspect. Therefore, political speeches are, under such circumstances, compelling to examine. The reason for choosing President Obama's and Martin Luther King's speeches is that they are interesting to observe for the following reasons;

First, both share specific common cognitive grounds in terms of racism and social inequality in their white-dominant societies.

Second, both belong to the black race and share mental representations that form their ideology, social behavior and attitudes.

Third, both employ structures and strategies of discourse to tell their addressees about those ethnic or racial prejudices, ideologies or other social cognitions.

0.3 Objectives of the Study

This study attempts to provide a cognitive approach within critical discourse analysis (CDA) of Obama's and Martin Luther King's speeches through the following;

A) It applies the cognitive-linguistic interpretation of their political discourses in facing racism, and how particular forms serve strategic functions in the cognitive discourse. It also aims at defining and clarifying the relation between the concepts of cognition, ideology and discourse. Both cognition and ideology are important notions in CDA. They are closely related to one another as they are forms of manipulation and exercise of power. Therefore, this study attempts to apply mental models by which ideology can operate in discourse and the cognitive processes which are involved in the production and understanding of discourse.

B) It also attempts to show how ideologies can be examined both cognitively and socially. In other words, this study is to shed light on the main cognitive function of ideologies through organizing the social representations of African American discourses and their power to influence the audience.

C) Furthermore, this study attempts to distinguish more than one level of discourse in two different cognitive genres; the mental (abstract) level and the concrete (text) level in an attempt to show the interaction processing between both to produce persuasive discourse. In addition, it attempts to show different forms of linguistic power through the strategy of masking. Three different methods would be employed in masking; truncation, permutation and generalization.

D) Moreover, this study attempts to stress the function of modality and metaphor as linguistic tools to reveal power relations among participants in a speech situation. The various branches of modals are investigated as they have a significant role in exposing the ideology of the speaker and his degree of commitment to truth. By employing the previous linguistic devices, this study shows how Obama and King use their language to introduce some new concepts to their audience such as; confirming the equality rights, voicing freedom and concepts of change and hope. The power of their words lies in its inherent ability to change people's belief and behaviour. Obama's eloquent words and his penetrating thoughts moved countless Americans to take action and vote for him. Therefore, this study attempts to explain that their manipulation of language and ideology had been carefully planned through their skillful maneuvering of linguistic aspects in achieving their goals and persuading the minds of their audience.

0.4 Research Premises

Four questions are addressed in the study. **First,** what are the main characteristics of the cognitive models in political discourse? **Second,** what is the form of cognitive ideological discourse in the racist society? **Third,** what transformations does the discourse undergo over the course of racism? **Fourth,** what are the linguistic tools used by Obama and King throughout their discourses?

0.5 Rationale of the Study

The importance of the study lies in analyzing how the cognitive approach is linguistically reflected in Obama's and King's speeches. Their political discourses are chosen for analysis since they are successful and persuasive in their discourse. They succeed in forming a universal support for convincing their audience of their right to get equal rights and overcome racist ideologies. This study, therefore, attempts to provide a critical discourse study of selected speeches in an attempt to unravel the power cues and cognitive strategies, which are implicit in Obama's and King's skillful use of language.

0.6 Review of Literature

Many studies have discussed the notion of political discourse analysis, critical discourse analysis, and the notion of power and ideology in discourse. Most of these studies will be presented in chapter one. In addition, many studies have been conducted on cognitive linguistics. These will be also presented in the same chapter. However, there are some relevant studies that have been carried out both in Egypt and abroad on topics similar to the present one. Mazid (1999), for instance, handles the notion of ideology and control in some speeches and newspaper genre. In addition, he investigates how certain linguistic aspects can be discussed with various genres in Arabic and English. Allam (2002) elaborates more on the political discourse during the Gulf war. The main point of her study is to formulate a framework which postulates the relationship between President Bush Sr's attitudes and his beliefs with his propensity to use military force. She focuses on the linguistic description of political language through the analyses of the linguistic tools such as syntactical and lexical cohesion, and the pragmatic devices employed in his discourse.

On the other hand, Hassan (2003) handles the concept of ideology and power in some American newspaper texts. In her study, she discusses the relationship between pragmatics and syntax within the framework of ideology. I er tte t to   ow t e owerful   ect i Frederic Dou l '   eec e , Tawfik (2006) attempts to investigate the manipulation of both language and ideology as powerful devices employed by Douglass to subvert dominant power relations.

From a broad, there are review varieties of studies on Barrack Obama's political discourse. Dupuis and Boeckelman (2008) handle the concept of American politics in Barrack Obama's era. Leanne (2009) discusses the power of Obama in his speeches and his persuasive tactics to convince his audience. In the same track, Assmundson (200) reviews the persuasive tools in Barrack Obama's political discourse from a linguistic perspective in his first speech during his presidential campaign in 2008.

One may observe from the above review that, to the best of the knowledge of the writer of this study, there is no study that handles the cognitive linguistic aspects of the political discourse of Martin Luther King and Barrack Obama.

0.7 Research Methodology

The main approach adopted for analyzing the selected speeches of president Barrack Obama and Martin Luther King is within the framework of critical discourse analysis (CDA) described by Van Dijk's article "Critical Discourse Analysis" (2001). It is the framework, the selected data are analyzed in terms of the cognitive, ideological, and linguistic levels employed to produce a cognitive persuasive discourse focusing on the strategies of mental representation in the selected speeches. However, other related tools, such as persuasive techniques, are also used for their relevance to the analysis of the data.

Cognitive techniques cover specific concepts such as; social schemas, anchoring, objectification, ontologizing, figuration, personification. Social schema is considered as a mental representation, or information stored in memory based on the past experience. Anchoring is a cognitive technique that allows new information in memory to be added to the old one.

Objectification is a mental process in which complex ideas are changed into concrete images, and understandable ideas. Objectification, as a cognitive strategy, is sub-classified into ontologizing, figuration, and personification. Ontologizing refers to using physical aspects to represent an idea. Figuration is based upon imaginations, while personification focuses on persons to explain an idea.

Cognitive persuasive tactics, used in the analytical part, are divided into three branches, namely; response shaping, response strengthening, response changing. Response shaping aims to shape some ideas about specific topics. Response strengthening attempts to enforce an idea in discourse, while response changing refers to the transformation of ideological concepts of the audience towards certain ideas.

Classification of Cognitive Tools

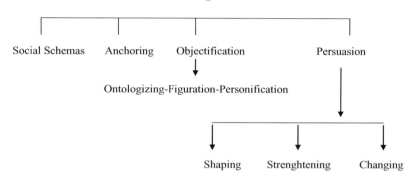

On the ideological level, there are certain concepts which are used in analyzing data, such as legitimation, unification, dissimulation, fragmentation, and reification. Legitimation is sub-classified into rationalization, universalisation, and narrativization. Unification is divided into standardization, and symbolization of unity. Fragmentation is sub-divided into differentiation, and expurgation. Reification is sub-divided into naturalization, and externalization. Explanation and detailed review of such ideological concepts are discussed in chapter one.

Classification of Ideological Tools

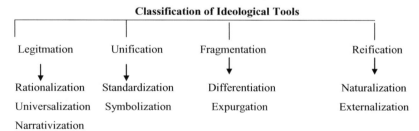

On the linguistic level, the devices, used in the analysis, are classified into lexical devices, including metaphors and modality, and pragmatic devices, covering speech acts concepts, ending with a computational program to figure out the frequencies of the words and their impact on understanding the meaning. The computer has been employed in preparing the selected data for analysis. Specifically, the selected data have been analyzed by using "concordance," a computational program which helps researchers to explore the word-frequency of any speech in a precise method.

Kennedy (1998:247) discusses the notion of concordance as "a formatted version or display of all occurrences or tokens of a particular type in a corpus." He explains that the particular type is called a keyword and sometimes referred to as a target item. Concordance has been used in this research at the end of each analysis for recognizing the distribution of words' frequencies. This frequency is simply a computational method which determines a clear distribution of the lexical items of the speeches of King and Obama.

The reason why concordance is employed in this study is that; concordance is the simple and precise use of computer in analyzing data. It shows various linguistic aspects of words, phrases and sentences. It also shows high and low levels of frequency and its relation to understanding the discourse. In addition, computational style is employed in the analytical parts of King and Obama speeches, as it shows the change of frequency of words. Such frequency is often indicative of a change in meaning, and the occurrence of new words for both leaders. In short, the computational approach is utilized in the analysis to show the following perspectives;

- Textual perspective: which identifies grammatical items through statistical frequencies, collocation patterns, context-sensitive meanings and uses of words
- Social perspective: which raises the awareness of how speakers' different discourse roles and power statuses are enacted in their grammatical choices.

0.8 The Data

The database is divided into two parts. The first part represents selected forms of King's speeches before and after winning the Nobel prize. In analyzing these speeches, they are further classified into two main sections. The first examines four of his speeches before being awarded the Nobel prize in 1964, while the second examines other four speeches after winning the Nobel prize in 1964 until his assassination in 1968. These speeches are selected as representative samples to undergo cognitive, ideological, and linguistic analyses.

The second part of the analysis tackles Obama's speeches before and after presidency. These are also divided into two sections. The first covers his speeches from January 2008 to August 2008 (pre-presidency). The second handles his speeches within the period of November 2008 to January 2010 (post-presidency). These speeches are chosen because they reflect three levels of analysis, namely; cognitive, ideological, and linguistic levels to deliver persuasive and strong message to their audience.

King's speeches are to be subdivided by the researcher into smaller sections according to the main topics discussed. Each subdivision is latter analyzed on the three levels mentioned above. The three levels "cognitive, ideological, and linguistic" overlap and interact together to give a communicative message to the audience. They are only divided for the purpose of analysis. Each speech is preceded by contextual orientation, obtainable from the online website of Wikipedia encyclopedia.

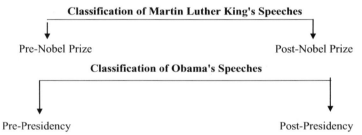

It is noteworthy to mention that the selected speeches of Martin Luther King are obtainable from the website, www.wikipedia.org. Obama speeches can be obtained from the following websites; www.nytimes.com, http://www.presidentialrhetoric.com/campaign2008., http://obamaspeeches.com,, http://www.whitehouse.gov/briefingroom/SpeechesandRemarks, http://usliberals.about.com/od/extraordinaryspeech2/a/ObamaIowaSpch.htm. A copy of the data is attached at the end cover of this dissertation on a CD.

0.9 Organization of the Study

This study is divided into five chapters, preceded by an introduction and followed by a conclusion. In the introductory part, the researcher lays out background of the study, statement of the problem, objectives of the study, research premises, , rationale of the study, review of literature, the data,. and organization of the study. Chapter one, which is entitled "an introduction to critical discourse analysis and cognitive linguistics," starts with the main concepts and different explanations of critical discourse analysis (CDA) theory. Then, it handles different approaches in CDA, and the relation between CDA and ideology. This chapter sheds light on the concept of racism, power, and persuasion. An emphasis is also laid in this chapter on the meaning of modality, speech acts, and metaphor as linguistic tools in CDA theory.

In addition, this chapter provides an attempt to bridge the gap between the linguistic level and cognitive level. Furthermore, this chapter presents a summarized overview of the theoretical concepts of cognitive linguistics, social schemas, the role of memory in comprehending discourse, and image schema theory. Chapters two and three are dedicated to the analytical part of Martin Luther King's speeches in the period (pre and post 1964). Four speeches are handled in chapter 2, and another four speeches are handled in chapter 3. Chapters four and five are dedicated to the analytical part of Obama's speeches in the pre and post presidency era. Four speeches are handled in chapter 4 and another four speeches are included in chapter 5. The conclusion provides a summary of the results and the findings of the study and suggestions for further studies.

Chapter One

A Theoretical Background of Critical Discourse Analysis and Cognitive Linguistics

1.0. Introduction

This chapter attempts to discuss the theory of critical discourse analysis (CDA) in terms of its linguistic origin, principles, and goals. The chapter sheds light on the role of ideology and power in discourse within the socio-political context. It also attempts to show how could the gap between the micro relations of language and the macro level of society be bridged. In addition, it reviews the role of CDA in making the study of language interdisciplinary.

Moreover, this chapter also explains how language has a paramount importance in the cognitive representation, as it is the main vehicle through which information is encoded. As a main cognitive medium of human life, language is defined as an instrument for manipulating objects, and for getting the others believe in what we want them to believe. It is, therefore, the object of CDA to manifest the patterns of beliefs and values which are encoded in language and below the notice of anyone who accept the discourse as natural.

1.1. Definition

Critical discourse analysis (CDA) is a branch of discourse analysis which, in the late of 1980s, has been discussed by many linguists such as Fairclough and Van Dijk. They view CDA as the field which is concerned with studying and analyzing written and spoken texts to reveal the discursive sources of power, dominance, inequality and bias. It examines how these discursive sources are maintained and reproduced within specific social, political, and historical contexts. In a similar vein, Fairclough (1992a:135) defines CDA as:

> Analysis which aims to systematically explore often (a) discursive practices, events and texts, and (b) wider social and cultural structures, relations and processes; to investigate how such practices, events and texts arise out of and are ideologically shaped by relations of power and struggles over power: and to explore how the opacity of these relationships between discourse and society is itself a factor securing power and hegemony.

Based on the previous utterance, Fairclough (1992a) sets the main pillars for CDA, which are; texts, ideology, power, and social practices. All these concepts are correlated to show how language reflects relations of power, reproduces dominance, and communicates ideology. In his agreement with the previous notion, Van Dijk (2001:35) mentions that critical discourse analysis is "a type of discourse analytical research that primarily studies the way social power abuse, dominance, and inequality are enacted, reproduced, and resisted by text and talk in social and political context." Such definition shows that critical discourse analysis is a socio-politically motivated approach which handles the concept of language in use. In this track, it assigns ideological significance to texts on the basis of their linguistic features.

CDA is significant because it explains the implicit ways in which language is involved in social life, including ideology, domination and possibilities of change. Crucial for discourse analysts is the explicit awareness of its role in society as it heavily focuses on social problems and political issues. Therefore, the core point in CDA is to show how language reflects relations of power, reproduces dominance, and communicates ideology.

Accordingly, the task of CDA is both deconstructive and constructive. In its deconstructive sense, it aims to disrupt the themes and power relations of everyday talk and writing. In its constructive meaning, it has been applied to the development of critical curriculum that aims at an expansion of analyst's capacities to criticize and analyze discourse and social practices. CDA may be seen as a reaction against the dominant uncritical paradigms of the linguistic theory. It requires multidisciplinary approach and an account of intricate relationship between text, talk, social cognition, power, society, and culture.

1.2. Historical Background of CDA

Since its foundation in the mid-1960s, several scholars have been engaged in critical or socio-political studies of text and talk. Some of the tenets of CDA can be found in the critical theory of the Frankfurt school before the Second World War. Its focus on language and discourse was initiated with isolated attempts at critical linguistics that emerged in the U.S. The main notion of such school was to combine the use of language in social institutions, and the ideological concepts. That is included in what is known as critical linguistics.

Fowler and Kress (1979:2) mention that critical linguistics is "a contribution to the unveiling of linguistic practices which are instruments in social inequality and the concealment of truth." This fact is confirmed by Teo (2000:11) as he confirms the core points of critical linguistics as it is "a branch of discourse analysis that goes beyond the description of discourses to an explanation of how and why particular discourses are produced." Such explanation shows that critical linguistics focuses on the details of the linguistic structure of the text under the coverage of the social and historical contexts.

One clear fact about critical linguistics is that, the concern of such field is to relate language to its users, and to seek different ways to bring out ideologies inherent in their communication. In this regard, Fowler (1996:6) elaborates that the importance of critical linguistics is in "its capacity to equip readers for analytical readings of ideology-laden text." That concept of critical linguistics also entails a certain notion of language as it is socially meaningful and embedded in social context.

If language is seen as action in social context, then certain consequences would follow. First, any interaction usually involves power and ideologies. No interaction exists where power relations do not prevail and where values and norms do not have a relevant role. Second, discourse is always historical, that is, it is connected synchronically and diachronically with other communicative events which are happening at the same time or which have happened before. This phenomenon is widely known as "intertextuality."

Over the years, CDA has been further developed and broadened. Recent works have raised some concerns with earlier ones. Among the concerns was, first, taking into consideration the role of audiences and their interpretations of discourse which could be different from that of the discourse analyst. The second concern has called for expanding the scope of analysis beyond the textual, to the intertextual.

In this respect, Fairclough (1995a) has raised both issues. He shows that the earliest work in CDA did not obviously focus on the interpretive practices of audience. In other words, he regards that critical linguistic analyses assumed that the audiences interpret texts the same way the analyst do. The other point that has been discussed by Fairclough (1995a:5) is that; while earlier contributions in critical linguistics were focused on the grammatical and lexical levels, they were less focused on the intertextual analysis of texts as he explains that "the linguistic analysis is very much focused upon clauses with little attention to higher level organization properties of whole texts."

Van Dijk (1998a) asserts that CDA is not a specific direction of research; therefore, it does not have a unitary theoretical framework. That means that there is a strong link between CDA and ideology, power, language, and discourse. Central to CDA is the belief that language is a social phenomenon that can not be handled without its socio-historical context. It is employed in a functional form to perform many tasks. Therefore, language can be used for directing, hurting, accusing, discriminating, marrying, and divorcing. In doing all these things, we produce consciously and unconsciously our ideas beliefs, i.e., our ideologies.

Framing language as a social phenomenon confirms that language is a socially situated mode of action. Fairclough (1995a:54-55) comments on that be explaining that language is not only socially shaped, but also socially shaping. In other words, CDA "explores these two sides of language use, the socially shaped and socially shaping"

Fairlclough (1995a:54) explains that the influence of language in society is carried out by three ways. The first is social identities, the second is social relations, and third is the systems of knowledge and beliefs. Language helps to reproduce and maintain existing social identities, relations, and systems of knowledge and beliefs. CDA's preference in analyzing language and social structures is manifested in the choice of topics and domains of analysis. CDA specialists tend to work on applied topics and social domains such as the following:

1- Political discourse and ideology: discourse is seen as a means through which ideology itself is a topic of considerable importance in CDA.
2- Racism: particular attention within CDA is given to racism. Van Dijk (1993c) stands out as prolific author in this field.
3- Media language and gender: particularly when it comes to the representation of women in media.
4- Institutional discourse: language plays a role in institutional practices such as doctor-patient or teacher-student communications.

CDA obviously conceives discourse as social phenomenon and seeks to improve the social foundations for practicing and situating discourse in society. A fundamental aspect of CDA is that; it claims to take its starting point in social theory. In this respect, CDA displays a vivid interest in the theories of power and ideology. Most common in this track is the use of Foucault's (1977) formulations of "orders of discourse" and "power-knowledge." In his agreement with Foucault's view, Gramsci (1971) focuses more attention on hegemony and the concepts of ideological directions in analyzing discourse.

All of these concepts are given a linguistic translation and projected in discourse field for two reasons. First, it attempts to account for the relationship between linguistic practice and social structure. Second, it provides linguistically grounded explanations for changes in these relations. It is important to mention that CDA does not have a single theoretical framework, but rather there are different approaches that can be applied. Three main approaches of CDA are related to each other; which are Fairclough, Wodak, and Van Dijk approaches. All of these scholars agree on certain concepts of analysis and tackle the same issues. In other words, such approaches attempt to make a clear link between discourse practices and social realms. The following is general review of such approaches.

1.3. Different Approaches to CDA

1.3.1. Van Dijk (Socio-Cognitive) Approach

Van Dijk is regarded as one of the most quoted scholars in the field of critical studies especially in media discourse. He applies his theory to media texts mainly focusing on the representation of ethnic groups and minorities in Europe. What distinguishes Van Dijk (1988) approach to analyze the news discourse is his comprehensive analysis not only of the textual and structural levels of media discourse, but also for the analysis and explanations at the production and reception level.

Van Dijk's approach to CDA

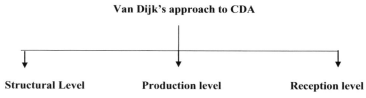

Structural Level   **Production level**   **Reception level**

By structural level, Van Dijk (1988) shows that the structures at various levels of description include not only the grammatical, phonological, morphological and semantic levels, but also the higher level of properties such as overall themes, and topics of news stories. Van Dijk (1988) adds the context and the social aspects of the event in his approach. He (1988:2) confirms this view by mentioning the following;

> Discourse is not simply an isolated textual or dialogic structure. Rather it is a complex communicative event that also embodies a social context, featuring participants as well as production and reception processes.

According to the previous view, by production processes, Van Dijk (1988) means journalistic and institutional practices of news-making and the economic and social practices. Reception processes involve the comprehension, memorization, and reproduction of information in the short and long term memories. In this respect, Van Dijk (1983:17) handles the notion of evaluative beliefs or opinions associated with general models. Generalized models and schemata formation entail generalizations and abstractions of these evaluative beliefs in the reception process, and thereby lead to the formation of general opinions of any social groups.

Van Dijk (1988) shows in his cognitive theory of information processing the social aspects of discourse. Personal memories are based on our own experiences "models," along with the conceptual content, which have more general shared social basis. Van Dijk (1983:25) explains that to understand the socio-cognitive approach in CDA, we have to tackle the notion of experiences in our memories. He shows that large part of such models "experiences" have social representations of events, time, location, participants and actions, which are represented in terms of socially acquired conceptualizations.

This means that despite individual differences in the understanding of a situation, there will be important similarities in the ways people of the same culture form models of such a situation. Van Dijk (1995a:17) perceives critical discourse analysis as ideology analysis because "ideologies are typically, though not exclusively, expressed and reproduced in discourse and communication, including non-verbal semiotic messages, such as pictures, photographs." His approach for analyzing ideologies in CDA has three parts: social analysis, cognitive analysis, and discourse analysis. (1995a:30).

Van Dijk's approach to analyze ideology in CDA

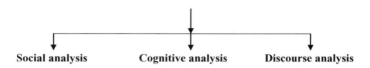

Social analysis   Cognitive analysis   Discourse analysis

Social analysis has to do with social aspects of discourse like the context. Van Dijk (1995a:17) asserts the significance of taking into consideration the historical and cultural aspects of discourse when conducting CDA. As for the cognitive analysis, it is the cognitive process involved in the production of discourse. The socio-cognitive approach, in Van Dijk's, perspective (1995a:18) is "the system of mental representation and processes of group members," and therefore, it mediates between society and discourse.

In this sense, Van Dijk (1995a:18) shows the link between such mental representation and abstract concepts of ideology as "ideologies are the overall, abstract mental systems that organize the socially shared attitudes." In his understanding of discourse, Van Dijk (1995a:2) calls the mental representations of individuals during such social actions and interactions "models." In his view, such mental representations or models influence the way in which people act, speak, write, or understand the social practices.

Van Dijk attempts to combine cognitive senses with racism. He views that the cognitive mental representations of racism and prejudice are articulated in US versus THEM dimension, in which specific group tends to present themselves in positive terms and other groups in negative terms. Van Dijk realizes that attitudes can not be mentioned through cognition only, rather it is also through the linguistic practice. Thus, he links his cognitive models of racism with the study of CDA. Van Dijk (1998b:61) defines certain elements for an ideological analysis of racism discourse based on the following:

A) Examining the context of the discourse: historical, political or social background of a conflict and its main participants.

B) Analyzing groups, power relations and conflicts.

C) Identifying positive and negative opinions about US versus THEM.

D) Making explicit the presupposed and the implied meanings.

E) Examining all formal structure: lexical choice and syntactic structure, in a way that helps to de emphasize group opinions.

Van Dijk (1998b) also focuses on the formation of racism in discourse through different strategies as the following:

A- Justification as an indirect way of legitimizing racist acts.

B- Vagueness: by avoiding outright accusation by adding modalities like probably, likely.

C- Repetition: to emphasize certain concepts.

1.3.2. Wodak (Historical-Socio Approach)

One of the directions of Wodak in CDA is the social historical approach. According to Wodak (1996:3);

> Discourse sociolinguistics is a social linguistics which not only is explicitly dedicated to the study of the text in context, but also accords both factors equal importance. It is an approach capable of identifying and describing the underlying mechanisms that contribute to those disorders in discourse which are embedded in a particular context.

Based on her previous view, one of the most important characteristics in her approach is the text analysis, within social and historical context. She points out that beliefs and notions, which are based on evaluations and judgements, require much context knowledge. Wodak has started researches in various institutional settings such as courts, schools, and hospitals, and on a variety of social issues such as, racism. Wodak's work in CDA led to a development of an approach she termed as historical discourse. The term historical denotes an attempt to integrate systematically all available background information in the analysis and interpretation of the many layers of a written or spoken text. Focusing on the historical contexts of discourse in the process of explanation and interpretation is a feature that distinguishes this approach from the previous approach of Van Dijk.

In the historical approach, Wodak & Ludwig (1999:12) believe that language "manifest social processes and interaction." According to Wodak & Ludwig (1999:12), viewing language this way entails three concepts at least.

First, discourse "always involves power and ideologies. No interaction exists where power relations do not prevail and where values and norms do not have a relevant role." Second "discourse ......is always historical, that is, it is connected synchronically and diachronically with other communicative events which are happening at the same time, or which have happened before."

The third feature of Wodak's approach is that of interpretation. According to Wodak & Ludwig (1999:13), readers and listeners, depending on their background knowledge and their position, might have different interpretations of the same communicative event. One of the most salient distinguishing features of Wodak's discourse-historical approach is its endeavor to work interdisciplinarily, and on the basis of a variety of different empirical data as well as background information. Depending on the object of investigation, it attempts to transcend the pure linguistic dimension to include the historical, political, sociological or psychological dimension in the analysis and interpretation of a specific discursive occasion.

In her approach, Wodak together with Reisigel (2003), pay attention on how to detect the implicit racist ideologies in the discourse. They specified four steps. First, investigating linguistically how people are referred to. Second, examining what qualities, characteristics are attributed to them. Third, investigating whether the utterances are intensified or mitigated. Fourth, from which point of view are these nominations expressed, (Wodak & Reisigl, 2003:385). Wodak and Reisigel (2003) show that discursive practices are socially constitutive in a number of ways. First, they play a decisive role in the genesis and production of certain social conditions.

This means that discourse may serve to construct collective subjects like races, ethnicities. Second, Discursive practices might reproduce, justify a certain social status quo. Third, they are instrumental in transforming the status quo, like racializing concepts. Fourth, discursive practices may have an effect on the dismantling or even destruction of the status quo. It is obvious that Wodak and her colleagues in CDA focus on the sociological dimension of the texts. The discourse historical approach is based on combining historical and socio-political aspects together with the linguistic approach to detect social inequality.

1.3.3. Fairclough (Critical Approach)

The third approach in CDA is that of Fairclough whose theory has been central to CDA. Fairclough calls his approach to language and discourse "critical language study" (1989:5). He describes the objective of such approach as "a contribution to the general raising of consciousness of exploitative social relations, through focusing upon language." (1989:4). Fairclough (1989) attempts to bring social science and linguistics together within a single theoretical and analytical framework, setting up a channel between them.

Chouliaraki and Fairclough (1999:30) argue that "the past two decades or so have been a period of economic social transformation on a global scale." They believe that such social changes reflect significant change "in the language and discourse." (1999:4). Therefore, CDA can help by theorizing transformation and creating an awareness of such changes. In this respect, Chouliaraki and Fairclough (1999:113) assert that:

> CDA of a communicative interaction sets out to show that the semiotic and linguistic features of the interaction are systematically connected with what is going on socially, and what is going on socially is indeed going on partly or wholly semiotically or linguistically.

According to the previous view, Fairclough (1995a:57) puts three analytical elements in analyzing any communicative event or interaction. They are text like news report, discourse practice (e.g. the process of production and consumption), and socio cultural practice (e.g. social and cultural structures) which gives rise to the communicative event. These elements closely resemble Van Dijk's three dimensions of analysis: discourse, socio-cognition and social analysis.

What seems to be the main difference between Fairclough's and Van Dijk's approach is the second dimension. Whereas Van Dijk perceives social cognition and mental models as mediating between discourse and social aspects, Fairclough (1995a:59) believes that this task is assumed by discourse practices, text production, and consumption. Fairclough fixes his framework for analyzing a communicative event as follows:

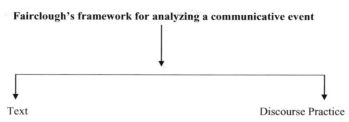

The first analytical point of Fairclough's model is text. Analysis of text involves linguistic analysis in terms of vocabulary, grammar, semantics, the sound system, and cohesion-organization above the sentence level (Fairclough, 1995a:57). Fairclough also views text from a multi-functional perspective. Any sentence in a text is analyzable in terms of the articulation of these functions, which he describes as:

A) Representation of social practices, which carries particular ideologies.
B) Particular construction of the relationship between writer and reader.
C) Particular construction of writer and reader identities.

According to Fairclough (1995a:58-59), the previous functions have two important aspects: institutional processes (e.g. editorial procedures), and discourse processes (changes the text go through in production and consumption). Fairclough (1995a:60) argues that discourse practice "removes the division between society and culture in the one hand, and discourse and text on the other." In this analytical framework, while there is a linguistic analysis at the text level, there is also linguistic analysis at the discourse practice that Fairclough calls "intertextual analysis."

According to Fairclough (1992b:16), "linguistic analysis is descriptive in nature, whereas intertextual analysis is more interpretative." Fairclough (1992b:84) defines intertextuality as "basically the property texts have of being full of snatches of other texts, which may be explicitly demarcated or merged in." Fairclough (1992b:85) identifies two types of intertextuality: "manifest intertextuality," and "constitutive intertextuality."

Manifest intertextuality refers to the heterogeneous constitution of texts by which "specific other texts are overtly drowned upon within a text." This kind of intertextuality is marked by explicit signs such as quotation marks. A clear example of manifest intertextuality is what Obama mentions about Martin Luther King in his speech on January 20, 2002 in Atlanta, Georgia. Obama, in this speech, combines overtly between the concept of civil rights era, the sufferings of African-Americans, and the dreams of Dr. King as he mentions the following;

> As I was thinking about which ones we need to remember at this hour, my mind went back to the very beginning of the modern Civil Rights Era. Because before Memphis and the mountaintop; before the bridge in Selma and the march on Washington; before Birmingham and the beatings; the fire hoses and the loss of those four little girls; before there was King the icon and his magnificent dream, there was King the young preacher and a people who found themselves suffering under the yoke of oppression.

On the other hand, constitutive or implicit intertextuality refers to the heterogeneous constitution of texts out of elements of discourse "interdiscursivity," (Fairclough 1992b:104). Fairclough views CDA as a type of reflection of social interactions. He calls for a critical combination of social aspects in daily life, combined with language. Therefore, Fairlcough (1992a: 8-9) bases his critical approach to language on few principles which he represents as follows:

1- Language uses "discourse" shapes and is shaped by society.
2- Discourse helps to constitute and change knowledge and its objects, social relations, and identity.
3- Discourse is shaped by relations of power, and invested with ideology.
4- The shape of discourse is a reflection of power struggle in society.

Fairclough (1992a:10-11) explains that there are three approaches used within CDA to be considered through the process of any analysis. First, "a text" whether spoken or written. Second, the interaction between people "processes of production and interpretation of the text." Third, the social action. Hence, Fairclough's CDA involves three analytical dimensions: description of the text, interpretation of the interaction processes, and their relationship to the social actions.

According to what has been mentioned, CDA functions as unraveling any concealed ideology or racism. Since terms such as ideology, racism, persuasion, power/dominance, are important common notions among CDA practitioners, it is worth shedding light on the meaning of these concepts.

1.4. CDA and Ideology

According to Williams (1976:126), the word "ideology," first appeared in English in 1796, as a direct translation of the new French word "ideologie" which had been proposed in that year by philosopher Destutt de Tracy to denote the "science of ideas." A contentious argument in CDA has been how discourse may manifest or at least implicate the ideologies of the discourse participants. By restoring the focus upon discourse in society, CDA offers an occasion to subject ideology to new methods of investigation and to formulate an explicit ideology in discourse.

Van Dijk (2004:42) explains that ideology is primarily some kind of ideas, which is "belief systems." This implies that ideology not only contains certain ideological practices, but it also includes a cognitive component that is able to account for the notions of belief. In addition, ideologies consist of social representations that define the social identity of a group. Secondly, based on the socio cognitive foundation of any group, ideologies are gradually acquired through life experiences. Fairclough (1992a) shows that ideology is an important feature in CDA as it is the key means through which social relations of power and domination are sustained. The function of ideologies is to establish, sustain, or change power relations in society.

For Fairclough (1992a), the concepts of ideologies are constructions of reality which are built into various dimensions of discursive practices. Through power relations implicit in discourse, ideology can appear. This makes the discourse a mode of producing, reproducing, or transforming social identities, social relations, and systems of knowledge and belief. Fairclough (1992a) makes three claims about ideology, based in part on the French Marxist philosopher, Althusser. Fairclough (1992a) explains that ideology functions in discourse in the following points:

1- Ideology has a material basis in the social practices of institutions, as a form of social practice, discourse practices are material forms of ideology.

2- Ideology and control appear through dominant discourse in terms of what the Marxist theorist and activist Gramsci called "hegemony."

Hegemony is a form of control through consensus, as contrasted with control based on coercion (force or threat of force). For Fairclough (1992a), hegemony operates through orders of discourse of a society and institutions such as education, media, business. Belsey (1980:5) shows that ideology is "inscribed in discourse.....it is not a separate element which exists independently in some free-floating realm of ideas.... but away of thinking, speaking, experiencing." It is generally assumed in CDA that innocent and neutral form and substance of discourse appears on the surface, it is thoroughly charged with the biases, constraints, opinions and variable judgements.

Macdonell (1986:59) believes that all discourses are "ideologically positioned: none are neutral." Ideology plays a crucial role in Van Dijk's analytical method. He offers a schema of relations between ideology, society, cognition and discourse. Within social structures, social interaction takes place. This social interaction is presented in the form of text, which is then cognitized according to the memory system. This system consists of two levels. First, short-term memory whereby strategies process or decoding and interpretation take place.

Second, long-term memory serves as holder of socio-cultural knowledge, which consists of knowledge of language, discourse, communication, groups existing in the form of scripts. Social attitudes reside within long-term memory. Each of these attitudes can represent an array of ideologies which combine to create one's own personal ideology that conforms to one's identity, goals, social position, values and resources (Van Dijk, 1991:44-45). In this respect, Van Dijk (1995c:248) elaborates:

> Ideologies are basic frameworks of social cognition, shared by members of social groups, constituted by relevant selections of socio-cultural values, and organized by ideological schemata that represents self-definition of a group. Besides their social function of sustaining the interests of group, ideologies have the cognitive function of organizing the social representations, attitudes, knowledge, of the group, and thus indirectly monitor the group-related practices, and hence also the text and talk of its members.

As one can understand from the previous quotation, Van Dijk (1995c) shows that ideologies have a cognitive function of systemizing the social representation and attitudes of the group in society. Thus, according to Van Dijk (1995c:243), "ideologies" can be viewed as "basic systems of fundamental social cognitions." They form the socially shared, valued based framework, and they are used by members of social groups. Van Dijk (1995c:244) identifies seven characteristics of ideology. First, ideologies are cognitive and are based on belief systems. Although they are social, political, and related to groups, ideologies involve mental objects such as ideas, thoughts, beliefs, judgments and values. They are the abstract basis of the socially shared belief systems of any group.

Second, ideologies are social, that is they have been defined in sociological or some economic terms. They have been related to groups, or group conflicts, and hence to "social power and dominance as well as their legitimation." Van Dijk (1995:245), however, claims that dominant groups are not the only possessors of ideology, dominated groups also have their ideologies that control their self-identification.

Third, ideologies are socio-cognitive, that is, they are both cognitive, involving basic principles of perception, judgments, knowledge, and understanding and social values, shared by members of groups or institutions, and related to the socio-economic or political interests of these groups. Fourth, ideologies are not true or false, rather they represent the partisan, self serving truth of a social group. They are efficient frameworks of interpretation of such groups if they are able to further the interests of these groups.

Fifth, ideologies may have various degrees of complexity. They range from simple and basic propositions to complex and well-organized frameworks such as, the ideologies of democracies or socialism. Sixth, ideologies have contextual variable manifestations. Personal and contextual variation of ideological discourse may be due to the existence of several groups with several ideologies, general social norms or laws.

Lastly, ideologies are general and abstract. They are situation-independent. Their expressions may be locally produced and contextually constrained. It is important to mention that ideology can be also manipulated for the abuse of power since our mental representation and misrepresentation of the distribution of power in our society is governed and sustained by ideology.

Ideology is generally viewed as the set of shared values and beliefs established in a certain community, but not necessarily esteemed by all the members of that community. Moreover, ideology is a social concept that controls the thinking of the different social groups whether ethnic, class or gender groups. It is also relative in the sense that what seems true for one group may appear false for the other. According to Thompson (1990:7), ideology is used in the critical sense to refer to "the ways in which meaning serves, in particular circumstances, to establish and sustain relations of power."

In this sense, ideology is closely linked to power because when we rely on the ideologies set in our mind, we tend to naturalize things such as existing power relations believing that they are legitimate while they are not. Thompson (1990:56) suggests that "ideological phenomena are meaningful symbolic phenomena in so far as they serve, in particular social-historical circumstances, to establish and sustain relations of domination."

1.4.1. Classification of Ideology in CDA

Thompson (1990:64) proposes five modes by which ideology can operate in discourse, naming them "modus operandi," and classifying them as the following:

Unification: such ideological strategy, according to Thompson (1990:64), involves dissolving differences between individual and putting them in a collective unity that overcomes racial, religious, social, gender or political differences, such strategy can be employed by two ways. It can be achieved by *standardization* whose symbolic forms that are used to deliver the message (1990:64). The second way is achieved by the *symbolization of unity* which involves binding individuals together by producing symbols of unity and collective identity.

Both Martin Luther King and Obama employ such strategy in the speeches to convince their audience of their goals. They attempt to overcome differences among individuals and to put them in the mode of unity that disregards social, religious, or political differences. King focuses on the strategy of *symbolization* on mentioning the concepts of dreams, justice, and freedom in the following speech, delivered on August 28, 1963:

> I have a dream that one day this nation will rise up and live out the true meaning of its creed: "We hold these truths to be self-evident: that all men are created equal." I have a dream that one day on the red hills of Georgia the sons of former slaves and the sons of former slave owners will be able to sit down together

> at a table of brotherhood. I have a dream that one day even the state of Mississippi, a desert state, sweltering with the heat of injustice and oppression, will be transformed into an oasis of freedom and justice. I have a dream that my four children will one day live in a nation where they will not be judged by the color of their skin but by the content of their character. I have a dream today.

Obama shares the same ideological strategy of King's *"unification"* by employing common symbols to break the barriers and refresh the memory of his audience. Obama shows his skills in organizing his ideas, and creating dynamic images, and employing effective repetitions. He delivers a moving speech in Iowa, January 3, 2008, after he gets the feelings and solid confidence that King's dream can be fulfilled by saying the following:

> Thank you, Iowa. You know, they said this day would never come. They said our sights were set too high. They said this country was too divided; too disillusioned to ever come together around a common purpose. But on this January night - at this defining moment in history - you have done what the cynics said we couldn't do. You have done what the state of New Hampshire can do in five days. You have done what America can do in this New Year, 2008.

President Obama gives this above-mentioned speech to unify people to vote for him and to persuade those who have not yet voted that he is the right candidate to vote for. His slogan during the campaign is "Change We Can Believe In", and his speeches most often carry that message alongside the call for hope. In his speech, Obama addresses his own supporters face to face, although, he is also addressing an external audience since the speech is broadcasted via the media to the rest of the American people and to other peoples as well

The second mode of operation, *legitimation* strategy, aims at representing relations of power and domination by three sub-branches. *Rationalization*, "whereby the producer of a symbolic form constructs a chain of reasoning which seeks to defend or justify a set of social relations or institutions, and thereby to persuade an audience," Thompson (1990:61). The second sub-way is *universalization*, where certain concepts held by few individuals are represented as serving the interests of all. The third sub-way is *narrativization* which involves stories that "recount the past and treat the present as part of cherished tradition." Thompson (1990:610. *Narrativization* involves reference to the traditions and history of the community to create a sense of belonging.

A clear example of the previous concept is what Dr. King contributes in his speech. As King looks for strengthening his position, he attempts to use universal concepts like in saying "*death comes to innocent and it comes to the guilty. Death is the irreducible common denomina*tor *of all men."* King applies two strategies which are *rationalization* and *universalization*. He deliberately uses the rationalization as he attempts to create symbolic forms that lead to reasonable and convincing arguments. King attempts to show up as a persuasive speaker, so he attempts to use the emotional and psychological appeals as they motivate the listeners to accept the proposed arguments. Since most African-Americans suffer from the social inequality at that time, King is skillful by choosing the concept of death to play on the right emotions which sway them as he wants.

The third ideological mode of operation is *dissimulation*, whereby power is maintained by "being concealed, denied or obscured, or by being represented in a way which deflects attention from existing relations." (Thompson, 1990:62) One of the strategies used for activating this ideological mode is displacement which is a process where 'a term customarily used to refer to one object or individual is used to refer to another." *Euphemization* is another strategy used to achieve *dissimulation,* where "actions, institutions or social relations are described or re-described in terms which elicit a positive valuation." (Thomspon 1990:62)

Tropes "figurative language" plays a great role in achieving *dissimulation.* Examples of tropes would be synecdoche (using a part to refer to the whole or vice versa) or metaphor. Each of these techniques is used to dissimulate social relations by different methods. One obvious example of the previous concepts is what Obama shows in his speeches. Obama employs this ideological approach of using the concrete to abstract metaphor by using the dynamic and concrete words, and combines it with the concept of ideas. In contrast to *unification* mode, *fragmentation* maintains power relations. In this track, Thompson (1990:65) affirms the following:

> Fragmentation is achieved not by unifying individuals in a collectivity, but by fragmenting those individuals and groups that might be capable of mounting effective challenge to the dominant group, or by orienting forces of potential opposition towards a target which is projected as evil, harmful or threatening.

Based upon the previous utterance, fragmentation is used when there is mounting challenges to the controlling group in society. Such strategy is employed by two ways, *differentiation*, which focuses on the differences and divisions between groups of potential power, thus preventing them from challenging existing relations or individuals of power. The other strategy in this mode is *expurgation* of the other, which involves constructing an evil and threatening enemy which calls individuals to unite together in order to challenge, resist and expurgate the threats and evil of that enemy.

Thompson (1990) observes that this strategy often overlaps with strategies of unification since it calls for uniting individuals in the face of the enemy creating a unified strategy. The last mode of ideological operation is *reification*. *Reification* establishes and sustains relations of domination by representing a transitory, historical state of affairs as if it were permanent, natural, outside of time" (Thompson 1990:65). There are different methods that refer to reification. First, *naturalization*, which occurs where a state of affairs may be treated as a natural event. Second, *externalization*, which portrays a state of affairs as permenant unchanging. Third, *passivization*, which focuses the attention of the hearer or reader on certain themes at the expense of others.

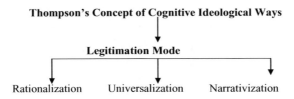

Thompson's Concept of Cognitive Ideological Ways

Legitimation Mode

Rationalization   Universalization   Narrativization

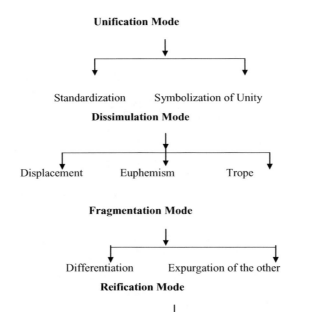

Unification Mode

Standardization   Symbolization of Unity

Dissimulation Mode

Displacement   Euphemism   Trope

Fragmentation Mode

Differentiation   Expurgation of the other

Reification Mode

Naturalization   Externalization   Passivization

In his agreement with Thompson's view of ideology, Van Dijk (2006:117) reviews the cognitive-socio function of ideology in discourse as ideologies organize and ground the social representations shared by members of groups. Secondly, they are ultimate basis of the discourses and other social practices of the group members. Thirdly, they allow members to organize and coordinate their joint actions and interactions in view of the goals and interest of the group as a whole. Finally, they function as the apart of the socio-cognitive interface between social structures of groups on the one hand, and their discourses on the other hand.

Therefore, some ideologies may function to legitimate domination, but also to articulate resistance in relationships of power. Van Dijk (2006) argues that the link between ideologies and discourse is indirect, because between ideologies and discourse, there is the presence of social cognitions, such as attitudes, opinions and knowledge, as well as personal cognitions, such as models.

Opinions are typically used, expressed, acquired and changed by discourse in communicative interactive contexts. It is important to mention that ideology is a concept that has to do with judgments, attitudes, and beliefs. It is a psychological framework that can be explained at various levels in discourse like the propositional, lexical and cognitive levels. The presence of ideology as an implied characteristic in language means that language can construct different views based upon shared beliefs and attitudes. What is related to ideology as a concept underlying the notion of shared beliefs and attitudes is the notion of racism in discourse.

1.5. CDA and Racism

As pointed out by Essed (2002:185), racism can be viewed as an ideological social process in which a social group intentionally treats another one with inequality for seeing it as being biologically and culturally different. Since racism can be practised in every day situations throughout practices of power relations, Essed (2002:177) employs the term "everyday racism" to illuminate the systematic nature of racism. Yet, it is important to mention that many approaches handled the notion of racism within discourse.

The first approach is the social cognitive approach. Wetherel and Potter (1992: 38) focus on social categorization and stereotyping, relying on the cognitive concepts of "schemas," "stereotypes," and "object classification." This approach confirms that the way our minds work, the way we process information may itself be sufficient to generate positive or negative image of a group. The second approach is the social identity theory which places the concept of social identity in the center of its social psychological theory of intergroup relations. It recognizes the importance of socialization and group experiences in the development and acquisition of social categories.

In this approach, racism is seen as the interpersonal result of psychological effects created by social inequality in a society. It is clear that the system of racism consists of a social and a cognitive subsystems. The social subsystem of racism is constituted by social practices of discrimination at the micro level, and relationships of power abuse by dominant groups, organizations and institutions at a macro level of analysis.

On the other hand, the symbolic elites, that is, those elites who literally have everything to say in society, as well as, their institutions and organizations, are examples of groups involved in power abuse or domination. The second subsystem of racism is cognitive. Whereas the discriminatory practices of members of dominant groups and institutions form the visible manifestations of everyday racism, discourse plays a clear role for this cognitive dimension of racism. Ethnic prejudices are not innate and do not develop spontaneously in any interaction. They are acquired and learned, and thus usually happens through communication. That is, through text and talk.

If racism is a behavioral manifestation of one's ideology or identity, then denial of racism is another manifestation of one's behavior. Denials of racism have both an individual and social dimensions. Whereas the former is a characteristic of informal every day conversations, the later "social" is typical for public discourse, for instance, politics, the media, education, and other organizations. Because public discourse includes a large audience, it is the social form of denial that is influential. Denial of racism takes different types as the following:

1- Act-denial "I did not do."
2- Control-denial "I did not say that a purpose, it was an accident."
3- Intentional-denial "I did not mean that" "you got me wrong"
4- Goal-denial "I did not do/say that, in order to…

1.5.1. Classification of Racism

One of the most systematic and radical approaches to the issue of racism types is that of Robert Miles. In his view, in order to analyze racism, one must understand that racism constitute an element of common sense. Miles' (1993:74-77) analysis of racism refers to key concepts. First, the notion of "racialisation" denotes the dynamic representational process of categorization and meaning construction in which specified meanings are ascribed to real features. Second, in order to avoid a semantic overstretch of the term, Miles (1993) regards "racism" in discourse as an ideological and representational phenomenon, distinguished from "exclusionary practice." The concept of exclusionary practice is thought to refer to concrete intentional action as well as to unintentional consequences. Third, key concept in Miles' theory (1993) about racism is that of institutional racism.

Van Dijk (2005:4) explains that institutional racism "is associated with a more macro approach to racism. That is, dominant groups usually do not exercise their power only at the level of personal interaction, but tend to organize their domination." Van Dijk (2005:4) gives a clear example of institutional racism that is the contemporary legal restrictions to immigration which is an obvious example of treating others differently by trying to keep them out. Among the prominent institutional examples of racism in politics are found in political organizations and in racist parties.

Van Dijk (2005:5) argues that media is another flourishing area for institutional racism. That can be achieved through the selection of topics, issues, sources which are biased in favor of a dominant group over other groups. In addition, the stereotypes and prejudices find their way in the media probably more blatantly than any other areas. Van Dijk (2005:6) points out that the third area where institutional racism can be found in education and research fields. In this respect, Van Dijk (2005:6) affirms the following:

> Institutional racism is implemented in schools and universities, in lessons and textbooks, in assignments and research projects. Although schools have much freedom to implement multicultural aims and values, and official curricula may have been formulated in such a way, the practice of everyday schooling is to impart not only dominant social ideologies in general, but also the dominant ideologies of gender and race in particular.

In his previous view, Van Dijk (2005) connects between the practices of racism and institutions as it is the process of purposely discriminating against certain groups of people through the use of biased laws or practices. Often, institutionalized racism is subtle and manifests itself in various ways. Van Dijk (2005) shows that media can play an important role in revealing racism. A clear example of the influence of media and its role of exposing racism is what George Staphanopoulos did with President Obama, when he asked Obama about the issues of race and racism, during an interview on ABC 's "This Week" TV show on September 18, 2009. The interviewer and the interviewee show key points from their words. First, they confirm that racism is an ideological phenomenon, practiced in a society. Second, the ideological stereotypes are blatantly exposed in media circles than any other area. Below is part of the interview;

> **George Staphanopoulos**: Let me ask you about the broader debate around this ... and see the issue of race being injected after Joe Wilson's outburst. This week, President Carter. And you know we've talked about this in several interviews, about these kinds of issues. So I'm just wondering: Does it frustrate you when your own supporters see racism?
> **President Obama**: Look, I think that race is such a volatile issue in this society. Always has been. That it becomes hard for people to separate out race being sort of a -- part of the backdrop of American society versus race being a predominant factor in any given debate. And what I've said, what we talked about during the campaign, are there some people who don't like me because of my race? I'm sure there are. Are there some people who vote for me only because of my race? There are probably some of those too.

In their agreement to Van Dijk's approach of racism, Reisgil &Wodak (2001:9-10) gave more attention to the types of racism. The first type is institutional racism, which has been discussed before. The second one is the inegalitarian racism which denotes the legitimization of domination and discrimination on the basis of clear concepts supporting genetic and biological inferiority. The third one is differentiated racism which is concerned with cultural differences, as customs and habits. This type is also described as cultural racism. Van Dijk (1984:40), on the other hand, specifies six levels in which racism can take. These levels are:

1. Differentiation: by seeing others differently.
2. Distance: keep specific people
3. Diffusion: diffusing beliefs and prejudices about certain people.
4. Diversion: attributing social or cultural problems to certain group of people.
5. Depersonalizing: treating them as inferior.

6. Destruction: hurting or destroying a group of people.

1.6. CDA and Power

Power is one of the most important notions that links discourse and society. The concept of power has been discussed by linguists, such as Fairclough (1989), Van Dijk (1984, 1993b, 1998A, 2001, 2005) Stark (1996). All confirm the close link between CDA and power in the sense that CDA attempts to reveal hidden power relations in discourse. There have been various definitions of the word "power" suggested by Pennycook (2001). He (2001:91) summarizes the concept of power in discourse as:

A) Power is not something owned or possessed, but rather something that operates throughout society.
B) Power does not have some ultimate location or origin.
C) Relation of power is not outside other relations, but is part of them.
D) Power is always linked to resistance where there is power, there is resistance.
E) Power is not just repressive, but is also productive.

Van Dijk (1993b:154) points out that power is the exercise of control by members of one group over another one. This exercise of power could take the form of controlling other's social actions and mental cognition. Control of others' actions is achieved through limiting the freedom of their actions, while control of cognition is employed by influencing others' minds by applying persuasive techniques. Fairclough (1989:2) attempts to find a close relation between power as a mental representation and ideology by confirming the following:

> The nature of the ideological assumptions embedded in particular conventions, and so the nature of those conventions themselves, depends on the power relations which underlie the conventions; and because they are means of legitimizing existing social relations and differences of power.

Based on the previous statement, power, as understood in CDA, is neither a unitary force nor an exclusively political phenomenon. Power is woven throughout all our practices and ideas. It is exercised in every relationship, and it is not necessarily abusive social order, but relies on the ability of one person or group to coerce another person or group. Van Dijk (1997:17) classifies the notion of power into two types: the coercive power "use of force" and the mental power "controlling others' minds."

Van Dijk (1997:17) describes the mental power as social power which he defines as "a specific relation between social groups or institutions." Social power is often described as being hegemony or hegemonic power. As some may confuse the notion of power with oppression, Hodge and Kress (1993:153) point out the distinctions between both in the following:

> What makes power hold good, what makes it accepted, is simply the fact that it does not only weigh on us as a force that says no, but it traverses and produces things, it induces pleasure, forms knowledge, produces discourse. It needs to be considered as a productive network which runs through the whole social body, much more than as a negative instance whose function is repression.

From the previous utterance, power can be used to produce pleasure, knowledge and discourse, and it can simply be more than as a negative notion. As Hodge and Kress (1993) clarify the notion of power in discourse, Bloor and Bloor (1995:233) argue that language and power are linked since "political or national power can be reflected in the language and language in turn can reinforce such power." They explain that "the exertion of power by individuals with certain social roles in particular social situations is often revealed in the form of the language," Bloor and Bloor (1995:234).

The use of language in everyday life contributes to the realization of goals. Language, as a power-related concept, provides conventional resource for influencing people attitudes and behaviour. Influence attempts may take the form of persuasion, argumentation, or use of threats, promises. Van Dijk (1996:24-85) suggests the following framework for the study of power, especially in the social domain:

1- Power is a property of relations between social groups, institutions or organizations. Therefore, only social power, not individual power, is more important in the social domain.

2- Power is based on privileged access to valued social resources, such as wealth, status, or jobs.

3- Social power and dominance are often organized and institutionalized, to allow more effective control.

1.6.1. Classification of Power

Wrong (1995:22) develops the concept of power which should be based on the individual's capacity, i.e. a person, who possesses the capacity to exercise any form of power and who is able in turn to produce an intended effect, is an example of a powerful person. Wrong (1995:22) distinguishes between different forms of power: force, manipulation, persuasion, and authority.

Wrong's Concept of Power

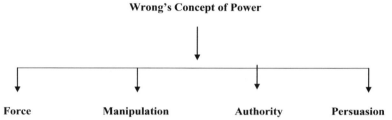

| Force | Manipulation | Authority | Persuasion |

Force refers most commonly to physical or biological force. The ultimate form of force is violence, but the methods of non-violence adopted by some recent social movements like Ghandi movement in India, or Martin Luther King's non-violent movement against racial segregation laws, exemplify force as a form of power. In non-violence approach, people use their bodies as physical objects to present or restrict actions by others rather than acting directly on the bodies of others. Force, according to Wrong (1995:27)), is more effective in preventing or restricting people from acting than in causing them to act in a given way. Force can achieve negative effects, the destruction, prevention, or limitation of the possibility of action by others.

Force, however, is often employed not just to eliminate someone's capacity to act, but to establish in the mind the future credibility of the power holders' willingness and capability to use force. It would not be accurate to confine the term force to physical aspects, as there is also a form of conduct, often described as psychological or moral force. The psychological form of force and violence may have institutionalized forms like ritual ceremonies, and the pronouncement of curse. Damage to the psyche is surely as real as damage to the body. Psychological violence, in which the intended effect of the perpetrator is to inflict mental or emotional harm, is connected with physical violence and has the same effect or stronger than the physical one.

Manipulation, according to Wrong (1995:28), is the concept of power holder concealing his intention to influence his listeners to follow his wishes. Such an exercise of power is unlikely to evoke resistance of power as a person is unaware of the effort to influence him. Yet, such apparently positive uses of manipulation have not escaped the suspicion that cling to this form of power, a suspicion aroused by the person's ignorance as to whether he has been manipulated and the manipulator's concealed purpose.

Manipulation may also occur where there is no social relation between the power holder and the power subject and the latter may not even be aware of the power holder's existence. This can take the form that power holder may exercise concealed control over the power subject through symbolic communications designed to make veiled suggestions, to limit or determine selectivity of the power subject. Many commercial advertising forms involve this kind of manipulation.

Manipulation has a more negative reputation than perhaps any other form of power, suggesting cunning and malign purpose on the part of the manipulator. It is a form of power that can not be openly resisted by the power subject, since he is unaware of the power holder's intent.

If the essence of persuasion, (see below), is the presentation of arguments, the essence of authority is the issuance of commands. Authority is the untested acceptance of other's judgment, whereas persuasion is the tested acceptance of other's judgment. In authority, there are sub branches as the following:

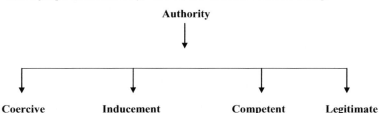

Wrong (1995:41) explains that coercive authority means "for A to obtain B's compliance by threatening him with force, B must be convinced of both A's capability and willingness to use force against him." Coercive authority is considered as the most effective form of power in extensiveness, comprehensiveness and intensity with the exception of the actual force. Coercive authority is potentially the most extensive form of power, because it requires bare minimum communication and mutual understanding between the power holder and power subject to compel the latter's obedience.

Authority by inducement is the counterpart of coercive authority based on inducement, or the offering of rewards for compliance with a command rather than threatening deprivations. Authority by inducement employs positive sanctions to bring about obedience on the part of the power subject rather than the threat of negative sanctions. Authority by inducement resembles a reciprocal, implicitly egalitarian exchange relationship in which A promises B a reward or service in return for B's performance of an action desired by A.

Competent authority is a power relation in which the subject obeys the directions of the authority as he believes in the authority's superior competence or expertise to decide which actions will serve the subject interests and goals. The most common illustration of competent authority has been the physician-patient relationship. The authority of doctors' orders may be taken as the prototype of competent authority. The doctor who says "stop drinking or you will be dead within a year" is not threatening to kill the patient should the patient refuse to comply. The doctor's authority does not rest on the ability to impose any coercive sanctions, nor is the doctor appealing to moral obligation to be obeyed by the patient.

Legitimate authority is a power relation in which the power holder possesses an acknowledged right to command and the power subject has an acknowledged obligation to obey. The source rather than the content of any particular command endows it with legitimacy and induces willing compliance on the part of the power subject. The shared norms that constitute a legitimate authority relation are not shared exclusively by two parties. They are shared within a larger group or community to which both belong.

Two friends or lovers may create a set of reciprocal expectations in which one comes to take for granted a right to command and the other an obligation to obey, but such interpersonal relationship may not be of legitimate authority. Although it may be properly described as one of personal authority, the authority of a parent over a child or master over a servant is a relation of legitimate authority because the norms of the larger society uphold it.

1.7. CDA and Persuasion

Persuasion is not only considered an essential tool in achieving the power of a speaker, but also for its prominent role in being the goal of any public or political speech. Both Barrack Obama and Martin Luther King deliver their speeches about specific topics that concern their audience at a certain time and place. The purpose of their speeches is to inform, impress, move the emotions of the audience, or persuade and call them for action. Simons (2001:7) defines persuasion as "human communication designed to influence the autonomous judgments and actions of others."

Persuasion is a form of attempted influence in the sense that it seeks to alter the way to think, feel, or act, and it differs from other forms of influence. The speaker makes use of certain rhetorical devices in conducting his speech to appear persuasive. A persuasive speech achieves power, influence, and dynamism. However, it is not sufficient to study the speaker's task, as persuasion is transactional process that involves both the speaker and the audience. The audience's position must be also taken into consideration since they can be holding very different beliefs, making the task of persuasion difficult in discourse.

1.7.1. Levels of Persuasion

Simons (2001:29) branches persuasion into three levels:

Simon's levels of persuasion

↓

| Response shaping | Response reinforcing | Response changing |

↓

| Neutralization | Crystallization |

Response shaping occurs when people acquire new beliefs on controversial matters or when they are socialized to learn new or acquire new values.

Shaping may involve, for example, teaching a child to become a patriot or democrat. Political campaigns may shape voter's attitudes toward previously unknown candidates. The key characteristics of shaping are that, it leads to the formation of new beliefs, values and attitudes. Response reinforcing consists of strengthening currently held convictions and making them more resistant to change. A campaign on behalf of a charity might begin by transforming verbal commitments into strongly felt commitments, then transforming those commitments into donations of money, then working to maintain strong behavioral support.

Response changing involves converting others, and getting them to switch parties, such as change cigarette brands, or perhaps quit smoking. The persuader's goal on any occasion may be neutralization, bringing an audience from the point of disagreement to a point of ambivalence or indecision. The second sub-branch of response changing is crystallization, getting those persons, who are uncommitted because of mixed feeling about an idea, to endorse the persuader's position or his proposal. This is what Obama contributes when he gives his speech in Iowa, after winning the Iowa caucus as the first step in the U.S. presidential elections. Obama succeeds in persuading the voters to vote for him to be the first African American president for the U.S. Within the three levels of persuasion, Obama and King activate certain persuasive techniques which are based on logic and facts, called "quasilogical," or which are based on emotions, called "presentational", or which are based on comparisons and evaluations, called "analogical."

1.7.2. Branches of Persuasion in Discourse

There are various approaches of persuading people. Pardo (2001:98) mentions that the type of persuasion is determined by "the use and the type of argument in verbal behavior." The first element of persuasion is the Speaker's credibility "ethos." Ethos is the primary element in persuasive speech, i.e. credibility should be achieved first since the recipients tend to accept the message if they accept the speaker. Ethos is defined by Aristotle as the credibility that the author establishes with his audience. Therefore, it is obviously related to the speaker, his character and his stance towards the issue he is talking about.

Speaker's credibility is an important element in persuasion since the beliefs the speaker is trying to convey will not be accepted by the audience unless he is first accepted personally by them. There are some elements which could contribute to establishing speaker credibility like "occupation, personal looks, respect for others, general expertise, knowledge of the problem" (Berko and Wolvin: 1989: 469).

Acquiring credibility on the part of Martin Luther King was a difficult task, still he succeeded to create credibility by combining his personal experience as an anti racism activist, with his competence and knowledge of his society, his logical and well-formed arguments. In addition, his personal image added a positive perception of him as a charismatic public speaker.

The second element is pathos, which is related to affecting the audience emotionally. It urges the listeners to believe in the proposed ideas as it appeals to their emotional and psychological motives. Therefore, a skillful speaker is one who is able to play on the right emotions, controlling them as he desires. Hence, the speaker has to know his audience and adapt his ideas according to his audience's beliefs and ideology.

In this respect, Berko and Wolvin (1989:482) explain the way for creating credibility "just as you must select your arguments and enhance your credibility on the basis of what you know about your listeners, so you must select psychological appeals on the basis of what you think, which will stir their emotions." Some of the motivating psychological appeals are directed to the senses of fear, humor, pride and are classified by Gronbeck (1990: 130-137) into three branches:

1- Affiliative motives, e.g., sympathy, loyalty, companionship.
2- Achievement motives, e.g., success, prestige.
3- Power motives, e.g., authority, defence, independence.

The third element of persuasion is logos, which stands for logic and reason as it appeals to the minds of the audience and has a great persuasive role. In this track, Berko and Wolvin (1989:474) assert such notion by the following:

> The effective speaker should remember that all factors in the persuasive situation ought to be centered on the audience and that an audience is influenced by clarity of ideas, vividness of language,

for example, and specifics that illuminate the reasons
for the chosen solution.

Based on the previous quotation, there are other factors that can influence the completion of persuasion, such as clarity of ideas and the directness of language. Persuasion which is based on logic can be classified in three sub branches, pure, manipulation and coercive persuasion. Pure persuasion depends on the rhetorical dimension of language. Speakers in this pure persuasion employ logic, facts and past experiences. The purpose of this type is to make a recipient have a freedom of choice. Pinto (2004:654) views manipulative persuasion as "a distinct form of persuasion and control." This type of persuasion presupposes that the person "who is in power hides his intention from subject of power," (Pardo, 2001:97).

In other words, the persuader attempts to hide the effect he wishes to produce in a way that does not allow the persuadees to understand the real goal of the persuader's argument. Manipulative persuasion is usually based on false information, lies and brainwashing. This type leads to producing a controlled-will recipient who has no freedom to choose. Coercive persuasion is the third sub branch of logo persuasion. This type depends on logic mixed with fear, threats and violence. This type leads to creating a controlled-will recipient. Coersive persuasion restricts the freedom of recipients and forces them to take only one choice.

Modal of Persuasion Branches

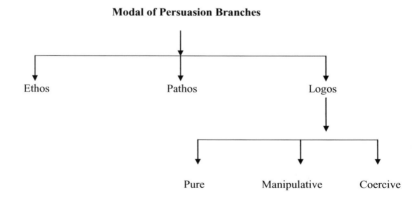

Persuasion, in the cognitive framework, has certain elements that clarify the concept of persuasion in discourse. The first element is that; persuasion is a symbolic process. It means that persuasion involves the use of symbols, with messages transmitted primarily through language with its rich, cultural meanings. Symbols include words like freedom, justice, and equality. Such linguistic symbols are King and Obama's tools, harnessed to change attitudes and mold opinions. The second element is that; persuasion involves an attempt to influence. Such element is activated by breaking down barriers and winning hearts and minds. Breaking down barrier, as Leanne (2009:42-54) explains, is achieved by the following points:

A) Stressing common dreams and values.
B) Illuminating shared experiences.
C) Employing words that resonate.

Leanne (2009: 66-78) argues that to activate the strategy of winning the hearts and minds, certain elements should be applied as the following:

1- Knowing the audience
2- Employing details effectively
3- Personalizing the message : "I" and Experience
4- Connecting one to one : "You and I"

The main point here is that; persuasion represents a conscious attempt to influence the audience along with an accompanying awareness that the persuadee has a mental state that is susceptible to change. It is a type of social influence which includes the behavior of one person who alters the thoughts or actions of another. Persuasion occurs within a context of intentional messages that are initiated by a communicator in hopes of influencing the recipient. The third element is that; persuasion involves the transmission of a message, the message could be verbal or non-verbal. Persuasion is a communicative activity; thus, there must be a message for persuasion, as opposed to other forms of social influence.

It is worth noting that Dr. King has a pioneering skill in convincing his audience. To convince his audience about his beliefs, King employs three important ways of persuasion. The first one is which is based on the logical structures of his speech. King uses such strategy when he starts in most of his speeches with generalised statements of the long journey of African Americans, then he moves in details by showing what happens in different southern states. King moves to universal concepts of violence and civilization on saying. In addition, King employs another persuasive tactic, presentational, that is based on the concepts rooted in his audience's consciousness by raising the degree of emotions and involvement.

It is important to mention that both persuasion and attitudes are linked together in the cognitive domain in discourse. That is because both are psychological contracts. Fishbeina & Ajzen (1975:6) define attitudes as "a learned predisposition to respond in a consistently favorable or unfavorable manner with respect to a given object." Perloff (2002:39) has also a similar definition of attitude as it is "learned, global evaluation of an object (person, place, or issue) that influences thought and action."

In his classification of attitudes, Perloff (2002:39) fixes a number of characteristics of attitudes in discourse. First, attitudes are learned. People are not born with attitudes; however, they acquire attitudes over the course of socialization. Second, attitudes are global, typically emotional evaluations. Attitudes invariably involve affect and emotions. They express passions and hates, attractions and repulsions, likes and dislikes. Affect usually plays an important role in how attitudes are formed or experienced. Third, attitudes influence thought and action. That is because they organize our social world, and categorize people, places, and events. In this respect, Sherif (1967:2) asserts the importance of shaping attitudes in discourse as the following:

> When we talk about attitudes, we are talking about what a person has learned in the process of becoming a member of a family, a member of a group, and of society that makes him react to his social world in a consistent and characteristic way, instead of a transitory and haphazard way. We are talking about the fact that he is no longer neutral in sizing up the world around him; he is attracted or repelled, for or against, favorable or unfavorable.

According to the previous view, attitudes influence behavior as they guide our actions in the direction of doing what we believe. They come in different shapes and sizes. Some attitudes are strong, others are weaker and susceptible to influence. Attitudes have different components and are formed in different ways. These components are thoughts, feelings, and behavior. Martin Luther

King and Obama's attitudes in their discourses reflect large evaluations of issues and topics. Their attitudes in their society are composed of beliefs, affect and intentions to behave one way or another.

To sum up, one can figure out that persuasion is an ancient art, as it dates back to ancient Greece. Yet, there are important aspects of contemporary persuasion in discourse that are unique. It includes the subtlety, volume, and complexity of modern messages as well as different types of persuasion that can be practised explicitly or implicitly by the speaker to convey his message to his audience. Another linguistic device that will be tackled in the following section is modality and its function in King and Obama's discourse.

1.8. Modality

Modality reveals the speaker's attitude and stance towards what he says in his speech. It also reveals his power over his audience. Therefore, it is an indicator of the speaker's ideology in relation to his recipients. The concept "modality" subsumes a wide range of tools that reflect the orator's attitudes to their topics and to their receivers. Such attitudes vary from predictability, desirability, obligation, and permission. The relation between such modal meanings and the concepts of power and persuasion is quite clear. This will be explained later in the analytical part of Martin Luther King and Barrack Obama's speeches.

The numerous considerations of validity, predictability, and desirability constitute an important part of legitimization of the authority, and persuasion to the speaker. Speaker's reliability is indicated in Obama and King's speeches through the system of modality. Modal adverbs or adjectives such as "possibly, certainly, necessarily" indicate the speaker's attitude. Modal auxiliaries like "I should explain, she has to have," can be used to indicate the speaker's relationship towards his argument as well as imply something about his authority.

1.8.1. Classification of Modality

Fairclough (1989:129) explains that modality can be either influence modalities or knowledge modalities.

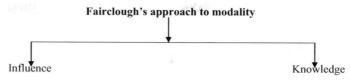

Influence modalities are those that direct and influence the behavior of others, while knowledge modalities are cognitive acts of assessment. In other words, modals are employed to indicate the power and authority of the speaker, his persuasive impact. It also refers to the certainty level of the speaker of what he utters. Fairclough (1989) confirms the significance of modality in representing both relational and expressive features of language.

Relational modality refers to the social power, while expressive modality discloses the speaker's own evaluation by his use of probability or certainty. In other words, it expresses the speaker's commitment to the truth. In his classification of modality, Fowler (1991:85) divides modality into the following branches:
1- Truth
2- Obligation
3- Permission
4- Desirability

Fowler (1991:85) explains truth modal means that a speaker/writer must always indicate or imply a commitment to the truth of any proposition he utters or to a prediction of the degree of the likelihood of an event. Truth modality varies in strength from hedges or mitigators like "might" to emphatics "certainty markers" like "will". Second, obligation reveals the amount of authority and power the speaker has. Permission is expressed by means of "can" and "could" which also are power markers because those in authority can provide such permission.

Desirability expresses less authority by using ought to or should. On the functional level, modality is subjected to classification and scrutiny by different linguists. They offer different labels for the different modes of modality. Palmer (1979:41) classifies modality into the following three kinds:
1- Epistemic modality: the primary function of modality here is to denote the speaker/writer's judgment about the possibility that something is or is not the case. In epistemic modality, there are three degrees. First, the degree of

possibility indicated by "may." Second, the degree of certainty denoted by "must." Third, the degree of probability expressed by "will" to express a reasonable inference, and might, should, would to express probability.

2- Deontic modality: it may also be labeled as performative, since "by uttering a modal, the speaker/writer gives permission, makes a threat, or even lays an obligation (Palmer 1979:41).

3- Dynamic modality: which is connected with ability and volition

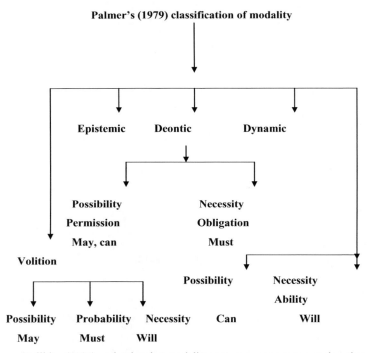

Halliday (1985) maintains that modality system expresses two scales; those of probability and usuality. The main points on the scale of probability are possible, probable, and certain. The main points on the scale of usuality are sometimes, usually and always. Modalization is expressed by one of three ways: by a finite modal operator like "he may be aware of the situation" or by a modal adjunct such as "he is possibly aware of the situation" or by both together such as "he may be possibly aware of the situation." According to modality functional level, modals are divided into "root" modals which reveal social interaction, and "epistemic modal" which deals with logical probability. This is clear in the two examples: you *may* leave the room "social" and it *may* rain tomorrow, "Probability." In this respect, Celce-Murcia and Larsen Freeman (1983:40) assert that:

> Modals which have a social interactional function require that a person using them properly take into account the characteristics of the social situation. In our first example, the speaker has sufficient authority to be able to grant permission to the listener. Furthermore, we can also infer that the context is likely to be a formal one, since the speaker chose to use may rather can in his or her grant of permission.

Based upon the previous concept, there are some factors that can influence the use of modals, like the authority of the speaker, knowledge of context. Obviously, root modals "social interactional models" express human control over events in permission, obligation, and volition, according to the social situation in which they occur. Modality explains the implicit ideology and the power relations hidden in texts. As far as King and Obama's discourse is concerned, modality system expresses the speakers' attitudes towards themselves and towards their subject matter. It also shows their social and political relations with their audience, and the actions which are performed by their language to push people confront social inequality and make something positive. That is obvious in King's "I have a dream" and in Obama's Iowa speech on January 3, 2008 to push the voters to vote for him. Obama, in his victory speech, November 4th, 2004, employs the modality as he says:

> The road ahead will be long. Our climb will be steep, But I will always be honest with you about the challenges we face. I will listen to you, especially when we disagree. And above all, I will ask you join in the work of remaking this nation the only way it's been done in America for two-hundred and twenty-one years - block by block, brick by brick, calloused hand by calloused hand.

Obama uses the modality as it reveals a relative power status between the participants in the speech situation. In addition, modals have a significant role in exposing the ideology of the speaker and his degree of commitment to truth. On saying, "the road ahead will be long, our climb will be steep, we as a people will get there," Obama employs "will" to reveal his power of certainty and ability. First, the use of "will" embodies a specific level of inference on "the road ahead will belong," Obama is certain that the road to restore the image of America as a land of dreams. Obama also certain that there will be set backs and the starting point would not be an easy task.

According to Hodge and Kress (1993), modality is related to power. What the powerful says is taken to be right just because it is said by those who have power, and not necessarily knowledge. The relation between knowledge and power is discussed in the system of modality in English. The modal auxiliaries (may and can) have their bases on knowledge or power. For example, *she can talk*, means either she is able to talk "expressing the speaker's knowledge about his capabilities", or she is allowed to talk "expressing the speaker's power of giving her the admission to talk.

Yet, modals are not only social nor logical as they can be categorized under ability (can/ able to), desire (would like to), offer (would you like), preference (would rather). As to the linguistic concept of modality, it is not only restricted to modal verbs, but also include modal like verbs of knowledge and evaluation such as think, believe, dislike, and nouns as ability, demand, adjectives like sure, certain. Language not only reflects the degree of power the speaker has, but it is also used to persuade, control and overwhelm the thoughts and behavior of others. The next section deals with pragmatic role of language in communication by employing speech act theory.

1.9. Speech Acts Theory

Speech act theory is usually attributed to the Oxford philosopher J. L. Austin. The basic ideas, which were formed by him in the late 1930, were presented in his lectures given at Oxford in 1952-1956. These lectures were finally published posthumously as *how to do things with words* in 1962. After his death in 1960, Austin's ideas were refined, systematized, and advanced especially by his Oxford student, the American philosopher John R. Searle. The concept of this theory defied the generally accepted tenets that unless a sentence can be verified as true or false, it is meaningless.

Austin differentiates between two types of sentences or utterances. Constatives, which describe states of affairs and which can be evaluated in terms of truth condition, and performatives, which are produced with aim of fulfilling a specific action. In Austin's view, performatives can not be regarded as true/false, but rather felicitous or infelicitous. In other words, they can be assessed in terms of felicity condition. These conditions are rules under which words can be used properly to perform actions. Schiffrin (1994:56) explains that Austin's classifications of such conditions are in the following manner:

A) The conditions should include the existence of "conventional procedure, having a certain conventional effect.
B) They should have particular persons and circumstances.
C) They should include the correct and complete execution of procedures.

However, the constative/performative distinction does not always hold. Any sentence can describe both the state of affairs and perform an action, such as: *"Law college is tough."* This example shows a fact in the education field "describing a truth in the academic world" and performs an action "warning the addressee." Austin shows that there is no clear distinction between the two concepts.

Therefore, any sentence, in addition to its meaning, does perform an action. The concept that an utterance performs an action is called "force." In other words, it is the ability to perform actions via communicative force. In this track, Austin introduces a three fold distinction of utterances produced by a speaker.

1.9.1 Classification of Austin's Speech Acts

Based on Austin's classification of speech acts, Schiffrin (1994:53 points out that there are three branches that confirm the notion of force in speech acts theory.

1- A locutionary act which involves the utterance of an expression with sense and reference, i.e. using sounds and words with meaning.
2- An illocutionary act which is performed in saying the illocution that has the force associated with an utterance.
3- Perlocutionary act which is the production of efforts on the audience by means of uttering the sentence.

The first type, which is locutionary act, is explained by Austin as producing certain noises, words in different construction. The second type, which is illocutionary acts, is conveyed by what Searle (1969:32) called on illocutionary force. The most familiar type of illocutionary force is an explicit performative.

Huang (2007:96) classifies performatives into two main types: explicit and implicit. Explicit performatives are performative utterances which contain a performative verb that makes explicit of act being performed. Explicit performative like, I order you to do that. Implicit performatives are performative utterances in which there is not such explicitness in the verbs. Such as: I will come to your talk tomorrow.

The third type "perlocutionary act" is performed through the impact of using illocutionary acts. Another way to put it is that a perlocutionary act represents a consequence or by-product of speaking. There are two major distinctions between illocutions and perlocutions. Firstly, illocutionary acts are intended by the speaker, while perlocutionary acts are occurred by the words or sentences. Secondly, illocutionary acts are under the speaker's will, while perlocutionary impacts are not under the speaker's control.

1.9.2. Searle's Theory

Searle's theory of speech acts is a systematization of Austin's notion of speech acts. Searle asserts that one can use language to do a lot of things. Searle divides illocutionary acts into five basic branches:

1- Representative or assertive: a representative is an utterance that describes some state of affairs such as "the earth is round" by asserting, concluding, claiming.
2- Directives: which aim at getting the addressee to do something, e.g. ordering, requesting, advising.
3- Commissives: which commits the speaker to do something in the future like offering, promising, vowing, threatening ……etc.
4- Expressives: express the speaker's psychological state, e.g. thanking, promising, blaming.
5- Declaratives: which are performed by someone especially authorized within institutional framework, e.g. declaring war, passing a sentence, appointing, firing……etc.

One obvious example of the pervious concept is what Obama uses in some of his speeches. On saying "*to reclaim the American dream*," Obama uses a representative speech act as he asserts the concept of restoring the American dream. This utterance holds another indirect speech act which is commissive as he promises his audience to get back the brightful image of the U.S. In the cognitive domain, the speech act is based on four levels. In the first level, the addresser produces an utterance and the addressee receivies it based on his hearing abilities.

In the second level, the addressee understands that the addresser relies on the first level based on the linguistic presumption (i.e the fact that the addresser must be using the langauge commonly used in society) plus the mutual contextual beliefs. In the third level, the addressee recognizes that the addresser says something to him or her based on the second level, which is the lingusitic presumption and the mutual contextual beliefs. In the final level, the addressee is able to realize the actual purpose of the addresser's utterance, relying on the third level, the communicative presumption, in addition to mutual contextual knowledge.

Part of speech acts theory is the notion of indirectness. Blum-Kulka (1997:44) asserts that indirectness is considered as "one of the most intriguing features of speech act performance." Indirectness, in her view, is classified into a conventional and non-conventional. The conventional type falls within a specific and known context. Blum Kulka (1997:40) gives a clear example for conventional type like if a child says to parent, "can you mend this toy for me?" And the parent replies with "not now." The child may say "I just wanted to know" denying any requestive intent. What can be concluded from such examples is that; the requestive interpretation is part of the utterance's meaning, and it is related to the literal interpretation.

The interpretation in the previous example is negotiated in the context. On the other hand, the second type of indirectness, non-conventional, which has an open-ended interpretation. The sentence "I am hungry" may be pronounced from a beggar who requests money or be said from an adult enter the dining room as a statement for food pleasures to come. In his explanation of indirectness, Thomas (1995:119) classifies indirectness into two points:

1- Intentional indirectness
2- Non-intentional indirectness

By employing indirectness, speakers behave in a rational manner as they contain some social or communicative advantage. Thomas (1995:121) handles the negative aspects of indirectness. She asserts that indirectness could be costly and risky. It is costly in a sense that indirect utterance takes longer for the speaker to produce and longer for the hearer to comprehend. It is risky in a sense that the hearer may not understand what the speaker wants to say exactly.

Two important elements should be handled in indirectness. First, indirectness is a rational way to convey meaning. That is because the speaker obtains some advantages or avoids some negative consequence by employing indirectness. The speaker can avoid the negative consequence by using the indirect way to avoid hurting someone else, and at the same time, it enables the speaker to achieve his goal. The second important element in indirectness is that; it is universal in a sense that it occurs to some degree in most languages.

Individual and groups from different cultural backgrounds vary in how, when, and why they use indirect speech acts in preference. Indirectness is always linked with social distance. The relation between them is that; the speaker uses a greater level of indirectness with people who have power or authority. Thomas (1995:142) explains that we use in our life indirectness to achieve the following reasons:

1- To increase the desire to make one's language more or less interesting.
2- To increase the force of the message.
3- To confirm goals.
4- To achieve politeness.

To sum up, the main contributions of speech acts and indirectness are that; they focus on the notion that words and sentences are not only used to show meanings, but also to convey specific different linguistic actions in specific contexts. Such actions that are done through utterances are called performative speech acts. Performatives can be explicit or implicit. It is important to view the link between the levels of meaning in speech acts and the concept of metaphor in discourse, as both have various levels of meaning structure.

1.10. Defining Metaphor

Metaphor has been defined in a variety of ways. According to Merriam Webster's Dictionary (1999), metaphor is "a figure of speech in which a word or phrase denoting one kind of object, or idea is used in place of another to suggest likeness or analogy between them, like drowning in money. Charteris-Black (2004:21) shows metaphor as "a linguistic representation that results from the shift in the use of a word or phrase." In this respect, Ross (1952:1457) views metaphor as "giving the thing a name that belongs to something else." The etymological origin of the word metaphor is from the Greek *meta* which means with and *phor* which means carry.

Clearly, the central notion of metaphor is one in which meaning is transferred. It is clear that all of these definitions attribute certain similar defining characteristics to metaphor despite the fact that they use different terms in description. First, they all define metaphor as a process of transference where words are transferred from one domain to another. Second, such transference is not haphazard; it must be based on a kind of analogy or similarity between the transferred referents. Third, the underlying structure of a metaphorical expression is a comparison where one word is likened to another. In general, metaphor is a process of substitution where one word substitutes for another on the basis of similarity between them.

Metaphor is considered as an important concept as it influences our beliefs, attitudes, and values. This is clear since metaphor uses language to activate unconscious emotional associations and influences the value that we place on ideas and beliefs on a scale of goodness and badness. It does this by transferring positive or negative association of various source words to a metaphor target. Metaphorical meaning is determined by sorts of connotations aroused by the words in their normal non-metaphorical or literal use. On the conceptual level, Richards (1936:92) shows that metaphor is "the omnipresent principle of language." Richards (1936) explains that language on a general level is full of metaphors, as they are integral component of any language. He further explains that metaphor is the outcome of an interaction between two variant ideas, simultaneously activated by a single word or phrase. He elaborates that these two ideas are; tenor and vehicle.

Richards (1936:96) describes the tenor as the literal meaning of the words, while the vehicle is the figurative or non-literal one. Black (1979:28) attempts to shed lights on the conceptual level of metaphor as he identifies two parts within metaphor; the primary and secondary subjects. The primary subject is basically the element that metaphorically identified. The second subject is not to be regarded as an isolated entity, but rather a scheme of relations. In this track, one can find that the significance of decoding meaning of metaphor is that; metaphor is pervasive in language and it is a basic process in the formation of words and word meanings. Such concepts and meanings are lexicalized, or expressed in words, through metaphor.

Secondly, metaphor is important because of its functions in explaining, clarifying, describing, evaluating. We choose metaphors in order to communicate what we think or how we feel about something. Chilton (1996) asserts that metaphor plays a cognitive and interactive role. It is employed cognitively as a means to interactively facilitate communication among individuals. Chilton (1996) shows that metaphors are employed in face-to-face interactions to ease the harshness of contact among individuals. He explains that people activate metaphors when they tackle sensitive topics to set up communicative path with recipients.

The concept of conceptual meaning of metaphor is common among cognitive linguists for many reasons. First, metaphor is a cognitive tool and it is part of the conceptual system. Such conceptual system is activated throughout the process of understanding and production of experience. Secondly, metaphor is part of thought. Third, it is part of everyday language which means metaphor is the contact point of everyday language. This means that metaphor is the contact point between language and mind. The mind recruits metaphors to interpret and understand daily experiences, and language functions as a tool through which metaphor is expressed.

1.10.1. Types of Metaphor

There are different types of metaphors. Ullmann (1975:242) shows that the first type is "concrete to abstract metaphors." This is the case of metaphorical extension of the usage of images drawn from the abstract sense to the concrete entity. Under this type, metaphor conveys sense impression to describe abstract experiences, for instance, "bitter feelings", "warm reception." The second type of metaphor is "synaesthesia metaphor" where words are transferred from one sense to another, from touch to sound and from sound to sight, like, "cold voice" or "piercing sound." The third type is called "anthropomorphic metaphor" where parts of the human body are used to refer to inanimate objects.

The obvious example for this type is "the neck of the bottle," "the mouth of a river." Leech (1974:150) states that the fourth type of metaphor is the "animistic metaphor" which attributes characteristics of animates to the inanimates. This is the case of the metaphorical utterances "an angry sky." Obama employs metaphor as a cognitive way of memorizing and refreshing his audience minds about his goals. When Obama says in one of his speeches that is analyzed in detail in the analyzed data, "*our promise live alive,*" Obama moves from something that is animistic or humanizing to something that is not inanimistic "inhuman" which is "promise." Obama uses that kind of metaphor to create new meanings and ideas, and to find a possible way to provide expressible thought. Obama generally employs metaphor to facilitate memorizing, and to communicate thoughts through his speeches.

Leech (1974:158) identifies another type which describes the "humanizing" type that attributes characteristics of human beings. It is important to mention that every metaphor employs two domains. The source domain and target domain. According to Lakoff & Johnson (1980:5), source domain represents the equivalent figurative meaning. To understand different levels of meaning, we have to understand that it is the mind which is naturally embodied.

Lakoff and Johnson's view is that, the mind gets from and makes uses of bodily experiences such as perception and movement. In addition, the concepts are embodied in the sense that they are entrenched in the brain's nervous system. Lakoff and Johnson (1999:20) explain that concepts are neural structures in our brains. These neural systems are responsible for mental activities and for the process of conceptualization and reasoning. Richards (1936:96) mentions two elements that interact with each other during the metaphorical process; "tenor" and "vehicle."

On the one hand, tenor is the original element that is compared to another object from a different domain. On the other hand, "vehicle" is the borrowed entity in terms of which tenor is presented. In the same track, Black (1962:28) elaborates that metaphor works via a kind of interaction between its two elements. Richards (1936) explains that these elements are "tenor" and "vehicle", while Black (1962:28) calls them "focus" and "frame." "Focus" is the word used non-literally "metaphorically" and "frame" is the surrounding literal meanings.

However, Black (1962:39) re-defines these elements as principal and subsidiary and explains that metaphor works by applying to the principal subject certain characteristics associated with the subsidiary one. For example, "John is a computer," is a metaphorical utterance, composed of a principal subject "boy" and a subsidiary subject " computer". These two subjects interact with each other through applying to the principal subject certain common characteristics of the subsidiary one (i.e., that he is prone to intelligence, good skills, and various talents).

1.10.2. The Conceptual Types of Metaphor

Lakoff and Johnson (1980:5) show that there are various types of metaphor from the cognitive perspective. They are divided into three types: structural, orientational, and ontological. Lakoff & Johnson (1980:5) explain that structural metaphors are cases "where one concept is metaphorically structured in terms of another." The concept that needs explanation is understood via the corresponding source domain. They argue that the example, ARGUMENT IS WAR, is a clear example of this type. They explain that an ordinary activity like argument is understood in terms of war.

They affirm that this metaphor can be found in a lot of ordinary utterances like, "your claims are indefensible, he attacked every weak point in my argument." In all these expressions, the concept of war structures the activity of argument. They contend that in the metaphor, "argument is war," the argument is only understood in terms of war, but it is not war. They explain that if one engages in an argument, one does not use any kind of weapons.

The second conceptual type of metaphor is the orientational metaphor which has a certain approach on a concept. Lakoff & Johnson (1980:14) define this type of metaphor as it "gives a concept a spatial orientation." The source domain infuses the target domain with certain direction. In the utterance "HAPPY IS UP," they explain that the target domain of happiness is structured via the source domain of verticality. In other words, people draw the picture of happiness in their minds as a vertical axis. Lakoff and Johnson (1980:14) state that orientational metaphor emerges from bodily experience. They clarify that the physical basis is the cornerstone of such metaphors.

So, when we say "I AM FEELING UP," the fact that upright position is associated with healthy attitude. A lower position is a reflection of unhappiness and desperation. Hence, the metaphor "SAD IN DOWN" or "I FELL IN DEPRESSION" is a reflection of specific meaning. Upward orientation tends to go together with positive evaluation, while downward orientation goes with a negative one. But positive-negative evaluation is not limited to the spatial orientation up-down.

Thus, the words like whole, balance, goal, front are mostly regarded as positive, while their opposites like, not whole, imbalance, no goal, and back are regarded as negative. An obvious example for that the phrase, "HALF THE MAN," which denotes someone who is not positively viewed, as in the example, "HE IS HALF MAN IN HIS DISCUSSION." Obviously, the "whole" versus "not whole" opposition is at work here.

The third type is the ontological "abstract" metaphor, which is a matter of viewing an abstract concept in terms of a physical entity. Lakoff & Johnson (1980:27) view this type as a way of describing "non-physical thing as an entity or substance." They explain that such abstract entities are ideas, feelings and events. They provide an example in the metaphor, "INFLATION IS UP" Here, inflation is regarded as an entity that makes one confront it and feel opposite against it.

1.10.3. Functional Approach to Metaphor in Discourse

Mac Cormac (1985:47) classifies metaphors into two main types, conveyance and basic. A metaphor that is employed to convey a general idea is called conveyance. Conveyance metaphor is a common type which is used in discourse. On the other hand, basic metaphor is employed for more specific purposes. It is basically employed to express concepts which confirm theories. The producer of in both types is required to understand the comprehensive context of the meaning.

Lakoff and Johnson (1999:60) divide metaphor as primary and complex ones. Primary metaphors are "atoms that are put together to form molecules." They form the building blocks of complex metaphors. Lakoff & Johnson (1999:60) give an example about the complex metaphor "LIFE IS A JOURNEY." They explain that it consists of three primary metaphors: a person living a life is a traveler, a life plan is an itinerary, and life goals are destinations.

These three metaphors, according to Lakoff and Johnson (1999), are held together by the pervasive cultural belief that one should have a purpose in life. Therefore, culture takes a significant position in shaping metaphors. Deese (1974:214) shows that metaphors are determined by culture which is embedded in the minds of its user. He mentions that "there must be a fine tuning of a metaphor to the structure of particular human minds in their cultural settings before it will work" (214). He argues that mind is shaped by the particular culture which is situated in; therefore, the metaphor should adapt to the culture-bound mind to be able to function. In other words, a metaphor's functionality is determined by culture.

Carter (1997:147) shows other two types of metaphor which are "creative," and "dead" or "frozen" metaphors. He believes that "creative" metaphors are those which seem to depart from the literal meanings of the words. One example for this type is when the producer says "she is fishing in troubled waters." This kind of metaphor has no fixed meaning but meanings depending on contextual considerations. Creative metaphor's producers aim at inviting the audience to exert effort and use their minds to interpret the intended meaning. On the other hand, "dead" or "frozen" metaphors as those whose meanings are so familiar to language users, so that their interpretation requires no act of creativity on the part of the receiver. One clear example for this type is when a producer says "head teacher." The interpretation that can be understood from such example does not require much effort to comprehend it.

Carter's concept of metaphor

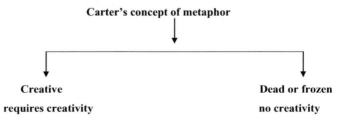

| **Creative** | **Dead or frozen** |
| requires creativity | no creativity |

Carter (1997: 145-147) distinguishes between these two types on the basis of what he calls "taking risk." He supports the notion that major characteristics of metaphor in general is that they involve "taking risk" because the addressee may not get the metaphor or may think of its producer as a liar. Since "creative" metaphors are those whose meanings are not previously encountered, they are characterized by being of high risk. On the other hand, since the meanings of "dead" or "frozen" metaphors are established in the language and their producers do not intend to convey additional meanings, they are of low or even no risk.

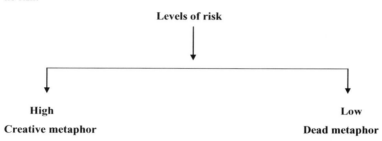

High   **Low**
Creative metaphor   **Dead metaphor**

Unlike the above-mentioned theory which tends to agree with regard to identifying "dead" and "creative" types of metaphor, Black (1979:26) criticizes the so-called "dead" metaphors and does not admit their existence. He argues that "a so-called dead metaphor is not a metaphor at all, but an expression that has no metaphor use." In addition to his classification of metaphor, Carter (1997:147) sheds lights on the significance of metaphor, which lies in being an instrument of communication. Metaphor conveys meanings and thoughts that may be difficult to be employed in non-metaphorical language. In this respect, Black (1962) points out that metaphor may be employed when there is no literal equivalent in the language. For example, engineers use the metaphor "the leg of an angle" because there is no literal expression for a bounding line.

In support of the view that metaphor is a fundamental device of human communication, Clark (1973:77) points out that children produce and create metaphors while acquiring language. On the basis of experimental observation of the behavior of a child, Clark finds out that having learned the word "mooi" for "moon," the child uses it to describe nearly all objects that are similar to the moon in that; they have the same round shape: cakes, circles, and the letter O.

From this view, it is clear that the mental aspects and mechanisms are involved in the metaphor's understanding process. Both Turner and Fauconnier (1998) propose that the concept of conceptual integration is the mental representation which is automatically activated at the moment of thinking. Such mental spaces are created as thinking and speaking for the purpose of understanding and reasoning. They (1998) explain that such mental network comprising an array of mental spaces which are classified into three types: inputs, generic spaces, and blends.

Classification of mental spaces of metaphor

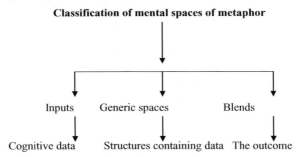

Input spaces contain the cognitive data prior to the processing stage, the generic space contains structure common to all input spaces involved in the network, and the blended space is the outcome of a mapping process from the input process. In the mental operations, there are three conceptual levels for the integration process: composition, completion and elaboration. Composition is the process of combining conceptual material from the input spaces. Completion takes place when the structure in the blend matches information in long-term memory. Elaboration happens when the blend triggers further additional information.

Conceptual operations

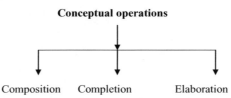

1.10.4. Persuasive Power of Metaphor in Discourse

Metaphors have a persuasive effect on the recipients, as they are able to persuade and influence attitudes. Politicians employ metaphors to persuade their audience of their views on any issue. In this respect, Miller (1979:155) argues that political speeches, which include metaphors, are more convincing to the audience. Political metaphors enforce the strength of the message on the political situation, as well as on the audience.

Another significant factor in the process of persuading the audience by metaphors is the leaders need to establish and confirm their credibility. Credibility is the criterion against which leaders' efficiency is judged as it shows whether or not politicians are able to deal with the political situation in which they are involved. On the other hand, Swanson (1978:164) confirms that metaphor "propels us on a quest for the underlying truth." He explains that the use of metaphor in political discourse urges us to search for the hidden truth. He affirms that the metaphor provokes the audience to search for both the explicit and implicit messages.

To sum up, metaphor in discourse has a strategic function as it convinces the audience about the speaker's messages. It also helps the speakers to create new meanings and ideas to find an appropriate way of expressing the inexpressible thought. It also has a cognitive function as it facilitates the memorizing process for the audience. In addition, it enables the speaker to communicate meanings and thoughts.

In short, the role of metaphors deserves to be explained as it shows that language is not only a medium of statements. Rather, it is also a tool of communicating, expressing, and creating new ideas and meanings in the conceptual domain. To get more understanding of the conceptualization and the conceptual domain, one has to start examining the basic principles of cognitive linguistics.

1.11. Defining Cognitive Linguistics

Cognitive linguistics is a modern school of linguistic thought and practice. It is concerned with the relationship between human language, the mind, and socio-physical experience. It originally emerged in the 1970s (Fillmore 1975, Lakoff & Thompson 1975) and has many approaches in the disciplines of linguistics and philosophy. While its original roots were in part philosophical in nature, cognitive linguistics has always been influenced by theories and findings from other cognitive sciences as they emerged during the 1960s and 1970s, particularly in cognitive psychology.

Cognitive linguistics deals with the notion of how human beings understand their world. The process of understanding, according to Johnson (1992), is based on the body and the surrounding environment. He explains that the way things can be understood depends on the kinds of bodies we have and the way we interact with our physical and social entities. Cognitive linguistics is described as a movement precisely because it does not constitute a single theory. Instead, it is an approach that adopts a set of commitments and leads to a diverse range of theories.

1.12. Classification of Cognitive Linguistics

There are two fundamental commitments that underlie the orientation of cognitive linguistics. The first one is generalization commitment, and the second one is a cognitive commitment. Lakoff (1990) explains the first principle in cognitive linguistics "generalization" as a dedication to characterizing general principles that apply to all aspects of human language.

Cognitive linguistics acknowledges that it may be often useful to treat areas such as syntax, semantics and phonology as being distinct. However, given the generalization commitment, cognitive linguists do not start with the assumption that subsystems of language like "syntax, phonology, morphology…etc" are organized in divergent ways. Therefore, the generalization commitment represents a commitment to openly investigate how the various aspects of linguistic knowledge emerge from a common set of human cognitive abilities which they draw. According to Evans (2007), cognitive linguistic studies focus on what is common among aspects of language, seeking to employ successful method, and explanations across these aspects.

The second commitment is termed the cognitive commitment. From Lakoff's (1990) point of view, it represents a commitment to providing a characterization of the general principles for language that accord with what is known about the mind from other disciplines. It is this commitment that makes cognitive linguistics to be an approach which is fundamentally interdisciplinary in nature. Just as the generalization commitment leads to the search for principles of language structure, the cognitive commitment represents the view that principles of linguistic structure include other cognitive branches, particularly psychology, artificial intelligence, philosophy, and social cognition.

1.12.1 Cognitive Commitment Branches

For any understanding of discourse within cognitive commitment, three important elements should be highlighted as the following:

B   **Elements of cognitive commitment**

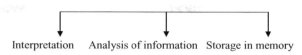

Interpretation   Analysis of information   Storage in memory

In the interpretation process, information we receive is given meaning often by the social context and our previous experience and cultural values. For example, we do not interpret another person's behaviour in a vacuum. What we interpret about the person is related to associated stereotypes and social values.

All of these concepts are involved the interpretation process. Second, social information is analyzed, which means that an initial interpretation may be adjusted, changed, or even rejected. For example, while the first impression we make of another person may be influential, further acquaintance and interaction with the person may dramatically change this impression. Third, social information is stored in memory from which it may be recalled or retrieved.

All of these elements are combined together to make social perception which both Baron and Byrne (2000) view as a process through which we seek to know and understand other persons. This is clear to what is known as the implicit personality theories in cognitive discourse, which is a general expectation that what an individual has about a person resulting from knowledge about central traits. According to Pennington (2000:65), implicit personality theory implies that people hold preconceptions about what an individual is like.

Inside this theory, the preconceptions are divided into primacy effect and recency effect. Primacy effect is where information about another person has greater influence on the impression formed than information which comes later. The second one is recency effect where information presented last has the greatest influence on the impression formed. Both Barrack Obama and Martin Luther King activate that kind of effect in addressing their audience, persuading them to start with their notions and beliefs.

Obama and King cognitive effect

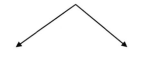

King's primacy effect   Obama's recency effect

1.13. Social Schemas

Part of the cognitive effects is linked with social schemas. In this track, Fiske and Taylor (1991:98) define social schemas as "cognitive structures which represent knowledge about a concept or type of stimulus, including its attributes and relations." Social schemas, as a cognitive concept, reflect organized collections of information stored in memory and based on past experience. A clear example of social schemas is what Obama said in his speech on January 20, 2008 in Atlanta, Georgia, during his presidential campaign, as he mentions the following;

> As I was thinking about which ones we need to remember at this four. My mind went back to the very beginning of the modern civil rights era. Because before Memphis and the mountaintop, the bridge in Selma and March on Washington; before Birmingham and the beatings: the fire hoses and the loss of those little girls.

What Obama does here is that; he attempts to refresh the memory of his audience by retrieving the information and social cognitive structures "social schemas" of his audience based on past experience. He does that to facilitate new conception in their mental representation that a black candidate can do what the white candidate can do. Therefore, in such strategy of social schemas, Obama is efficient in categorizing information and paying attention to what is important and influential. He also employs consistent information which is stored in the memory as the following:

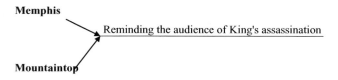

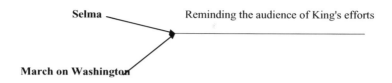

Birmingham events	The African American sacrifices
The beatings	
The fire hoses	
The loss of little girls	

Obama mentions the name of Dr. King, later in his speech, to create person schemas based on expectations about other people. Obama, in this way, activates other cognitive ways like I) Self schemas which are based on generalizations. II) Event schemas which create expectation in social situations. Obama employs all such strategies as he says in the same speech;

> What Dr. King understood is that if just one person chose to walk instead of ride the bus, these walls of oppression would not be moved. If a few more women were willing to do what Rosa Parks had done, may be the cracks would start to show. May be if white folks marched because they had come to understand that their freedom too was at stake in the impending battle, the wall would begin to sway.

In the previous part, Obama employs very specific cognitive strategies in his discourse. He uses different types of mental representations of social knowledge based on previous experiences "social schemas" to convey his message persuasively. He uses person schemas, self schemas, role schemas, and event schemas. Person schemas reflect a number of behaviours and personality traits together with certain attitudes and beliefs. Obama embodies this style by claiming that he wants to make a change in the American politics, and his behavious with his attitude show that. According to Pennington (2000), person schemas help any person to create a full expectation of behaviours and judgments. Person schema is viewed by Markus (1977) as cognitive generalizations about the person, derived from past experience, that organize and create the cognitive image of any one.

Role schema is defined, according to Fiske and Taylor (1991:119), as "the set of behaviours expected of a person in a particular social situation." People have a large number of role schemas mentally represented. These include, for example, the roles of student/teacher, husband/wife, father/mother, politician/his audience. In role schemas, there are two different branches; ascribed and achieved roles.

Achieved roles are those by which a person has actually managed to acquire such as teacher, salesman, and politicians. When a person achieves a role, others may have quite strong expectations. Ascribed roles are ones that person acquires automatically because of birth or age or race. In other words, role schemas are behaviours expected in a social situation. Event schemas are mental representation of what we normally expect in a multitude of social situations.

King activates the concept of *role schemas* by taking the *ascribed role* as well as the *achieved role*. His *ascribed role* is the defender of all African Americans because he, as a human, does not agree with any kind of oppression. *Achieved role* is obtained through his charismatic personality in gaining the appreciation of not only his followers, but also the international institutions that qualify him to win Noble award.

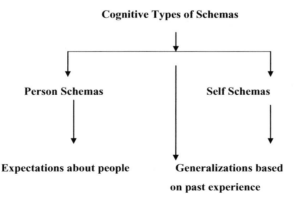

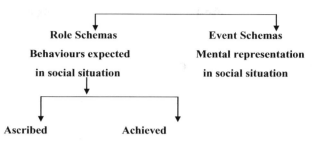

One important notion within the framework of social schemas in discourse is the concept of social representation. Moscovici (1981:181) defines the concept of social representation as the following:

> A set of concepts, statements and explanations, originating in daily life in the course of inter-individual communications. They are the equivalent, in our society, of the myths, and belief systems in traditional societies; they might even be said to be the contemporary version of common sense.

According to the previous definition, it is clear that social representation is based on ideological ideas and social interactions. In his comments on the previous definition, Pennington (2000:48) explains that four points can be concluded from such definition. First, everyday social events are only given meaning through our interaction with other people. Second, meanings are determined by the culture in which we live, hence, different cultures will have different values about what is and what is not socially acceptable.

Third, the more persons are engaged or identified as part of a culture, the better able they are to interact and communicate with other people who are part of the same culture. Fourth, the social representation approach attempts to understand everyday, common sense aspects of our social life. A clear example of such element is that; different cultures have different social representation for what is acceptable to eat, how to dress, how to greet people, how to use the appropriate social non-verbal behaviour in the social interaction.

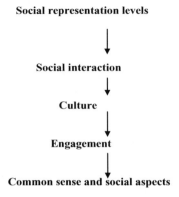

1.14. Classification of Social Representation

Moscovic (1984) explains that social representations are the product of two key processes: anchoring and objectification. Anchoring is a process which allows new or novel information to be categorized as belonging to a particular social category we possess. Anchoring functions to render the unfamiliar feelings, like strange, frightening, to be familiar and understandable. Objectification is the process that turns complex and abstract ideas into specific, concrete images, thus, making them easier to be understood. Moscovici and Hewstone (1983) identify three processes within objectification which turn complex ideas into social representations. Objectification, as cognitive strategy, is classified into three branches:

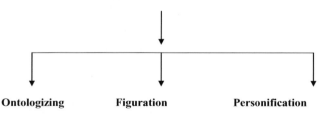

Ontologizing refers to physical properties, represented by ideas. This is what Obama in his speech did in Atlanta, GA, on January 20, 2008, which is handled in detail in the following analytical chapter. In the following part, Obama reflects the cognitive strategy of ontologising by saying the following:

> We will have to fight to fix our schools, but we will also have to challenge ourselves to be better parents, we will have to confront the biases in our criminal justice system, but we will also have to acknowledge the deep-seated violence that still resides in our communities and marshal the will to break its grip. That is how we will bring about the change we seek.

In the previous quotation, Obama used physical aspects like "our schools" to show what kind of change that should be done inside the American society. So, the idea of change is explained by the physical entity "school." The second strategy of objectification is the figuration, which refers to the usage of pictures and concrete image. The third strategy is personification, which refers to the usage of a person to represent an idea. This is what Obama did in many of his speeches. In his speech in Atlanta, GA, on January 20, Obama applies such a strategy by mentioning the following:

> That is how Dr. King led this country through the wilderness. He did it with words. Words that he spoke not just to the children of slaves, but the children of slave owners. Words that inspired not just black but also white: not just the Christians, but the Jews: not just the Southners, but the Northerners. He led with words, but he also led with deeds. He also led by example. He led by marching and going to jail and suffering threats and being away from his family. He led by taking a stand against a war, knowing full well that it would diminish his popularity. He led by challenging our economic structures, understanding that it would cause discomfort.

In the previous utterances, Obama applies the cognitive strategy of personification as he attempts to use a person as a model to represent certain ideas. When he mentions Dr. King's efforts, he shows a sense of unity and conviction about King's ideas to unite the country. Obama employs two different levels of his social thought; social representations and social schemas. Social representations are at macro level and encompass cultural beliefs, values and social traditions.

By contrast, social schemas operate at a micro level and focus much more on the individual and the schemas developed from experience. In a sense, they are complementary to each other since a more complete explanation and understanding of social thought and behaviour is provided when taken together. The cognitive process of conceptual comprehension of discourse takes place at several levels. It is crucial in the process of discourse comprehension to understand the cognitive role of memory, which will be explained in the following parts.

1.15. The Cognitive Role of Memory in Discourse Comprehension

Memory is classified into short term memory (STM) and long term memory (LTM). Short term memory, which has limited capacity, is the place where all incoming information from various senses is analyzed and interpreted. In discourse comprehension, this means that in short term memory, we analyze sound sequences as phonemes, morphemes and syntactic structures of a particular language which we assign conceptual meaning. Short term memory apparently functions as so-called working memory. That includes the process of perception, understanding, thinking, etc. In this track, Bower and Cirilo (1985:75) confirm the following:

> The STM is the active part of the central processor that holds the internal symbols currently in the focus of attention and conscious processing. The STM need not to be viewed as a place or register physically distinctfrom LTM. STM and LTM may only be two different states or levels or current activation of the same memory schemata.

According to previous utterance, Bower and Cirilo (1985:75) observe a number of characteristics for STM as the followings:

1- STM is the active partition of the memory system.
2- It makes the information to have faster access to the items in STM than items to the LTM.
3- STM has a limited capacity for all stored information.

Verbal items "words, sentences" can be maintained in STM by focusing on them and by rehearsing, covertly going over the item repeatedly. This rehearsal serves to maintain items in STM and to transfer some information about those items to LTM. Bower and Cirilo (1985:76) pay attention to another level of memory called "working memory" or intermediate-term memory. This type of memory refers to memory structures that maintain information with context, but information is neither in the focus of active memory nor in the distant edges of LTM.

Working memory constructs and keeps an internal model of the immediate events of the past few minutes. Working memory holds the plan that the person follows in performing some task. The plan is typically a structured set of goals, sub goals, and anticipated actions. In reading text, one can have various goals to comprehend every sentence, or extract certain specific facts from the texts, or look for grammatical errors.

Long term memory, however, is the storage room where the information from short term memory eventually is deposited. Although much information gets stored in this way in LTM, this does not mean that we can remember all information, because recalling or recognition of information depend on processes of retrieval. Bjork and Bjork (1996:14) elaborate a number of processes for copying and maintaining information as the following.

The process of maintaining information in cognitive discourse

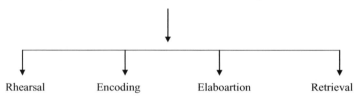

Rhearsal   Encoding   Elaboartion   Retrieval

Rehearsal refers to the overt and covert process that refreshes information in STM. Encoding refers to any mental operations performed on information arriving in the sensory systems that form memory traces of that information. Elaboration refers to the establishing of linkages between new information and previously stored information, a process that seems to be especially effective at promoting long-term storage of new information. Retrieval refers to the process of bringing information out of memory for use.

Van Dijk (1998:79) shows that mental models play an important role in the contruction of memory. Mental models, based on his view, are representations in personal memory of events, or as the term "episodic memory" suggests, representations of episodes. Therefore, when we witness, participate in, or hear/read about a car accident, people construct a model of such an event. This model is subjective as it reflects or represents the personal experience and interpretation of the event by the participant. So, what people know personally about such an event is represented in their subjective, individual models of the event. The notion of the model is attrative, since it is responsible for the personal/subjective interpretation of the discourse by language users.

When language users begin their discourse production, the model is the starting point for text and talk. Model is the personal knowledge, experience or opnion about an event that is being used as input to the discourse production processes. These models are essentially personal and subjective. They embody personal interpretations and experiences of actions, events and all social practices. This personal dimension may be the result of earlier experience, which is based on old models that are being activated or updated.

This dimension constitutes the personal history of each person, as well as other general or abstract personal representations. People are engaged in the ongoing interpretation of the episodes of their everyday lives from the moment they wake up until they fall asleep. Such interpretations should be based upon relevant constructions of such episodes in mental modes, stored in episodic memory. These models account for the familiar notion of an experience. Therefore, it is not the episodes that play a role in our lives, but rather personal interpretation or construction as models, and that is the way episodes are experienced.

In addition to the subjectivity of everyday understanding of our environment, experience models also account for the nation of consciousness. The word "conscious" means that we are aware of ourselves and of our environment. Van Dijk (1998) handles another branch of models, which is description models.

Van Dijk's approach of cognitive models

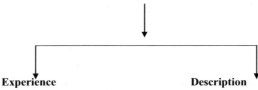

To put it simply, description models show that people do not build models of episodes in which they are engaged, but also models of those episodes they witness and especially those they hear and read about. Description models, which can be described as situation models, are needed as a basis for text production and comprehension. Description models are shaped by our experience models, because we tend to understand unfamiliar episodes in light of what we know personally.

Van Dijk (1998a) proposes a third model, which is the event models. Event models refer to any kind of models that interpret events or situations. This particular type of event model has a crucial influence on discourse and its structures, namely the communicative event or situation in which the current discourse is being produced or received. These models represent part of our personal experiences, namely, the one in which we are engaged when communicating. Context models are a specific type of experience models. That is as context models are personal, subjective and possibly biased and therefore, represent the personal interpretations of communicative events.

Context models also have the same structure as experience models, that of a setting, time, location, circumstances, participants and their various roles, and finally a communicative action. At the same time, context models explain how our personal knowledge about people, actions, events, or situations. Knowledge about an event, as represented in experience or event models, may be relatively stable across contexts. Context models typically represent the changing, ongoing nature of text production/comprehension and especially face-to-face talk.

Participants continually update and change their interpretation of the current situation and represent this in their context models. During the interpretation of discourse, context models may affect the way we represent the events talked or written about. One can figure out that models not only feature unique personal knowledge about events, but also opinions about them, That means that there is a link between ideologies and the actual social practices that construct or implement certain beliefs. It starts from the deep cultural beliefs, via group beliefs to their manifestations in social practices.

Mental Models

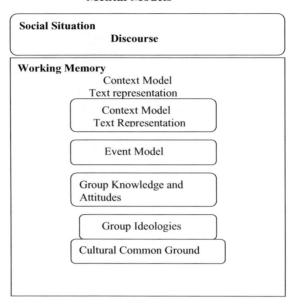

The above figure shows that mental models must be based on a system of cultural common ground, featuring shared general knowledge and attitudes and their underlying principles, such as values and cultural criteria. Groups select from this cultural base specific beliefs, and construe these beliefs with other basic principles of their group. These representations of the social mind monitor the formation of the social dimension of personal mental model in episodic memory.

Models which are controlled by group beliefs may be called ideologically "biased." The personal dimension of these mental models is monitored by old mental models "earlier experience" and by general representation of individuals. Under the constraint of context models, these personal event models and experience models may be expressed in discourse or enacted in other social practices.

Therefore, ideologies are the interface between the "social mind" shared by group members, on the one hand, and social structure, on the other hand. Models are the interface between social practices and the individuals, and so between the general embodiment and particular embodiment. Models occur between shared representations and the actual practices that appear in social and personal situations. To get more understanding of the cognitive structures in discourse, It would be important to describe the cognitive basis of social embodiment in discourse.

1.16. The Theory of Embodiment

Evans and Green (2006:44) consider embodiment as a central idea in cognitive linguistics, since the Seventeenth century French philosopher Rene Descartes developed the view that mind and body are distinct entities. There has been a common assumption within cognitive sciences that the mind can be studied without recourse to the body, and language can not be investigated in isolation from human embodiment. The idea that experience is embodied entails that we have a specific view of the world due to the unique nature of bodies. One obvious way in which our embodiment affects the nature of experience is the realm of colours. The white colours give a sense of peace and safety, while red colours give a feeling of blood and battles.

The fact that our experience is embodied through language in discourse has reflections in cognition. In other words, the concepts we have access to and the nature of reality we think and talk about are a function of our embodiment. Thus, we can only talk about what we can perceive and conceive, and the things that we can percieve derive from embodied experience. In his comment on embodied experience, Johnson (1987) proposes that there is one way in which embodied experience manifests itself at the cognitive level, which is image schemas. There are familiar concetps like, contact, container, which are meaningful because they derive from and are linked to human experience. Johnson (1987) argues that embodied concepts of this kind can be extended to provide more abstract concepts. This process is called "conceptual projection." For example, the conceptual metaphor is a form of conceptual projection. According to this view, the reason we can talk about conceptual meaning of the preposition *in* like, *in love* or *in trouble* is because of abstract concepts such as;

- A) George is in love.
- B) Amily is in trouble.
- C) The government is in deep crisis.

In the previous examples, the abstract concepts like LOVE or TROUBLE are structured and understood by virtue of the fundamental concept CONTAINER. In this way, embodied experience serves to structure more complex concepts and ideas. In this track, Mandler (2004) has made a number of proposals concerning how image schemas might arise from embodied experience. The CONTAINER image schema is supported by another enitity that contains it. In other words, the CONTAINER schemas are meaningful because containers are meaningful in our everyday experience. To explain notion of spatial scene, Tyler and Evans (2003:ix) shed lights on image schema and spatial scene as the following:

> The spatial scene relating to *in* involves a containment function, which encompasses several consequences such as locating the activities of the contained entity. Being conatined in the cup prevents the coffee from spreading out over the table.

According to the previous quotation, it is for this reason that the English preposition *in* can be used in scenes that are non-spatial in nature like the example, George is in love. It is because containers include activity that it makes sense to conceptualise power and all other abstract senses like love or crisis in terms of containment. In other words, it is experience, meaningful to all of us by our embodiment, which forms the basis of many of our most fundamental concepts. Mandler (1992:591) affirms that one of the basics of the conceptualizing capacity is the image schema. She further suggests that "basic recurrent experiences with the world form the bedrock of the child's semantic architecture." That direction of understanding the process of conceptual system obliges any researcher to have a look at the concept of image schema.

1.17. Image Schema's Theory

Johnson (1987) proposes that embodied experience gives rise to image schemas within the conceptual system. Image schemas derive from sensory and perceptual experience as we interact with the world. To explain the previous statement, humans walk upright, and we have head at the top of our bodies and feet at the bottom, given the presence of gravity which attracts unsupported objects. Therefore, we recognize HIGH as a positive word and LOW as negative word. Cognitive linguists argue that this is meaningful because of the way we interact with our environment. According to Johnson (1987), this aspect of our experience gives rise to an image schema: the UP-DOWN schema.

This means that because this experience is a function of our bodies and of our intercation in the world, this type of experience arises in conjunction with our physical and psychological development during our childhood. In other words, image schemas are most claimed to be innate knowledge structures. For example, in the early stages of development, infants learn to orient themselves in the physical world. They follow the motion objects with their eyes, and later use their hands intentionally to grasp those meaning objects. Thus, image schemas act as an interface between the body and the understanding process.

Johnson (1992: 349) explains that they are repeated patterns of physical experiences. These bodily experiences or rather micro experiences are in turn grouped into patterns which act as the raw material. For macro experience, schemas are created from the various experiences. According to Mandler (2004), image schemas like container, which is grounded in the embodied experience. They are related to and derived from sensory experience. This means that such schemas are pre-conceptual in origin, as they arise from sensory experiences in the early stages of human being's development that precede the formation of the concepts. In his comment of schemas, Johnson (1987:29) confirms that image schema is entrenched in the human body. Such schema spring from the bodily activities, and from the brain's nervous system. Schemas are active parts of one conceptual system because they are used frequently and automatically.

Thus, schemas are easily accessible cognitive tools, used unconsciously to structure one's experiences. Lakoff and Turner (1989:62) explain that schemas become conventionalized through their recurrent use, and it is a conceptual tool as it is used repeatedly, unconsciously and automatically. Image schema can not be tied to a specific image or mental picture as it is an abstract structure, grouping a number of features common to corresponding multifarious objects, actions, and activities.

In the same track, Chilton (1996:49) argues that the contact between the human body and the surrounding environment provides image schemas. He shows that such schemas act as the bases upon which human physical and social experiences are built. He also explains that social schemas are the raw material of human experiences as they organize one's experiences and infuse them with meaning.

1.17.1. Image Schema Properties

Evans and Green (2006:185) show a number of features of image schemas. First, they shed light on the relationship between mental image and image schemas as they are not the same. Mental images are detailed and resulted from conscious cognitive process that involves recalling visual memory. Image schemas are more abstract in nature, emerging from ongoing embodied experience. If a person closes his or her eyes and imagines the face of his father, child, or close friend, a specific image will come up through his or her mind. This is a mental image or image schema, which is more based on the previous experiences of any person through his social interaction.

Secondly, image schemas are multi-modals and they derive from experiences across different modalities, and hence are not specfic to a particular sense. In other words, image schemas are burried deeper within the cognitive system, being abstract patterns, arising from a vast range of perceptual experiences. For instance, blind people have access to image schemas for PATHS because the past experiences that give rise to these image schemas rely on a range of sensory-perceptual experiences in addition to vision, including hearing, touching, and other experiences of movement.

Evans and Green (2006:189) explain that there is a relation between image schemas and linguistic meaning, as image schemas can serve as the conceptual representation that underpins lexical items. For example, there is a relation between the FORCE schemas and the English modal auxiliary verbs (e.g. must, may, can). Johnson (1987) suggests that certain FORCE schemas underlie the basic or root meanings of these verbs. Such meanings are related to socio-physical experiences, as illustrated in the following sentences;

A. You **must** move your foot or the car will crush it.

   (Physical necessity)

B. You **may** now kiss the bride

   (No social barrier now prevents the bridge from being kissed by the groom)

C. John **can** throw a stick over 20 metres.

(he is physically capable of doing this)

Johnson (1987) argues that the root meaning of *must* (physical necessity) derives from the compulsion schema, while the root meaning of *may* (permission) relates to the REMOVAL OF RESTRAINT schema and the root meaning of *can* (physical capacity) derives from ENABLEMENT schema. Therefore, meanings associated with the modal verbs have an image-schematic basis which arises from embodied experience.

1.18. Conclusion

To sum up, this chapter provides a survey of critical studies and cognitive linguistics approaches in discourse analysis. First, it starts with giving a brief explanation of critical discourse analysis, historical background, as well as different approaches in critical analysis, which include; the socio-cognitive approach, historical-socio approach, and critical approach.

This chapter also sheds lights on the relationship between CDA and ideology, and the notion of racism in CDA and its classification. The concept of power and persuasion in CDA are also handled. This chapter discusses the idea of modality and its classification, the notion of speech acts and metaphor in discourse. The second part of this chapter clarifies the concept of cognitive lingusitics, the role of social cognition in discourse. It also discusses the role of memory in comprehending discourse, the mental models, and the theories of embodiment and image schema.

Chapter Two
Analysis of Martin Luther King's speeches pre-1964

0. Introduction

The language of Martin Luther King (1929-1968) is recognized around the world. The period from 1955 to 1968 has witnessed his linguistic capabilities and is described as the King years of American history. From the Montgomery bus boycott in 1955, the first civil disobedience in King's era, to the garbage workers' strike in Memphis, the last civil disobedience act in 1968, King's language occupied a central place in the American society. This is because it illuminates a set of interrelated issues that have not yet been fully investigated in his society. In addition, King employs different cognitive linguistic devices to shed light on such issues like racism, segregation and social inequality.

This chapter addresses the question of how King's mental perceptions and linguistic tools are constructed? What meanings are embedded in such constructions? In what ways are these meanings related to the creation of certain understanding of the struggle within the civil rights movement's discourse? And finally, what are the ideological meanings that can be implicitly found in his language? It is well-known that King was a brilliant orator and an activist who preached non-violence philosophy, who willingly went to jail, who had the linguistic abilities to make his society listen and take note of a problem, to understand that something was happening and led to a change in his society.

Moreover, King was a part of several historical contexts during the 1950s and 1960s in the U.S. Linguistically, King's language is a central point of the civil rights movement and it deserves attention both in the social and historical contexts. King mixes language with politics, religion, science, history to frame the images he drew in his civil rights rhetoric. Therefore, King positions himself between different cultures; not only between white and African-American cultures, but also between political, social, religious and academic cultures. Besides, King's ideological direction is placed between African-American's religious background and whites' Protestantism, between middle classes and lower classes, between the south and the north, between the spoken word and the written word.

Generally, there are two important tendencies in King's roots of his ideas, the first is based on King's focus on theology and philosophy he encountered during his graduate studies. The second tendency emphasizes his African-American heritage and affirms that any real understanding of King must involve philosophical traditions and look beyond his language to understand his view that is evolved from the black church.

2.1 The data

The data, analyzed in this chapter, and the following one consist of two main divisions of Martin Luther King's speeches which were delivered within the period (1955-1968). The selected eight speeches are classified as the pre-1964, and the post-1964. The pre-1964 speeches are analyzed in this chapter, while the post-1964 four speeches are analyzed in chapter 4. As mentioned before, The analysis is on three levels; cognitive, ideological, and linguistic.The reason for choosing the year 1964, as the dividing point, is that; King was granted the Nobel peace prize in 1964 for his efforts to make a change in his society. King's discourse became, after Nobel, more opened to international issues and handled different topics that had never been approached before.

This prize pushed King to make another shift in his thinking towards a greater understanding of the importance of the distinctive black heriatge, and a different conceptual understanding of the African-Americans' position in the U.S. society. Moreover, the strategy of King's discourse, post 1964, was to engage in a large-scale civil disobedience, make alliances among the poor in the society, regardless of race or ethnicity. In other words, King calls upon blacks to use political and economic power to achieve his discourse's goals.

The classification of King's speeches

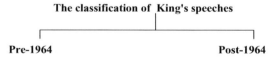

Pre-1964	Post-1964
1- Give us the ballot	1- Nobel Prize acceptance
2-The power of non-violence	2- Our God is marching on
3- I have a dream	3- Beyond Vietnam
4- Eulogy for the martyred children	4- I have been to the mountain top

2.2 The analysis of data

This chapter attempts to highlight the role of cognitive, ideological, and linguistic tools, employed by the addressor "King" to addressees "his audience" through his speeches. The analysis in this chapter follows the theoretical framework presented in chapter 1. The purpose of using cognitive, ideological, and linguistic tools is that; they help to explore how discourse participants employ such tools to influence and persuade the audience of specific ideas. Using these tools would also pave the way to understand how particular constructions serve strategic functions in the cognitive discourse. In short, these tools would help to distinguish more than one level of discourse in two different cognitive genres. The first is the mental (abstract) level and the second is the concrete (text) level in an attempt to show the interaction processes between both to create persuasive discourse.

2.2.1 Give us the ballot speech
May 17, 1957, Washington, D.C.

A) Persuading the audience

Three years ago the Supreme Court of this nation rendered in simple, eloquent, and unequivocal language a decision which will long be stenciled on the mental sheets of succeeding generations. For all men of goodwill, this May seventeenth decision came as a joyous daybreak to end the long night of human captivity. It came as a great beacon light of hope to millions of disinherited people throughout the world who had dared only to dream of freedom.

Unfortunately, this noble and sublime decision has not gone without opposition. This opposition has often risen to ominous proportions. Many states have risen up in open defiance. The legislative halls of the South ring loud with such words as interposition and nullification. But even more, all types of conniving methods are still being used to prevent Negroes from becoming registered voters. The denial of this sacred right is a tragic betrayal of the highest mandates of our democratic tradition. And so our most urgent request to the president of the United States and every member of Congress is to give us the right to vote. (Yes)

Contextual orientation

King delivers this speech in a non-violent demonstration, called The Prayer Pilgrimage for Freedom, in Washington, D.C. on May 17, 1957. It was delivered three years to the day since the United States Supreme Court had held racial segregation in public schools unconstitutional. The demonstration was held at the Lincoln Memorial in Washington, D.C. The event was chaired by Martin Luther King with the objective of accomplishing the following goals: co   e or ti   t e t ird   iver r of t e u re e Court' decision on school segregation, protesting terror and violence in the South, showing unity in the demand for civil rights legislation, and paying homage to Abraham Lincoln.

King linked the African-American struggle for human rights to independence and freedom. He also urged his listeners to be nonviolent, to love, to be understanding, to seek harmony, and to keep moving ahead with dignity, in spite of the hardships and obstacles. Martin Luther King was the main speaker and it was the first time that he addressed a national audience. It was his first Lincoln Memorial speech and he set the agenda for voting rights as an important part of the civil rights struggle against a reluctant administration. About 25,000 demonstrators attended the event to voice their opinion. At that time, the event was the largest organized demonstration for civil rights, albeit it did not fulfill the anticipated attendance.

The analysis

It is clear that Martin Luther King deliberately starts his speech by mentioning the ruling of the U.S. Supreme Court to end the racial segregation between African-Americans and White Americans in order to establish a persuasive startegy to his audience. On the cogntive level, King starts his speech by describing the decision as it comes in "*simple, eloquent, and unequivocal language,*" to show his stance that it is the right of all African-Americans to get their freedom through the ruling. On the other hand, King employs the psychological mode by saying "*decision came as a joyous daybreak to end the long night of human captivity,*" in order to win the hearts and minds of his audience by explaining that African Americans are as if they are in captivity in their society. King exploits cognitive persuasive techniques to support his arguments. On saying, *all types of conniving methods are still being used to prevent Negroes from becoming registered voters*, he attempts to build credibility "*ethos*" by using the abstract facts with reference to personal experience as an African American who does not have the legal right to vote.

Ideologically, King has in his long-term mental representation a number of social characteristics of his society like; the distinction between the African Americans and White Americans, and the suffering and oppression many African-Americans faced through the U.S. history. King employs certain ideological startegies that can be figured from his speech. On saying, *It came as a great beacon light of hope to millions of disinherited people throughout the world who had dared only to dream of freedom*, King activates an ideological strategy *rationalization* whereby King produces symbolic forms such as, *beacon light of hope*, to construct a chain of reasoning which seeks to defend and persuade his audience.

In other words, King employs a kind of mental representation to his audience through two ways, the image set by the speaker of himself as well as the content of his speech. King shows a modest image of himself as a way to be accepted by the audience. On the other hand, he manages to build credibility through cues in the message itself by means of references to real experiences of the society. King employs another way of persuasion by using the ideological strategy of *rationalization* based on self-evident truths which confirms the notion that all races are equal. King's cognitive representation is based on his episodic personal memory and his social memory. By saying *"this May seventeenth decision*," king focuses on the U.S. supreme court's decision which gives all blacks the legal rights to vote. King's cognitive level explains that his long-term memory has a social representation of racism and social inequality applied in his society.

Linguistically, King employs certain metaphorical expressions to make his message powerful to his audience and to show how strong is the decision of the supreme court in the minds of the African-Americans. He employs the process of transferrence from one domain to another by mentioning, *the mental sheets of succeeding generation, to end the long night of human captivity*. In the previous utterance, King employs anthropomorphic extension where parts of the human body are used to refer to inanimate objects. King also employs that kind of humanizing metaphorical expression in saying "*noble decision*" where he attributes a characteristic of human being to what is noble and sublime.

Clearly, all the metaphors employed in his speech are conventional ones, and it seems that King deliberately uses that style since he wants to make his message clear and vigorous without any need for an act of creativity. King uses another linguistic strategy which is indirect speech act. On saying, *It came as a great beacon light of hope to millions of disinherited people*, King employs an indirect speech act, overlapping with a direct one which is representative, as he tries to praise the decision of the US supreme court. King deliberately employs such strategy of indirect speech act and metaphorical expression to create new meanings and ideas and to find a possible way of expressing an otherwise inexpressible thought, to facilitate memorizing, to communicate meanings and thoughts, to constitute understanding, to link different domains, and to evaluate and persuade.

B) Call for political rights

Give us the ballot, and we will no longer have to worry the federal government about our basic rights. Give us the ballot (Yes), and we will no longer plead to the federal government for passage of an anti-lynching law; we will by the power of our vote write the law on the statute books of the South (All right) and bring an end to the dastardly acts of the hooded perpetrators of violence. Give us the ballot (Give us the ballot), and we will transform the salient misdeeds of bloodthirsty mobs (Yeah) into the calculated good deeds of orderly citizens.

Give us the ballot (Give us the ballot), and we will fill our legislative halls with men of goodwill (All right now) and send to the sacred halls of Congress men who will not sign a "Southern Manifesto" because of their devotion to the manifesto of justice. (Tell 'em about it) Give us the ballot (Yeah), and we will place judges on the benches of the South who will do justly and love mercy (Yeah), and we will place at the head of the southern states governors who will, who have felt not only the tang of the human, but the glow of the Divine. Give us the ballot (Yes), and we will quietly and nonviolently, without rancor or bitterness, implement the Supreme Court's decision of May seventeenth, 1954. (That's right)

The analysis

King starts the second part of his speech by using the imperative form on saying "*Give us the ballot*," in order to affirm the will and the desire of the African-Americans to make a sort of change. On ideological perspective, King addresses the minds of his white and black audience as a means to control and challenge their stagnant beliefs. He makes use of the reactionary mental techniques which is based on the action and its repercussions. When king says "*Give us the ballot*," he puts the result of giving the ballot to all blacks which is "*they will no longer have to worry the federal government, no longer plead to the federal government for passage of anti-lynching law, will transform the salient misdeeds of bloodthirsty mobs.*"

All of king's arguments are directed towards justifying the African-American rights, while his refutations attempt to eradicate the prevalent pro-segregation theories. King aims at legitimizing the blacks' rights to have their legal rights for voting, and he does so in the form of metaphorical expressions like "*we will transform the salient misdeeds of bloodthirsty mobs into calculated good deeds, their devotion to the manifesto of justice*," which play an important role of conveying conceptual levels of various meanings.

From a cognitive view, by showing his insistence on the African-American rights, king strongly confirms the concept of *social schemes*. This is clearly shown by the cognitive structures which represent king's knowledge of social schemas stored in his memory and based on past experience. King's cognitive style enables him to facilitate and determine encoding of new approach to handle specific issues in his society.

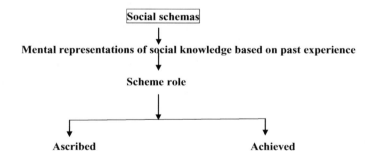

King employs both the ascribed and achieved roles. The ascribed role is acquired by King because of his race, thus he dedicated his speech to defend the rights of the African-Americans. The achieved role, on the other hand, is employed by King's efforts to organize such event to convey his message in a way that makes his audience acquire strong expectation. King employs the utterance "*give us the ballot*," six times as a kind of deliberate repitition to confirm his intention. He bases his strategy on four main principles: *rehearsal, encoding, elaboration and retrieval.*

By saying, *Give us the ballot, and we will no longer have to worry the federal government about our basic rights,* King employs the cognitive tachnique of *Rehearsal* in which King activates the initial information in his short-term memory. *Encoding* refers to the mental operations performed on information arriving in the sensory systems in his mind. By saying, *we will no longer plead to the federal government for passage of an anti-lynching law*, King establishes a linkage between the new information of demanding the legal rights for all African-Americans, and the previous stored information about slavery. This link represents the strategy of *elaboration*, which seems to be especially effective at promoting long-term storage of new information. By delivering these words, *Give us the ballot (Yes), and we will quietly and nonviolently, without rancor or bitterness, implement the Supreme Court's decision of May seventeenth, 1954*, King employs the strategy of *retrieval* in which he refers to the process of bringing information out of his memory for a specific target, that is equality.

On the linguistic level, modality is obviously employed to reveal his power of certainty and ability. First, the use of "*will*" in his utterance "*we will no longer have to worry the federal government, we will transform the slaient misdeeds, we will fill our legislative halls, we will place judges, we will quietly and nonviolently without rancor or bitterness implement the supreme courts,*" embodies certainty and power. He repeats such modal in paralleling structure as he presents his audience with the only key that could help in explaining the social situation. King employs clearly the root modal "*will*" to express the social interaction and his determination to confront the social status in his society. He uses a specific persuasive strategy in his speech which is *presentational* persuasion as he uses the metaphors, emotions and involvement.

King clearly uses creative types of metaphors such as "*bloodthirsty mobs, sacred halls,*" as their meanings are expanded in language and need an act of creativity. That means the bloodthirsty mobs could be those who deny the rights of the African-Americans and they are so determined on that denial. The speaker could also mean that those white southerners are very aggressive to the extent of being bloodthirsty creatures. Under any circumstance, King uses the metaphorical process "tenor" and "vehicle". Tenor is employed by referring to those who stand against the freedom and equality of African-Americans. In other words, tenor is the original element that is compared to another object from a different domain.

On the other hand, vehicle is the borrowed enitity in terms of which meaning is presented. In saying "*the manifesto of justice*," King uses that kind of concrete to abstract metaphor. He links the word "*manifesto*" with the word "*justice*" to show his deep appreciation to justice and equality. Obviously, King uses that kind of metaphors as they are very efficient tool in communication. They help in overcoming the human problems of limited active memory and also enable the speaker to convey large chunks of information through few words.

Table (1) Concordance of the pronoun "We"

Context	Word	Context
Give us the ballot	we	Will no longer have to
Give us the ballot (Yes)	we	And will no longer plead to
passage of an anti-lynching law	we	will by the power of
(Give us the ballot), and	we	will transform the salient misdeeds
(Give us the ballot), and	we	will fill our legislative halls
Give us the ballot (Yeah), and	we	will place judges on the benches of the South
and love mercy (Yeah), and	we	will place at the head
Give us the ballot and	we	will quietly and nonviolently,

Table (1) shows that the total frequency of "*We*" is 8, which is indicative in the production of mental persuasive strategy since it shows the shared responsibility of African Americans to face the social inequality.

C) The need for strong leadership

In this juncture of our nation's history, there is an urgent need for dedicated and courageous leadership. If we are to solve the problems ahead and make racial justice a reality, this leadership must be fourfold. First, there is need for strong, aggressive leadership from the federal government. So far, only the judicial branch of the government has evinced this quality of leadership. If the executive and legislative branches of the government were as concerned about the protection of our citizenship rights as the federal courts have been, then the transition from a segregated to an integrated society would be infinitely smoother. But we so often look to Washington in vain for this concern. In the midst of the tragic breakdown of law and order, the executive branch of the government is all too silent and apathetic. In the midst of the desperate need for civil rights legislation, the legislative branch of the government is all too stagnant and hypocritical.

This dearth of positive leadership from the federal government is not confined to one particular political party. Both political parties have betrayed the cause of justice. (Oh yes) The Democrats have betrayed it by capitulating to the prejudices and undemocratic practices of the southern Dixiecrats. The Republicans have betrayed it by capitulating to the blatant hypocrisy of right wing, reactionary northerners. These men so often have a high blood pressure of words and an anemia of deeds. [laughter]

In the midst of these prevailing conditions, we come to Washington today pleading with the president and members of Congress to provide a strong, moral, and courageous leadership for a situation that cannot permanently be evaded. We come humbly to say to the men in the forefront of our government that the civil rights issue is not an Ephemeral, evanescent domestic issue that can be kicked about by reactionary guardians of the status quo; it is rather an eternal moral issue which may well determine the destiny of our nation (Yeah) in the ideological struggle with communism. The hour is late. The clock of destiny is ticking out. We must act now, before it is too late.

A second area in which there is need for strong leadership is from the white northern liberals. There is a dire need today for a liberalism which is truly liberal. What we are witnessing today in so many northern communities is a sort of quasi-liberalism which is based on the principle of looking sympathetically at all sides. It is a liberalism so bent on seeing all sides, that it fails to become committed to either side. It is a liberalism that is so objectively analytical that it is not subjectively committed. It is a liberalism which is neither hot nor cold, but lukewarm. (All right) We call for a liberalism from the North which will be thoroughly committed to the ideal of racial justice and will not be deterred by the propaganda and subtle words of those who say: "Slow up for a while; you're pushing too fast."

A third source that we must look to for strong leadership is from the moderates of the white South. It is unfortunate that at this time the leadership of the white South stems from the close-minded reactionaries. These persons gain prominence and power by the dissemination of false ideas and by deliberately appealing to the deepest hate responses within the human mind. It is my firm belief that this close-minded, reactionary, recalcitrant group constitutes a numerical minority.

The analysis

King cognitively moves to another part of his speech which is the need for strong leadership to support the legal rights of his race. He explains that through his cognitive strategy of *quasilogical* persuasion which is based on the notion that the key to the persuasiveness of an argument is the logical sequence of ideas. That is strongly mentioned by using the ordinal number "*first, second, third.*" He confirms his persuasive strategy of *pathos*. By saying "*both political parties have betrayed the course of justice,*" he influences the audience emotionally by motivating the listeners to accept the proposed arguments. King succeeds in such strategy, especially the response of his audience is a positive one which is "*oh yes.*" Based on the mental representations and his previous experience, King employs a certain type of *social schemas*, which is the role schemes

Social schemas

Role schemes

By taking the position of the African-American leader, King takes the stance of *role schemes* which determine his expected behavior in a particular social situation. Being an African-American, King takes the *ascribed role* automatically because of his race. On the other hand, King activates the *achieved role* in this part of his speech as he shows himself as the pusher and supporter for the dreams and hopes pursued by his followers. He employs the body metaphors in saying "*soul force, matriculate into the university of eternal life*," which enforces a connection between the human body and the social affairs as a cognitive way in his episodic memory to shed lights on the moral and social problems in his society

On the ideological level, King employs the ideological strategy of narrativzation by repetition, which is also employed through the simple and complex lexical levels. King repeats the words "*government, liberalism, leadership, liberal*," as a simple lexical repetition. Simple paraphrasing strategy is also employed in using the word "*evaded*" in the utterance "*permanently be evaded,*" and the verb "*kicked*" in the utterance "*can be kicked about by reactionary guardian*," and the gerunds "*witnessing, seeing*." Obviously, King applies that kind of repetition, namely, lexical and paraphrase to confirm his strategy of *narrativzation* which involves reference to the historical and traditional aspects of a community in a society to create a sense of belonging and loyalty. By stating that "*both political parties have betrayed the cause of justice*," King asserts the strategy *naturalization* as he mentions the state of African-American affairs as a kind of natural status.

King explains clearly the distinction between the two main branches in his society as negro and white in the utterance "*whether he be negro or white*." It seems that King deliberately activates the use of the word *"negro"* to refer to a permanent and unchanging status of his race under the coverage of cognitive *externalization*. *Passivization* technique is another process that has been frequently employed in his utterance "*there is the danger that those of us who have been forced so long to stand, who have been trampled over, who have been kicked about,*" in which the attention of the hearer or the reader is focused on certain themes at the expense of the subject. King uses such strategy to focus the attention of his audience on the theme and strengthen their conviction that they must take a serious action towards the social prejudice.

On the linguistic level, King attempts to influence his audience, so he heavily uses the modal verb "*must"* as a root modal that might reveal his social interaction. It also expresses his control over events occurring in his society. King employs *"must*" to reflect the certainty of the fact that the African-

American race has potential power. The repetition of the modal verb shows a high degree of assurance. King employs the first person plural pronoun "*we*" to show the sense of group work and the joint responsibility that should be shouldered by all African-Americans. By saying, *This dearth of positive leadership,* king employs a direct speech act which is assertive, as he expresses a real fact in his society. He also activates in the same statement an indirect speech act, which is expressive, as he is blaming the federal government for being ineffective. This shows that speech acts types can overlap when they come to the functional approach.

D) A call for equality

We must meet hate with love. (Yeah) We must meet physical force with soul force. There is still a voice crying out through the vista of time, saying: Love your enemies (Yeah), bless them that curse you (Yes), pray for them that despitefully use you. (That's right, All right) Then, and only then, can you matriculate into the university of eternal life. That same voice cries out in terms lifted to cosmic proportions: "He who lives by the sword will perish by the sword." (Yeah, Lord) And history is replete with the bleached bones of nations (Yeah) that failed to follow this command. (All right) We must follow nonviolence and love. (Yes, Lord)

There is another warning signal. We talk a great deal about our rights, and rightly so. We proudly proclaim that three-fourths of the peoples of the world are colored. We have the privilege of noticing in our generation the great drama of freedom and independence as it unfolds in Asia and Africa. But we must not, however, remain satisfied with a court victory over our white brothers.

And those of us who call the name of Jesus Christ find something of an event in our Christian faith that tells us this. There is something in our faith that says to us, "Never despair; never give up; never feel that the cause of righteousness and justice is doomed." There is something in our Christian faith, at the center of it, which says to us that Good Friday may occupy the throne for a day, but ultimately it must give way to the triumphant beat of the drums of Easter. (That's right) There is something in our faith that says evil may so shape events that Caesar will occupy the palace and Christ the cross (That's right), but one day that same Christ will rise up and split history into A.D. and

B.C. *(Yes),* so that even the name, the life of Caesar must be dated by his name. *(Yes)*

The analysis

In his mental representation, King shows that the struggle against segregation is not a struggle between white and black or between individuals, but is a struggle between the forces of good/light and the forces of evil/darkness. On saying "*our white brother,*" King expresses that the struggle is ultimately about values. The core of King's notion of describing whites as "*brother*s" and his tendency for getting the rights of African-Americans by non-violence strategy contains and creates this idealistic effect. The goal in his schemata is to reach the real conscience of the evil doer and thereby change him and his activities. Changing the conscience of the white is also another point for what social change is as expressed in King's notion of reality. King's objection to the white hegemony in the society reflects the ideological effects of this notion which is based on change. .

Cognitively, in his mental representation of change, King reflects his *person schemas* through his attitude which stresses the possibility of positive change and speaks of the creative ability of humanity to give birth to something new. In his perspective, man has the ability to make change as he can use non-violence strategy to make it real. King focuses on the religious concepts in his speech for certain purposes. Not only does he employ that to legitimize his view, but also to symbolize, and in some cases, to serve as the core of his argument. He also uses an idealistic level of meaning to place the struggle of the movement in the right directions. Therefore, he uses the words "*Christ, Caesar,*" to reinforce the image of himself as a leader who both embraces and represents his beliefs and knowledge.

King speaks from a position where he has access to the knowledge in the same way that the preacher has access to the word of God and is able to interpret it to his audience. He employs the imperative forms in saying "*Go out with that faith today, stand up for justice, let nothing slow you up,*" to strengthen the strategy of *unification*. King's practice of using repetitions and imperative forms is ultimately tied to the dichotomy between sameness and differences that is central in King's mental level. If he is to be an effective leader, he needs to balance between two concepts in his society. The first concept is the American achievement to evoke the common identity of humanity, and the second is the racial discrimination in the American society.

When King delivers this speech, his long term memory is full of the concepts of segregation and racism in his society. He clearly activates certain types of schema to convey his view to his audience. On repeating the pronoun *"we"* in the utterance *"We proudly proclaim that three-fourths of the peoples of the world are colored. We have the privilege of noticing in our generation the great drama of freedom and independence as it unfolds in Asia and Africa,"* King refers to the African American character as *person schema*. He creates the strategy of *categorization* by describing them as one people. King attempts to use another cognitive strategy of *self-schemas* as he employs the generalization of social imbalance in the structures of American society.

King uses the *retrieval* strategy in which he reminds his audience of religious senses and links them with racism to evoke the emotional aspects of his audience. So, he links what he has in his mind with the current situation and connects the old information in his long-term memory (slavery, segregation, oppression) with the information in the short-term memory (racism and social inequality). That kind of describing the mental operations by connecting the short and long-term memories is known as encoding,

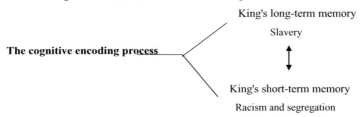

It is important to mention that King uses the religious sense by quoting certain verses from the bible. God is a constant reference point in the definitions of King's identity and is present in King's rhetoric, either through himself as "*God*" or through the concepts that are explained in his speech like "*love, justice and absolute morality.*" When King mentions that "*There is something in our faith that says to us, never despair; never give up; never feel that the cause of righteousness and justice is doomed,*" he shows his insistence on the divine principles which helps him in many aspects to persuade his audience.

The most typical example of such aspects is the strong link between evil and segregation since it deprives the individual of his or her worth as a person. When King uses such religious values, they enable him to attack segregation not only morally but also in a cognitive religious sense that went beyond the daily life experiences of whites and blacks. King combines the social schemas represented by his mental categories about the tragic events and his use of religious representation as ethical strategy.

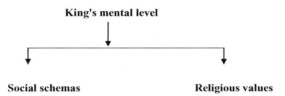

King simply mentions such combination of social and religious values and then places them before his audience as an example of how a truly righteous life should be lived. This strategy works as an incitement to act against the social inequality and as a confirmation that the ways of the struggle and the struggle itself are righteous. King defines the role of religious concepts on the macro level, and the prestigious position of the church in the context of racial tension to show that church is the source and upholder of divine ethics and morality.

From ideological view, King activates the stored information in the long-term memories of his audience. He employs the ideological strategy of *unification* by employing the symbols of unity based on the historical and legal rights in saying "*we talk a great deal about our rights and rightly so.*" He uses the grandiose words to describe their rights as important and motivate the masses of civil rights activists and to interpret the struggle in such a way that it can be accessible to as many as possible. King's use of rhetoric expresses a logic that in a comprehensive way defines real social stance in all its aspects. That clearly proves that King employs the *quasilogical persuasion* based on creating rhetorical impression that makes his argument to be logically incontrovertible

One of the ideological effects of King's discourse is that; it is connected with equality and justice. On saying *"go back to your homes in the southland to that faith, go back to Philadelphia, to New York, to Detroit and Chicago, Egypt and Red Sea,"* King reveals another area of his cognitive level, which contains definitions of what history is. Historical change is closely associated with progress, which King ties to a sense of the rationality of history. King uses that strategy to uphold and construct the assumption that right and wrong "*good and evil*" are real entities. King's insists on the concept of determined personality on saying *"But I say to you this afternoon: keep moving. Let nothing slow you up. Move on with dignity and honor and responsibility*," as he shows that the divine value of personality provides him with many ways to be used in several aspects of the civil rights movement discourse. The most typical being the strong link between evil and segregation since it deprives the individual of his worth as a person

Therefore, when King delivers this speech, he shows two major responsibilities. First, is to heal the broken-hearted people, and second is to free the people. By saying, *We proudly proclaim that three-fourths of the peoples of the world are colored,* King uses the persuasive tactics by combining the emotional aspects of Jesus' story with the logical concepts. Thus, King employs the *positive self-presentation* strategy by using the direct speech act "assertive", which is based on historical facts, religious concepts. King shows the threads of power that become more evident and quite stronger in the second part of his speeches.

King creates a link between himself, as a participant in the struggle, and the educated white north. This leads to further expansion of the mental representation regarding the position of the white ideology explained by King's discourse. To put it bluntly, he speaks the language of the oppressor and thereby become identified with it. It seems that King's struggle as a leader of the civil rights movement took place in a context that was larger than the fierce opposition of the white mobs who confronted the activists. This context includes an America divided into a supposedly racist south and a supposedly anti-racist liberal north.

Table (2): Concordance of the modal verb "Must"

Context	Word	Context
We	must	meet hate with love
We	must	meet physical force with soul
We	must	follow nonviolence and love.
But we	must	not, however, remain satisfied with a court victory
ultimately it	must	give way to the triumphant beat
the life of Caesar	must	be dated by his name

Table (2) shows that the total frequency of "must" is 6, which is indicative in the discourse of calling for equality to achieve his purpose of encouraging his followers of their rights and increases his cognitive ideological strategy of unification.

2.2.2. The power of non-violence speech
June 4, 1957

A) Calling for non-violence strategy

From the very beginning there was a philosophy undergirding the Montgomery boycott, the philosophy of nonviolent resistance. There was always the problem of getting this method over because it didn't make sense to most of the people in the beginning. We had to use our mass meetings to explain nonviolence to a community of people who had never heard of the philosophy and in many instances were not sympathetic with it. We had meetings twice a week on Mondays and on Thursdays, and we had an institute on nonviolence and social change. We had to make it clear that nonviolent resistance is not a method of cowardice. It does resist. It is not a method of stagnant passivity and deadening complacency. The nonviolent resister is just as opposed to the evil that he is standing against as the violent resister but he resists without violence. This method is non aggressive physically but strongly aggressive spiritually.

Another thing that we had to get over was the fact that the nonviolent resister does not seek to humiliate or defeat the opponent but to win his friendship and understanding. This was always a cry that we had to set before people that our aim is not to defeat the white community, not to humiliate the white community, but to win the friendship of all of the persons who had perpetrated this system in the past. The end of violence or the aftermath of violence is bitterness. The aftermath of nonviolence is reconciliation and the creation of a beloved community. A boycott is never an end within itself. It is merely a means to awaken a sense of shame within the oppressor but the end is reconciliation, the end is redemption.

Contextual orientation

According to the online encyclopedia "Wikipedia," on December 1st, 1955, Rosa Parks, a 40 year old black seamstress, was arrested for refusing to give up her seat to a white man on the bus in Montgomery, Alabama. Park's was a violation of the city's racial segregation laws. The successful Montgomery Bus Boycott, organized by Martin Luther King, was followed by Park's historic act of civil disobedience.

According to a Montgomery city ordinance in 1955, African Americans were required to sit at the back of public buses and were also obligated to give up those seats to white riders if the front of the bus filled up. Parks was in the first row of the black section when the white driver demanded to give up her seat to a white man. Because of her refusal, Parks was put in jail at the end. Meanwhile, local civil rights' leaders had been planning for a boycott as a challenge to Montgomery's racist bus laws for several months.

The boycott stretched on for more than a year, and participants carpooled or walked miles to work when no other means were possible. As African Americans previously constituted 70 percent of the Montgomery bus ridership, the municipal transit system suffered gravely during the boycott. In November, 1956, the U.S. Supreme Court declared that Alabama state bus segregation's laws as being in violation to the U.S. Constitution. On December 20, 1956, Montgomery's buses were desegregated and the Montgomery Bus Boycott was called off after 381 days.

The boycott resulted in the activation of the U.S. civil rights movement which received one of its first victories and gave Martin Luther King the national attention that made him one of the prime leaders of the cause. The black community did not use violence to protest bus segregation, but rather a non-violent strategy. They simply stopped using the bus system to show that they weren't going to be treated unfairly, by the community, government and bus system. Every week the black community used to meet at the First Baptist Church and have a meeting about the protest. These gatherings were the inspiration and the backbone of the Boycott.

When Martin Luther King delivers such speech, he captures the attention of the nation with his philosophy and commitment to the method of nonviolent resistance. Based on King's evaluation, this was the only solution that could cure ociet ' evil d cre te ju t ociet . A i e er ed   leader in the civil rights movement, he put his belief into action and proved that this was an effective method to combat racial segregation.

The analysis

On The cognitive level, King moves from the physical struggle to the cognitive one by mentioning, *this method is non aggressive physically but strong by aggressive spiritually.* King shows that the cognitive structures which represent the whites' knowledge about African Americans are that; blacks use the physical power to get their ends meet. By saying, *There was always the problem of getting this method over because it didn't make sense to most of the people in the beginning,* King activates self schema which is obviously used through the generalizations based on the past experiences of the African Americans.

In his mental representation, King attempts to transform the ideas of non-violence struggle by winning the friendship of the whites and activating the real concepts of reconciliation into concrete concepts. He employs the strategy of *objectification* through two main channels. The first one is ontologising, which means that the physical properties are represented by abstract ideas. That is clear on saying, *a cry that we had to set,* as he attempts to make "cry" to be a physical concept that needed to be set. The second one is *personification*, which is shown by the person to represent ideas. That is clear in King's way of personifying the concept of boycott with a human being who can awaken a sense of shame within the oppressor.

That kind of personification is employed to persuade his audience and mentally evokes their positive attitudes, feelings, and beliefs towards white people. Clearly, the ideological basis for using personification is to arouse empathy for a social group evaluated as heroic, or to arouse opposition towards a specific group that is evaluated as villainous. King uses this strategy by associating the black peoples and their beliefs that are positively evaluated, with heroic human attributes, such as friendship and reconciliation. King also associates negative specific ideas with villainous attributes such as violence and aggression. This process activates a mental representation comprised of three images;

A) The hero
B) The villain
C) The victim

King's use of cognitive frame is the one in which civil rights movement is the hero, racist whites are the villains, blacks and other colored people in the American society are the victims. It seems that what is important in King's value judgments is the creation of a polar contrast between forces of good, represented by blacks, and evil, represented by whites.

On the ideological level, by repeating the pronoun "*we*," King shows two processes which are employed in his speech. The first process is *standardization* in which he uses symbolic forms "*friendship, reconciliation*" to make his argument being acceptable. The second one is the *symbolization of unity* which involves binding the ideas of the people to face the segregation.

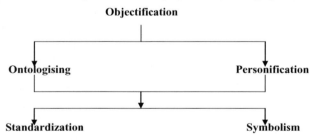

King stresses in his speech the importance and effectiveness of non-violence strategy to convince his black audience about it. Therefore, by saying "*From the very beginning there was a philosophy undergirding the Montgomery boycott, the philosophy of nonviolent resistance,*" he employs the ideological mode, *rationalization* and *narrativization* based on the common dreams, values, and shared history. His illumination of African American history is deliberately employed to get his audience's persuasion. When King says "*we had an institute on non violence, we had to make it clear,*" he employs the ideological strategy of *unification* by the constant reference to first person plural pronoun "*we.*"

On the linguistic level, King employs the functional level of the modal "*had to*" as a root modal, which shows his growing power as it expresses certain kinds of moral or ethical obligation on the part of the receivers (Palmer, 1979:121). This is clear in, *we had to make it clear,* in which king repeats the modal "*had to*" for two functions. The first expresses a high degree of certainty about non-violence philosophy which is the inevitable way for every African-American to get their rights. The second one denotes moral obligation which reveals the authority of the speaker. He directs his audience to a certain type of behavior, which is embodied in his utterance, *non-violent resister does not seek to humiliate of defeat the opponent but to win friendship and understanding.* King employs the cognitive strategy of positive presentation through certain features like the historical facts, spiritual power, and personification of non-violence strategy.

B) The philosophy of non-violence

Then we had to make it clear also that the nonviolent resister seeks to attack the evil system rather than individuals who happen to be caught up in the system. And this is why I say from time to time that the struggle in the South is not so much the tension between white people and Negro people. The struggle is rather between justice and injustice, between the forces of light and the forces of darkness. And if there is a victory it will not be a victory merely for fifty thousand Negroes. But it will be a victory for justice, a victory for good will, a victory for democracy.

Another basic thing we had to get over is that nonviolent resistance is also an internal matter. It not only avoids external violence or external physical violence but also internal violence of spirit. And so at the center of our movement stood the philosophy of love. The attitude that the only way to ultimately change humanity and make for the society that we all long for is to keep love at the center of our lives. Now people used to ask me from the beginning what do you mean by love and how is it that you can tell us to love those persons who seek to defeat us and those persons who stand against us; how can you love such persons? And I had to make it clear all along that love in its highest sense is not a sentimental sort of thing, not even an affectionate sort of thing.

The analysis

Ideologically, King starts the second part of the above mentioned speech by emphasizing two important concepts, the first one is that; the African-Americans' struggle should not be based on the explicit level, namely between blacks and whites, but rather between the justice and injustice or between *"the forces of light and the forces of darkness."* The second concept is that; non-violence strategy is not only external physical strategy, but also an internal spiritual philosophy which is based on love. King makes the best use of ideological strategy of *fragmentation* which is based on dividing concepts into various divisions *(explained more in Chapter1, P31)*.

He aims at making his audience conscious of the equal distribution of power by contrasting the privileges and rights of the white race with those of the blacks on saying, *between justice and injustice, light and darkness.* King uses these contrasting concepts as a means to illuminate the difference in status between the two races with the hope of changing the consciousness of the white audience to activate his cognitive strategy of *fragmentation*. King uses the differentiation style between blacks and whites by the contrasting terms *"darkness and light"* and the strategy of expurgating the others by saying *"to attack the evil."*

On the linguistic level, to make his speech persuasive and effective, King employs concrete to abstract metaphors in the phrases, *forces of light, forces of darkness, violence of spirit,* as they create feelings of solidarity and encourage resistance of short-term suffering for the purpose of achieving long-term political objectives. King uses his audience's familiarity with race as a way of predicting the success of non-violence strategy practiced by civil rights movement. The cognitive and ideological motivation originated in King's use of that kind of metaphors is that; African Americans are a chosen people who are escaping from a place of oppression and social inequality towards the Promised Land.

For King, concrete to abstract metaphors are used as an effective rhetorical strategy since they raise the expectations of confrontation and do not promise short-term attainment of political and social goals. When King says, *the struggle is rather between justice and injustice,* he uses the value of antithesis which activates our knowledge of African-American struggle to assess political choices. African Americans, in King's view, have the opportunity to decide between continuing on the journey to get their rights or stopping. King's rhetoric supports the first choice of continuing in favor of achieving, *victory for justice, a victory for good will, a victory for democracy.* In the previous utterance, there are three quite rhetorical techniques in combination; metaphor, repetition and contrast. It is the interaction of these different techniques that adds momentum to his argument in a way that is effective.

C) Determination to achieve the goal

I am quite aware of the fact that there are persons who believe firmly in nonviolence who do not believe in a personal God, but I think every person who believes in nonviolent resistance believes somehow that the universe in some form is on the side of justice. That there is something unfolding in the universe whether one speaks of it as a unconscious process, or whether one speaks of it as some unmoved mover, or whether someone speaks of it as a personal God. There is something in the universe that unfolds for justice and so in Montgomery we felt somehow that as we struggled we had cosmic companionship. And this was one of the things that kept the people together, the belief that the universe is on the side of justice. God grant that as men and women all over the world struggle against evil systems they will struggle with love in their hearts, with understanding good will. Agape says you must go on with wise restraint and calm reasonableness but you must keep moving.

We have a great opportunity in America to build here a great nation, a nation where all men live together as brothers and respect the dignity and worth of all human personality. We must keep moving toward that goal. I know that some people are saying we must slow up. They are writing letters to the North and they are appealing to white people of good will and to the Negroes saying slow up, you're pushing too fast. They are saying we must adopt a policy of moderation. Now if moderation means moving on with wise restraint and calm reasonableness, then moderation is a great virtue that all men of good will must seek to achieve in this tense period of transition.

But if moderation means slowing up in the move for justice and capitulating to the whims and caprices of the guardians of the deadening status quo, then moderation is a tragic vice which all men of good will must condemn. We must continue to move on. Our self respect is at stake; the prestige of our nation is at stake. Civil rights is an eternal moral issue which may well determine the destiny of our civilization in the ideological struggle with communism. We must keep moving with wise restraint and love and with proper discipline and dignity.

The analysis

King starts the third part by employing the ideological unified stance based on the fact that all peoples, whether they are religious or not, have the same concept of justice. King uses the ideological mode of unification through two elements, the first is standardization by saying, *We have a great opportunity in America to build here a great nation,* as he uses standardized unifying concepts for his audience. The second element is symbolism by saying, *Our self respect is at stake; the prestige of our nation is at stake,* as he attempts to use symbolic concepts like linking the self respect with the prestige of the nation. King builds mental representation by involving his audience in his cause. He establishes the mental control by making the two races share a common ground. King affirms that the common ground is represented by one concept which is justice, the greatness of America, moving forward to achieve the goal of equality. Moreover, King resorts to the *unification* strategy when he refers to his country and his people as, *where all men live together as brothers and respect the dignity and worth of all human personality.*

King moves on to another ideological strategy of universalization (Chapter 1, page 30) in which he uses certain concepts held by all individuals in the society. That is clear on saying, *we felt somehow that as we struggled we had cosmic companionship,* as he uses universal concepts which are shared by most strugglers. The essence of universalization is to identify a set of common values regarding the social status quo in his social background because these values form the basis for political action. Therefore, king tries to be persuasive by combining universal concepts with the moral struggle such as anger and resentment. These concepts evoke strong feelings of antipathy towards an entity which African-Americans identify as the enemy or the villain. King also evokes strong feelings of loyalty and affection towards a "*hero*" represented by black race.

On the linguistic level, when King says, *they will struggle with love in their hearts*, he employs synaesthesia metaphor in which the words are transferred from one sense to another. In the previous statement, King attempts to combine human features "*struggle*" with another sense "*love.*" It is important to mention that King uses that kind of metaphor on two levels; first by relating abstract notions of life experience into concrete realities and making the abstract ideology accessible. King is usually effective in making the abstract concepts seem concrete and responsive to real human emotions. Hence, he enhances his legitimacy and ability to persuade his audience.

2.2.3. I have a dream speech
August 28, 1963. Washington D.C.

A) Revolution against oppression

I am happy to join with you today in what will go down in history as the greatest demonstration for freedom in the history of our nation. Five score years ago, a great American, in whose symbolic shadow we stand signed the Emancipation Proclamation. This momentous decree came as a great beacon light of hope to millions of Negro slaves who had been seared in the flames of withering injustice. It came as a joyous daybreak to end the long night of captivity. But one hundred years later, we must face the tragic fact that the Negro is still not free. One hundred years later, the life of the Negro is still sadly crippled by the manacles of segregation and the chains of discrimination. One hundred years later, the Negro lives on a lonely island of poverty in the midst of a vast ocean of material prosperity. One hundred years later, the Negro is still languishing in the corners of American society and finds himself an exile in his own land. So we have come here today to dramatize an appalling condition.

It is obvious today that America has defaulted on this promissory note insofar as her citizens of color are concerned. Instead of honoring this sacred obligation, America has given the Negro people a bad check which has come back marked "insufficient funds." But we refuse to believe that the bank of justice is bankrupt. We refuse to believe that there are insufficient funds in the great vaults of opportunity of this nation. So we have come to cash this check -- a check that will give us upon demand the riches of freedom and the security of justice. We have also come to this hallowed spot to remind America of the fierce urgency of now. This is no time to engage in the luxury of cooling off or to take the tranquilizing drug of gradualism. Now is the time to rise from the dark and desolate valley of segregation to the sunlit path of racial justice. Now is the time to open the doors of opportunity to all of God's children. Now is the time to lift our nation from the quicksands of racial injustice to the solid rock of brotherhood.

Contextual orientation

This speech was delivered in a large political rally called the March on Washington for jobs and freedom that took place in Washington, D.C. on August 28, 1963. Martin Luther King delivered his historic "I Have a Dream" speech advocating racial harmony at the Lincoln Memorial during the march. The march was organized by a group of civil rights, labor, and religious organizations, under the theme "jobs and freedom." Estimates of the number of participants varied from 200,000 to over 300,000. About eighty percent of the marchers were African Americans and twenty percent were white and other ethnic groups. The march was extensively covered by the media, with live international television coverage.

The march is widely credited as helping to pass the Civil Rights Act (1964) and the National Voting Rights Act (1965). At the time of delivering such speech, American outrage was sparked by media coverage of police actions in Birmingham, Alabama, where attack dogs and fire hoses were turned against protestors, many of whom were in their early teens. Martin Luther King was arrested and jailed during these protests, writing his famous "Letter From Birmingham City Jail," in which he advocates civil disobedience against unjust laws. Dozens of additional demonstrations took place across the country, from California to New York, culminating in the March on Washington.

President Kennedy backed a Civil Rights Act, which was stalled in Congress. President Kennedy originally discouraged the march, for fear that it might make the legislature vote against civil rights laws. Once it became clear that the march would go on, however, he supported it. The march did, nevertheless, make specific demands: an end to racial segregation in public school; meaningful civil rights legislation, including a law prohibiting racial discrimination in employment. The demands also include protection of civil rights workers from police brutality; a $2 minimum wage for all workers.

The tangible manifestation of the change was quick in coming. Less than a year after the march, President Lyndon Johnson signed the 1964 Civil Rights Act, which banned discrimination in public facilities, such as hotels and restaurants, and also prohibited employment discrimination. The following year, the Voting Rights Act was enacted to ensure that African Americans had the right to vote. In 1968, Congress passed the Fair Housing Act to remove discrimination in buying and renting houses. This landmark legislation was complemented by new policies, such as affirmative action, designed to counter the legacy of discrimination and to promote African American advancement.

The analysis

King starts his greatest speech in his lifetime by using the cognitive strategy of *objectification* as he attempts to turn the complex and abstract ideas and social concepts of racism into specific concrete images, and thus making them easier to understand. King employs three ways of objectification; ontologising, figuration and personification (explained in Chapter1). Ontologising is clearly activated by showing the physical entities of certain cognitive ideas. That is clearly mentioned through using the words, *Negro, slaves, segregation, captivity*, which reveal the stored information in King's long-term memory.

Cognitively, King also employs cognitive images by describing the status of African-Americans as he mentions "*one hundred years later, the life of the negro is still sadly crippled by the manacles of segregation and the chains of discrimination, the Negro lives on a lonely island of poverty, the Negro is still languishing in the corners of American society.*" In the previous utterance, King uses the images and pictures he holds in his mind. So, he employs the *figuration* strategy to convey a mental level of his imagination to his audience. To make his strategy of objectification clearer, which is based on making complicated ideas to be understandable, King employs the personification mode by referring to specific persons "negro" to represent his ideas. King employs the two main branches of *personification*, namely the *strong positive evaluation* and *strong negative evaluation*. The positive one is represented through the words "*beacon light of hope, material prosperity, the riches of freedom,*" in which King carries strong expressive attitudes and apply them to the African-American ideological basis.

Therefore, the basis for using the positive evaluation is to increase empathy for his race and also to arouse opposition towards the whites. Within personification, King uses the second branch which is: *strong negative evaluation* in repeating the negative words in "*Negro, slave, captivity.*" King intelligently mixes legitimating strategy with unification concepts. In order to show his determination and power, King employs symbolic forms that construct a chain of reasonings to defend his view. On saying, *Negro lives on a lonely island of poverty in the midest of vast ocean of material prosperity*, King attempts to be very reasonable as he refers to a stark contradiction between the prosperous materialistic life in the U.S. and the terrible status of African-Americans. King also employs universal concepts of equality and freedom as he clearly opposes any kind of segregation and discrimination on saying, *the manacles of segregation and the chains of discrimination*.

To strengthen his ideology, king begins his speech by a historical reference to the African-American social status one hundred years ago as "*Negro, slaves.*" By using such words, King creates a sense of belonging and also promotes the struggle against oppression and racial inequality. Thus, he makes use of narrativization to motivate the audience in order to follow the footsteps of their forefathers as he mentions, *symbolic shadow we stand signed the emancipation proclamation*. King supports his arguments by using the word "*but*" as he refers to a certain contradiction between the real meaning of Emancipation Proclamation, and the current social status of African-Americans. What makes King persuasive is his usage of the strategy of *fragmentation* (explained in Chapter1) by repeating the utterances, *but we refuse to believe that, now is the time*. King aims at making his audience conscious of the equal distribution of power by making a comparison between the concepts of refusing the current status of African-Americans, and the responsibility of his audience to rise and move from one position to another.

In addition, King employs the opposite concepts to show the goal of the civil rights movement. King opposes the positive and negative realities in the speech. The positive keywords and phrases are "*equal, brotherhood, freedom, justice, be able to join hands.*" In opposition to these values and goals, King speaks of "*slavery, injustice, oppression, nullification.*" All of these key words, used by King throughout his speech, have a central position in the civil rights movement discourse as expressed in King's rhetoric. They reappear in one or another combination over and over again in King's speeches, sermons, and books. But this repetition explains what the struggle is really about. King also applies the strategy of using short slogans, such as, *Emancipation Proclamation, a great beacon light of hope to millions of Negro slaves,* to define larger concepts. That strategy is effective as it grabs the attention of listeners and readers and links the message with an uncontestable truth.

From a cognitive ideological perspective, these terms define the civil rights movement's discourse. The intimate relationship between the movement and the moral righteousness of the terms shows that the struggle has the feature of being generally desirable. Freedom, equality, brotherhood and justice are all used to define the concept of the struggle as a struggle that has universal moral authority. In the first section of the speech, King creates the frame for identity and destiny of the U.S.; the dream is about how, *this nation will rise up and live out the true meaning of its creed.* That premise asserts the cognitive frame based on the concept which is; the inherent ideals of the United States that all men are created equal. King speaks of actual American history and he mentions slavery and slave owners. Therefore, King uses various strategies of persuasion to convey his message.

On the linguistic level, King sounds persuasive in his speech as he employs three strategic persuasive tactics; quasilogical, presentational and analogical. Quasilogical persuasion is shown through the logical structure of the speech. When King starts his speech with a historic reference, he deliberately attempts to pave the way to make the rest of his speech logical for his audience. King also employs the presentational mode by using metaphors, emotions and the repetition through the utterance, *one hundred years later, but we refuse to believe, now is the time.* That kind of persuasion is used to call on the audience's emotions and to create their involvement in the experience. By comparing the stories of African-Americans with their current status, king uses the *analogical* persuasion in revealing the real status of his race in two different times.

King shows his implicit power and his certainty. First the use of "*will*" in, *a check that will give us, in what will go down in history*, expresses determination and certainty of the speaker. It expresses King's conviction of the fact that is; if

African-Americans obtain their freedom, they will be pacified. But if they do not, the resentment will kindle the anger of the all. King employs "*must*" as another *root modal* to express a high degree of obligation to the degree that African-Americans must face the painful fact that they are still not free. King activates a moral obligation which reveals the authority of the speaker and directs his audience to a certain course of behavior.

By employing the word "*Negro*," King activates the conceptual understanding of the social status of his race as they "*still languishing in the corners of American society.*" King associates the languishing style of life with the Negro life style to show the negative evaluation and to increase the emotional impacts to the extent that his audience responds positively.

B) The will to move forward

But there is something that I must say to my people who stand on the warm threshold which leads into the palace of justice. In the process of gaining our rightful place we must not be guilty of wrongful deeds. Let us not seek to satisfy our thirst for freedom by drinking from the cup of bitterness and hatred. We must forever conduct our struggle on the high plane of dignity and discipline. We must not allow our creative protest to degenerate into physical violence. Again and again we must rise to the majestic heights of meeting physical force with soul force. The marvelous new militancy which has engulfed the Negro community must not lead us to distrust of all white people, for many of our white brothers, as evidenced by their presence here today, have come to realize that their destiny is tied up with our destiny and their freedom is inextricably bound to our freedom. We cannot walk alone.

And as we walk, we must make the pledge that we shall march ahead. We cannot turn back. There are those who are asking the devotees of civil rights, "When will you be satisfied?" We can never be satisfied as long as our bodies, heavy with the fatigue of travel, cannot gain lodging in the motels of the highways and the hotels of the cities. We cannot be satisfied as long as the Negro's basic mobility is from a smaller ghetto to a larger one. We can never be satisfied as long as a Negro in Mississippi cannot vote and a Negro in New York believes he has nothing for which to vote. No, no, we are not satisfied, and we will not be satisfied until justice rolls down like waters and righteousness like a mighty stream.

I am not unmindful that some of you have come here out of great trials and tribulations. Some of you have come fresh from narrow cells. Some of you have come from areas where your quest for freedom left you battered by the storms of persecution and staggered by the winds of police brutality. You have been the veterans of creative suffering. Continue to work with the faith that unearned suffering is redemptive. Go back to Mississippi, go back to Alabama, go back to Georgia, go back to Louisiana, go back to the slums and ghettos of our northern cities, knowing that somehow this situation can and will be changed. Let us not wallow in the valley of despair.

The analysis

King starts the second part of his speech by activating the cognitive strategy of rehearsal (Chapter1: page 75) as he refers to the process of gaining their rights by legitimate ways, not by illegal ways. King uses certain words like *,thirst of freedom, drinking from the cup of bitterness and hatred,* to refresh the stored information in the short-term memory of most African-Americans. King moves to another mental mode which is elaboration in which he attempts to make a linkage between the new information he gives to the audience, and the previously-stored information.

Ideologically, King attempts to employ the strategy of unification by repeating the first person plural pronoun "*we*" in the utterances, *we must forever conduct our strong, we must not allow our creative, we must rise, we can not turn back, we can never be satisfied,* to consolidate his unified perspectives. King manipulates *pathos* to affect the audience's emotions and to achieve his goals. For instance, he appeals for their motive of freedom and pride in saying, *we must make the pledge, we can not turn back.* In addition, King reminds the African-Americans about their struggle which is based on, *the high plane of dignity and discipline,* and continues to increase their ambition by saying, *let us not wallow in the valley.* King's use of such descriptions is not only visual, but also psychological and emotional with the aim at arousing sympathy and motives.

When King mentions different southern states "*Mississippi, Alabama, Georgia, Louisiana,*" he employs the symbolization of unity which involves binding the peoples who live in these states by producing symbols of unity and collective identity. The repetition of the phrases, *some of you, go back*, activates a sense of strong positive evaluation that conceptualize the African-Americans as the victims.

On the other hand, he employs the strategy of depersonification by using the negative words like "*protest, physical violence*" to show strong negative evaluation about violence practised against the black race during the slavery time. In his mental level, King portrays the whites as the villains who take anti-black positions. In other words, he uses over lexicalization to show both the villains and victims as well as to show himself as a hero of his race.

On the linguistic level, King uses conceptual metaphor in saying, *palace of justice,* as he moves from the materialistic sense of justice to the conceptual level by combining the word justice with threshold. That sense of metaphorical meaning is a conventionalized one whose meaning is clear so that there is no much difficulty in interpreting it. King's source domain of such abstracted metaphor is a place for equality and freedom represented by the place, but the target domain is the place represented by his country whereby all Africa-Americans get their basic rights.

In saying, *thirst for freedom*, and, *drinking from the cup of bitterness and hatred,* King employs another conventionalized metaphor of humanizing type. He associates the humanistic aspects through the word "*thirst*" with freedom, and the word "*cup*" with hatred to show how urgent their rights are and to reveal the mental conception of the African-Americans.

C) Voice of freedom

I say to you today, my friends, that in spite of the difficulties and frustrations of the moment, I still have a dream. It is a dream deeply rooted in the American dream. I have a dream that one day this nation will rise up and live out the true meaning of its creed: "We hold these truths to be self-evident: that all men are created equal." I have a dream that one day on the red hills of Georgia the sons of former slaves and the sons of former slave owners will be able to sit down together at a table of brotherhood. I have a dream that one day even the state of Mississippi, a desert state, sweltering with the heat of injustice and oppression, will be transformed into an oasis of freedom and justice.

I have a dream that my four children will one day live in a nation where they will not be judged by the color of their skin but by the content of their character. I have a dream today. When we let freedom ring, when we let it ring from every village and every hamlet, from every state and every city, we will be able to speed up that day when all of God's children, black men and white men, Jews and Gentiles, Protestants and Catholics, will be able to join hands and sing in the words of the old Negro spiritual, "Free at last! free at last! thank God Almighty, we are free at last!

The analysis

It is obvious that King's mental representation through the short term memory and long term memory is the state of racism and social inequality in his society. King gave his speech in a society dominated by the white race, and he employs a specific cognitive level for achieving his purpose of equality and restoring the rights of African Americans in the society. In his mental representation, King employs the following ideological strategies ;

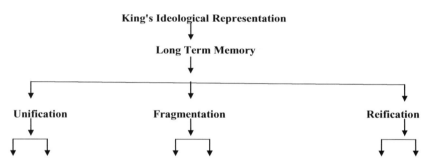

Through his introduction of the historical aspects of African Americans, King employs a self-identity description by explaining who they are, where they come from, what are their properties, and what is their history, and how they are different from the others in the society. This is typically the case for those groups and minorities whose identity is threatened or marginalized. He cognitively employs such description by using negative lexicalization such as "*negro, appalling*" to uphold the mental model of African Americans.

King shows a strategy of reification which establishes and represents a transitory, historical state of African Americans as if it is permanent and natural state. He employs two different tools to achieve his strategy; the first one is naturalization, which encodes a state of affairs that may be treated as a natural event or inevitable outcome. In his description, King employs externalization as he describes the Negro's life and his status of being languishing in the corners of American society and finds himself in an exile in his own land for hundred years. King portrays a state of affairs as permanent, unchanging to emphasize the cruelty of the whites against blacks. King uses a cognitive strategy which is concretization, which is used to describe the acts in details to strengthen the concept of racism against blacks.

In the second part, King employs the *unification* strategy which involves dissolving differences among individuals, and putting them in a collective unity that disregards racial, religious, social or gender differences. He employs two methods; *standardization* in which symbolic forms are adapted to standard framework which is promoted on the shared and acceptable basis. King shows another method of unification which is symbolization of unity in saying, *to work together, to pray together, to struggle together, to go to the jail together, to stand up for freedom together*, as he involves the concept of binding individuals together by producing symbols of unity and collective identity.

It is obvious that King employs a strategy of positive presentation to show the main principles of his country, the history and facts. On the other hand, King activates negative strategy by emphasizing the notion of slavery that comes in contradiction with the U.S. constitution. This way has a significant function on the cognitive aspects by forming the mental representations about the others. In this direction, Troutman and Smitterman (1997:116) contend the following:

> Indeed, we see that at all levels of discourse; this overall principle will remain the same, namely a strategy that combines positive self-presentation with negative other-presentation. Obviously, it is this strategy that plays a primary role in the socio-cognitive function of discourse about others, namely the formation of negative cognitions, specific mental models of concrete events.

King also employs a strategy of topicalization, in which he chooses what to put in the topic position, creating a perspective that influences the reader's perception. It determines how people understand and recall such text. That kind of topicalization is carried out by three strategies; rationalization, universalization and narrativazation. In rationalization, King appears as the producer of symbolic forms to construct a chain of reasoning which seeks to expose a set of relations and thereby persuade the audience. In universalization, he employs certain concepts like, social inequality, white domination, to serve his cognitive ideological purpose. In narrativization, he involves reference to the traditions and history of the community. Therefore, he uses the words, *to work together, to pray together, to go to jail together, to stand up for freedom together,* to create a sense of belonging and unity and overcome that kind of social inequality.

Table (3): Concordance of the noun "dream"

Context	Word	Context
I still have a	dream	it is a dream
It is a	dream	deeply rooted in the American dream
I have a	dream	this nation will rise up and live out
I have a	dream	that one day on the red hills of Georgia
I have a	dream	that one day even the state of Mississippi
I have a	dream	that one day the state of Alabama

The table shows that the approximate frequency of "dream" is 6, which is indicative in the discourse of calling for ambitious actions to achieve a social change and increases his cognitive ideological strategy of unification.

2.2.4. Eulogy for the martyred children speech
September 18, 1963, Brimingham, Alabama
A) A call for action

*And yet they died nobly. They are the martyred heroines of a holy crusade for freedom and human dignity. And so this afternoon in a real sense they have something to say to each of us in their death. They have something to say to every minister of the gospel who has remained silent behind the safe security of stained-glass windows. They have something to say to every politician [*Audience:*] (*Yeah) *who has fed his constituents with the stale bread of hatred and the spoiled meat of racism. They have something to say to a federal government that has compromised with the undemocratic practices of southern Dixiecrats (*Yeah) *and the blatant hypocrisy of right-wing northern Republicans. (*Speak)

*They have something to say to every Negro (*Yeah) *who has passively accepted the evil system of segregation and who has stood on the sidelines in a* *mighty struggle for justice. They say to each of us, black and white alike, that we must substitute courage for caution. They say to us that we must be concerned not merely about who murdered them, but about the system, the way of life, the philosophy which produced the murderers. Their death says to us that we must work passionately and unrelentingly for the realization of the American dream.*

*And so my friends, they did not die in vain. (*Yeah*) God still has a way of wringing good out of evil. (*Oh yes*) And history has proven over and over again that unmerited suffering is redemptive. The innocent blood of these little girls may well serve as a redemptive force (*Yeah*) that will bring new light to this dark city. (*Yeah*) The holy Scripture says, "A little child shall lead them." (*Oh yeah*) The death of these little children may lead our whole Southland (*Yeah*) from the low road of man's inhumanity to man to the high road of peace and brotherhood. (*Yeah, Yes*) These tragic deaths may lead our nation to substitute an aristocracy of character for an aristocracy of color. The spilled blood of these innocent girls may cause the whole citizenry of Birmingham (*Yeah*) to transform the negative extremes of a dark past into the positive extremes of a bright future. Indeed this tragic event may cause the white South to come to terms with its conscience. (*Yeah*)*

*And so I stand here to say this afternoon to all assembled here, that in spite of the darkness of this hour (*Yeah Well*), we must not despair. (*Yeah, Well*) We must not become bitter (*Ye , T t' ri t), nor must we harbor the desire to retaliate with violence. No, we must not lose faith in our white brothers. (*Yeah, Yes*) Somehow we must believe that the most misguided among them can learn to respect the dignity and the worth of all human personality.*

May I now say a word to you, the members of the bereaved families? It is almost impossible to say anything that can console you at this difficult hour and remove the deep clouds of disappointment which are floating in your mental skies. But I hope you can find a little consolation from the universality of this experience. Death comes to every individual. There is an amazing democracy about death. It is not aristocracy for some of the people, but a democracy for all of the people. Kings die and beggars die; rich men and poor men die; old people die and young people die. Death comes to the innocent and it comes to the guilty. Death is the irreducible common denominator of all men.

I hope you can find some consolation from Christianity's affirmation that death is not the end. Death is not a period that ends the great sentence of life, but a comma that punctuates it to more lofty significance. Death is not a blind alley that leads the human race into a state of nothingness, but an open door which leads man into life eternal. Let this daring faith, this great invincible surmise, be your sustaining power during these trying days.

Contextual orientation

Martin Luther King gave this speech after bombing the 16th Street Baptist Church. The bombing was a racially motivated terrorist attack on September 15, 1963, by members of a Ku Klux Klan group in Birmingham, Alabama. The bombing of the African-American church resulted in the deaths of four girls. Although city leaders had reached a settlement in May with demonstrators and started to integrate public places, not everyone agreed with ending segregation. Other acts of violence followed the settlement. The bombing increased support for people working for civil rights. It marked a turning point in the civil rights movement and contributed to support for passage of the Civil Rights Act of 1964.

The three-story Sixteenth Street Baptist Church was a rallying point for civil-rights activities and is where the students, who marched out of the church during the 1963 Birmingham campaign, were trained. The demonstrations led to an agreement in May between the city's black leaders and the Southern Christian Leadership Conference (SCLC) to integrate public facilities in the country. In the early morning of Sunday, September 15, 1963,, members of United Klans of America, a Ku Klux Klan group, planted 22 sticks of dynamite with a delayed-time release outside the basement of the church.

At about 11:22 a.m., when twenty-six children were walking into the basement assembly room for closing prayers of a sermon, the bomb exploded. Four girls were killed in the blast, and 22 additional people were injured. In addition, five cars behind the church were damaged, two of which were destroyed, while windows in the laundromat across the street were blown out.

Moderate whites condemned the bombing and the FBI took over the investigation from local authorities that had shown no real concern for solving the crime, though they held strong evidence pointing to the bombers. FBI failed to convict anyone for the crime by 1968. It was not until 1977 that the state convicted but one of the bombers. The tragedy came as a result of a month of tension following the desegregation of Birmingham's schools.

Black leaders and moderate whites alike had tried to prepare their communities for the inevitable mixing of the races in an effort to forestall any event like the riots that had taken place before, where police and firemen used dogs and fire hoses on demonstrating blacks. The bombing outraged the American people and the American public opinion. The blast was combined with other shameful Alabama events, such as the beatings of demonstrators as they began the Selma to Montgomery march in 1964. Such event contributed to the passage of the Civil Rights Act of 1964, the Voting Rights of 1965, and the end of segregation in the South.

The analysis

In the previous speech, King confirms his ideological morality in discourse. His discourse is constructed on the basis of right and wrong (good and evil). Good, represented by the martyred children and the African Americans, and evil, represented by the white racist murderers, are real entities in the society according to King's view. Such dichotomy shows that King's assertions of faith have two sides. The first side stands the belief that man and God share the same reality and God is an active participant in the reality of society.

The second side supports the freedom of man, who can act according to his own will, but must be aware that his actions are measured by an absolute right and absolute wrong. King made that clear by quoting words from the Holy Scripture "A little child lead them." Such words reflect the role of religion and church in King's ideology. On saying, *they have something to say to every negro who has passively accepted the evil system of segregation* , King attempts to win the hearts and minds of his audience by combining those children with the track of civil rights movement. King activates what Casey (2004:23) explains as collective memory and public memory. Casey (2004:23) defines collective memory as "a socially shared recollection of a particular event by different persons who do not necessarily know each other." He (2004:23) explains that in more details by saying:

> It is a plural remembering that has no basis in overlapping histories or shared places but is brought together only in and by a conjoint remembrance of a certain event, no matter where those who remember are located or how otherwise unrelated they are to each other.

What King activates is a collective memory, which simply based on remembering together in a collective way. The only necessary condition for collective memory is that a specific event is recalled by many. In the same track, King employs public memory, which is a style of remembering together occurring in a public place where "people meet and interact in a single scene of interaction," (Casey, 2004:32). Public memory is bound to a physical public space that allows for social interaction. It is socially negotiated enactment of collective memory.

Therefore, collective memory contributes to the formation of public memory. On saying, *Death comes to every individual. There is an amazing democracy about death. It is not aristocracy for some of the people, but a democracy for all the people,* King attempts to apply the strategy of unification by dissolving the differences among individuals and putting them in a collective unity that overcomes racial, religious, social differences. King applies influential symbols by saying, *kings die and beggars die; rich men and poor men die; old people die and young people die.* King uses the symbolic meaning of death as it has equal system for all the people regardless of their differences.

As King looks for strengthening his position, he attempts to use universal concepts in saying, *death comes to innocent and it comes to the guilty. Death is the irreducible common denomina*tor *of all men*. King applies two strategies which are rationalization and universalization. He deliberately uses the rationalization as he attempts to create symbolic forms that lead to reasonable and convincing arguments. King attempts to show up as a persuasive speaker, so he attempts to use emotional and psychological appeals as they motivate the listeners to accept the proposed arguments. Since most African-Americans suffer from the social inequality at that time, King is skillful in choosing the concept of death to play on the right emotions which sway them as he wants.

King attempts to influence his audience by using modality. On saying, *we must not despair, we must not become bitter, nor must we harbor the desire to retaliate with violence. We must not lose faith in our white brothers*, King repeatedly uses the modal verb "must" as a root modal that reveals his social interaction with his audience. King employs two speech acts; the first one is a direct directive. King may be understood as requesting his followers to do a specific action. On the other hand, King employs an indirect speech act, which is expressive, as he attempts to give his advices to his followers.

King employs the metaphorical expressions as he says, *death is not a blind alley*, in which King attributes characteristics of animates to the inanimates. In other words, King employs a humanizing type of metaphor, in which the speaker attributes the characteristics of the human beings to what is not human. King employs the same metaphorical expressions in saying "*mental skies*" as he attempts to link an animate feature with something inanimate.

Table (4) : Concordance of the noun "death"

Context	Word	Context
to each of	death	us in their death. They
produced the murderers. Their	death	says to us
oh yeah	death	the death of these little
this experience.	death	comes to every individual
democracy about	death	it is
die	death	comes
guilty	death	is the irreducible common
affirmation that	death	is not the end.
the end	death	is not a period
significance	death	is not a blind alley

The table shows that the approximate frequency of "death" is 10, which is indicative in the discourse of calling for emotional feeling to support his arguments for balanced social life in his society.

2.3. Conclusion

The analysis of Martin Luther King's speeches in the 1964 reveals certain features that King used for confirming his charismatic leadership. First, his ability to articulate certain idealized goals. Second, the inspiration, in which he shows an enthusiastic and optimistic display for shared goals for both African-

American and White Americans. Third, his intellectual simulation, which encourages his audience to question assumptions and reframe the racial problems in his society. Fourth, King's language elaborates the concept of fostering a collective identity, by abandoning individual self-interests for collective understanding. King employs various cognitive, ideological, and linguistic techniques.

The purpose of using cognitive, ideological, and linguistic tools is that; they help to explore how discourse participants employ such tools to influence and persuade the audience of specific ideas. King confirms the concept of breaking down the barriers with his audience and winning their hearts and minds by the following steps. A) altruistic calling, a deep-rooted desire to make a difference in the lives of others. B) Emotional healing, which is a commitment for fostering spiritual recovery from the hardships of social imbalances in his society. C) Wisdom, which is an awareness of surroundings and anticipation of consequences. D) Persuasive mapping, by influencing others through sound reasoning and mental frameworks.

Chapter Three
Analysis of Martin Luther King's speeches post-1964

0. Introduction

This chapter provides a cognitive linguistic analysis of King's speeches within the period (1964-1968). The analysis follows the theoretical approach explained in chapter one, using certain cognitive, ideological, and linguistic tools, within the theory of critical discourse analysis (CDA). Among these ideological tools are Thompson's (1990) ideological devices, including unification, legitimation, universalization, rationalization, symbolization of unity.

Among the cognitive tools are social schemas, person schemas, self schemas, role schemes "ascribed and achieved," event schemas. In addition, the cognitive strategy of objectification with the sub branches of ontologizing, figuration, and personification are handled in the analysis. Cognitive elements are also employed including; rehearsal, encoding, elaboration, and retrieval. On the linguistic level, speech acts, metaphor and modality are used in the analysis. In addition, this chapter shows the significance of applying such tools to political persuasion.

3.1. The data

The selected data to be analyzed in this section is the second part of Martin Luther King's speeches which falls within the period (1964-1968). Four speeches are randomly selected for the analysis. These speeches are:

1- Nobel Prize acceptance speech
2- Beyond Vietnam speech
3- I have been to the mountain top speech
4- Our God is marching on speech

Each speech is analyzed from a cognitive, ideological, and linguistic perspectives. The linguistic analysis is followed by a concordance analysis to show the frequency distribution of certain lexical items and its impact on meaning construction.

3.2. Analysis of Martin Luther King's speeches post-1964

One important feature found in this period of King's speeches is the dramatic change in his discourse orientation from the local topics to the international topics, such as the war against Vietnam and his opposition to its poverty across world, and dictatorship in different countries. This chapter tries to show how language, employed in King's speeches, reflects specific conceptual structures in the cognitive discourse. It also attempts to reveal the cognitive, ideological, and linguistic devices and their roles in demystifying power relations within the cognitive-socio context.

3.2.1. Nobel prize acceptance speech
December 10, 1964, Oslo, Norway

A) Increasing the awareness level

I accept the Nobel Prize for Peace at a moment when 22 million Negroes of the United States of America are engaged in a creative battle to end the long night of racial injustice. I accept this award on behalf of a civil rights movement which is moving with determination and a majestic scorn for risk and danger to establish a reign of freedom and a rule of justice. I am mindful that only yesterday in Birmingham, Alabama, our children, crying out for brotherhood, were answered with fire hoses, snarling dogs and even death.

I am mindful that only yesterday in Philadelphia, Mississippi, young people seeking to secure the right to vote were brutalized and murdered. And only yesterday more than 40 houses of worship in the State of Mississippi alone were bombed or burned because they offered a sanctuary to those who would not accept segregation. I am mindful that debilitating and grinding poverty afflicts my people and chains them to the lowest rung of the economic ladder.

Therefore, I must ask why this prize is awarded to a movement which is beleaguered and committed to unrelenting struggle; to a movement which has not won the very peace and brotherhood which is the essence of the Nobel Prize. After contemplation, I conclude that this award which I receive on behalf of that movement is a profound recognition that nonviolence is the answer to the crucial political and moral question of our time - the need for man to overcome oppression and violence without resorting to violence and oppression. Civilization and violence are antithetical concepts. Negroes of the United States, following the people of India, have demonstrated that nonviolence is not sterile passivity, but a powerful moral force which makes for social transformation. Sooner or later all the people of the world will have to discover a way to live together in peace, and thereby transform this pending cosmic elegy into a creative psalm of brotherhood.

If this is to be achieved, man must evolve for all human conflict a method which rejects revenge, aggression and retaliation. The foundation of such a method is love. The tortuous road which has led from Montgomery, Alabama to Oslo bears witness to this truth. This is a road over which millions of Negroes are travelling to find a new sense of dignity. This same road has opened for all Americans a new era of progress and hope. It has led to a new Civil Rights Bill, and it will, I am convinced, be widened and lengthened into a super highway of justice as Negro and white men in increasing numbers create alliances to overcome their common problems.

Contextual orientation

King was the second African-American and 14th U.S. citizen to win the Nobel Peace Prize, since it was first awarded in 1901 to Dr. Ralph Bunche, an United Nations official. After King was honored, hundreds of crowds, who waited for the Nobel ceremony to end, sent shouts of "Freedom Now" and "We Shall Overcome." As the first place for his itinerary to Sweden, King visited London where he and part of his party, which numbered 33 and was the largest entourage ever to accompany a Nobel Prize winner, stopped for several days enroute to Oslo.

There had been crowds and shouts of "King Yeah Yeah." After being in London, King flew to Stockholm where he met other Nobel laureates and was honored by hundreds of Swedes. Having honored in Stockholm, King preached to thousands, including Sweden's Queen, in the Stockholm Cathedral. King left Stockholm with a new and overwhelming sense of what the world was expecting of him.

At his hero's welcome in New York, King expressed his own intensified feeling of personal responsibility in speaking of individuals who will hold the torch firmly for others because they have overcome the threat of jail and death. Dr. King took the best use of this prize by validating his methodology of nonviolence and made the struggle for racial equality in America as internationally-recognized issue. He donated all of his prize money to organizations fighting for justice, in spite of the fact that he was not earning enough money to adequately support his family.

The analysis

King accepts the Nobel prize for peace, but also attempts to make racial injustice world issue. He speaks on behalf of the twenty two million African Americans who suffer in their society. He places the atrocities against blacks within the context of external arena. He does not speak of specific political context, but just gaining the emotional side of his audience. He details the Negro's place in America, the wrong doings of the past, the false intellectual proofs of the Negro's inferiority when he says "*this award which I receive on behalf of that movement is profound recognition that non violence is the answer to the crucial political and moral question of overtime.*" King clearly connects his introduction and thereby the framework of his ideology with the civil rights movement.

On the cognitive level, when King says, *I am mindful that only yesterday in Birmingham, Alabama, our children, crying out for brotherhood, were answered with fire hoses, snarling dogs and even death*, he attempts to explain his mental representation of social knowledge based on previous experiences. He shows that clearly in mentioning what happened of anti-black attacks in Alabama, Philadelphia, Mississipi. King uses that kind of *social schemas* to draw the world's attention to such atrocities in his society and to raise the degree of rationality and emotions.

King attempts to activate the strategy of ontologizing by showing ideas which reflect human features in his society. On saying, *poverty afflicts my people*, he attempts to link economic and social problems with the sufferings of the African-Americans as they are also afflicted with such problems. King also employs the figuration strategy by activating the images of certain social events in his audience minds. That is clear when King makes a comparison between the African-Americans and people of India. King creates here the image of unity and establishes a shared belief systems for both peoples.

When King says, *when twenty two million Negroes of the United States,* King activates the concept of role schemas by taking the ascribed role as well as the achieved role. His *ascribed role* is that the role he wants to assume as the defender of all African Americans because he, as a human, does not agree with any kind of oppression. The *Achieved role* is obtained through his charismatic personality in gaining the appreciation of not only his followers, but also the international institutions that qualify him to win Nobel award. Second, on saying, *Negroes of the United States, following the people of India, have demonstrated that nonviolence is not sterile passivity,* King strengthens the sense of non-violence ideology which is based on moral force to make social transformation.

In his mental representation, King considers that Gandhi and Gandhiism also have a more concrete function; the practicality of Gandhian non-violence in the struggle of the civil rights movement. When King says, *Negroes of the United States, following the people of India....all the people of the world,* he attempts to make a cognitive description of how successful non-violence was an effective method in India and can be applied to the American circumstances. It is through such concept that further meaning is created since the two fronts are established in one arguments; the factual success of non-violence in India and the impending success of non-violence in America.

To convince his audience with his beliefs, King employs three important ways of persuasion. The first one is quasilogical persuasion which is based on the logical straucture of his speech. He uses such strategy when he starts with generalised statements of the long journey of African Americans, then he moves in details by showing what happens in different southern states *"Alabama, Mississipi."* After that he moves to universal concepts of violence and civilization on saying, *civilization and violence are antithetical concepts.* In addition, King employs another persuasive tactic, *presentational,* that is based on the concepts rooted in his audience's consciousness by raising the degree of emotions and involvement.

King repeats the utterance, *I am mindful,* to raise the emotions of his audience in a way that is indirect. In repeating the word, *road,* in the phrases, *this tortuous road, this road over, this same road,* King evokes a positive feeling about his struggle for equality. By employing a strong positive evaluation, King activates personification in his speech. Cognitively, King shows three images in his speech; the hero, who is represented by human equality and freedom. The villain, who is represented by racist whites. The victim, who is represented by the African-Americans.

On the ideological level, King uses specific ideological modes, when he mentions the tragic events afflicted directly to his race by saying, *only yesterday in Birmingham, Alabama, our children, crying out for brotherhood, were answered with fire hoses, snarling dogs and even death.* King uses the strategy of narrativization which involves the reference to certain historical aspects of African-Americans and their sufferings.

This strategy justifies their rights for equality and real freedom since they are human beings like their white counterparts. King, to activate his legitimation strategy, employs another way to convince his audience about his beliefs. King produces very symbolic signs through rationalization on saying, *on behalf of a civil rights movement which is moving with determination and a majestic scorn for risk and danger to establish a reign of freedom and a rule of justice,* in order to persuade his audience. He explains that if one wants to be successful in facing inequalities, he has to change the minds of the people and their behaviour. This would never happen by using violence and oppression, but by using universal concepts that all people agree upon, and he details that on saying "*Negro and white men in increasing numbers create alliances to overcome their common problems.*"

On the linguistic level, King uses metaphors to express his ideas in a very powerful way and to provoke the curiosity of his listeners about certain implicit meanings by saying, *This same road has opened for all Americans a new era of progress and hope*. In the previous utterance, King employs a concrete to abstract metaphor. This is the case of metaphorical extension of the usage of images drawn from the concrete entity "road" to the abstract entity "progress." Under this type, King's style of using metaphorical expressions gives an impression that describes abstract experiences.

On the same track, King employs a direct speech act on saying, *I accept the Nobel Prize for Peace at a moment when 22 million Negroes,* which is declarative, as king declares his acceptance for the award. Kings also activates an indirect speech act which is expressive as he expresses his praise for the sacrifices of the African Americans. On saying *,I must ask why this prize is awarded to a movement,* King employs a direct speech act which is directive as he raises a question about the reasons for awarding the prize to the civil rights movement. King uses both the direct and indirect speech acts to broaden the mental horizons of his audience and deliver his message in a powerful way.

Table (1) Concordance of the pronoun "I"

Context	Word	Context
	I	accept the Nobel Prize for Peace
	I	accept this award on behalf of a
A rule of justice.	I	am mindful that only yesterday
	I	am mindful that only yesterday in Philadelphia
	I	am mindful that debilitating and
Therefore,	I	must ask why this prize is awarded
After contemplation	I	conclude that
this award which	I	receive on behalf of that movement
And it will	I	am convinced

The above table shows that the total frequency of "I" is 9, which is indicative in the discourse of personification and determination as a persuasive technique to break down the barriers between him and his audience and to get closer to them.

3.2.2. Our God is marching on speech

March 25, 1965, Montgomery, Alabama

A) Strenghtening the level of determination

The confrontation of good and evil compressed in the tiny community of Selma (Speak, speak) generated the massive power (Yes, sir. Yes, sir) to turn the whole nation to a new course. A president born in the South (Well) had the sensitivity to feel the will of the country, (Speak, sir) and in an-address-that will live in history as one of the most passionate pleas for human rights ever made by a president of our nation, he pledged the might of the federal government to cast off the centuries-old blight. President Johnson rightly praised the courage of the Negro for awakening the conscience of the nation. (Yes, sir)

On our part we must pay our profound respects to the white Americans who cherish their democratic traditions over the ugly customs and privileges of generations and come forth boldly to join hands with us. (Yes, sir) From Montgomery to Birmingham, (Yes, sir) from Birmingham to Selma, (Yes, sir) from Selma back to Montgomery, (Yes) a trail wound in a circle long and often bloody, yet it has become a highway up from darkness. (Yes, sir) Alabama has tried to nurture and defend evil, but evil is choking to death in the dusty roads and streets of this state. (Yes, sir. Speak, sir) So I stand before you this afternoon (Speak, sir. Well) with the conviction that segregation is on its deathbed in Alabama.

The only thing uncertain about it is how costly the segregationists and Wallace will make the funeral. (Go ahead. Yes, sir) [Applause]. Our whole campaign in Alabama has been centered around the right to vote. In focusing the attention of the nation and the world today on the flagrant denial of the right to vote, we are exposing the very origin, the root cause, of racial segregation in the Southland. Racial segregation as a way of life did not come about as a natural result of hatred between the races immediately after the Civil War. There were no laws segregating the races then.

And as the noted historian, C. Vann Woodward, in his book, The Strange Career of Jim Crow, clearly points out, the segregation of the races was really a political stratagem employed by the emerging Bourbon interests in the South to keep the southern masses divided and southern labor the cheapest in the land. You see, it was a simple thing to keep the poor white masses working for near-starvation wages in the years that followed the Civil War. Why, if the poor white plantation or mill worker became dissatisfied with his low wages, the plantation or mill owner would merely threaten to fire him and hire former Negro slaves and pay him even less. Thus, the southern wage level was kept almost unbearably low.

To meet this threat, the southern aristocracy began immediately to engineer this development of a segregated society. (Right) I want you to follow me through here because this is very important to see the roots of racism and the denial of the right to vote. Through their control of mass media, they revised the doctrine of white supremacy. They saturated the thinking of the poor white masses with it, (Yes) thus clouding their minds to the real issue involved in the Populist Movement. They then directed the placement on the books of the South of laws that made it a crime for Negroes and whites to come together as equals at any level. *(Yes, sir)* And that did it. That crippled and eventually destroyed the Populist Movement of the nineteenth century.

Thus, the threat of the free exercise of the ballot by the Negro and the white masses alike *(Uh huh)* resulted in the establishment of a segregated society. They segregated southern money from the poor whites; they segregated southern mores from the rich whites; *(Yes, sir)* they segregated southern churches from Christianity *(Yes, sir)*; they segregated southern minds from honest thinking; *(Yes, sir)* and they segregated the Negro from everything. *(Yes, sir)* That's what happened when the Negro and white masses of the South threatened to unite and build a great society: a society of justice where none would prey upon the weakness of others; a society of plenty where greed and poverty would be done away; a society of brotherhood where every man would respect the dignity and worth of human personality. *(Yes, sir)* We've come a long way since that travesty of justice was perpetrated upon the American mind. James Weldon Johnson put it eloquently. He said:

We have come over a way

That with tears hath been watered. (Yes, sir)

We have come treading our paths

Through the blood of the slaughtered. (Yes, sir)

Out of the gloomy past, (Yes, sir)

Till now we stand at last

Where the white gleam

Of our bright star is cast. (Speak, sir)

Today I want to tell the city of Selma, *(Tell them, Doctor)* today I want to say to the state of Alabama, *(Yes, sir)* today I want to say to the people of America and the nations of the world, that we are not about to turn around. *(Yes, sir)* We are on the move now. *(Yes, sir). Yes, we are on the move and no wave of racism can stop us. (Yes, sir)* We are on the move now. The burning of our churches will not deter us. *(Yes, sir)* The bombing of our homes will not dissuade us. *(Yes, sir)* We are on the move now. *(Yes, sir)* The beating and killing of our clergymen and young people will not divert us. We are on the move now. *(Yes, sir)* The wanton release of their known murderers would not discourage us. We are on the move now. *(Yes, sir)* Like an idea whose time *has come, (Yes, sir) not even the marching of mighty armies can halt us. (Yes, sir) We are moving to the land of freedom. (Yes, sir).*

Contextual orientation

King gave this speech, after the historic Selma marches took place and had its impact on the Civil rights track. The Selma to Montgomery marches were three marches in 1965 that marked the political and emotional peak of the American Civil Rights Movement. These marches were the culmination of the voting rights movement in Selma, Alabama, and were led and supported by Martin Luther King. After the Civil Rights Act of 1964 forbade discrimination in voting on the basis of race, efforts by civil rights organizations to register black voters were met with fierce resistance in southern states such as Alabama.

In early 1965, Martin Luther King Jr. and other non-violence organizations decided to make Selma, located in Dallas County, Alabama, the focus of a voter registration campaign. Alabama Governor was a notorious opponent of desegregation, and the local county sheriffs in other Counties had led a steadfast opposition to black voter registration process. As a result, only two percent of Selma's eligible black voters had managed to register.

After King had won the Nobel Peace Prize in 1964, his higher profile helped to draw international attention to Selma during the eventful months that followed. On February 18 1965, white segregationists attacked a group of peaceful demonstrators in nearby town in Alabama. In the ensuing chaos, an Alabama state trooper fatally shot a young African-American demonstrator. In response to his death, King and civil rights activists planned a massive protest march from Selma to the state capitol of Montgomery. A group of 600 people set out on March 7, but didn't get far before Alabama state troopers wielding whips, sticks and tear gas rushed the group and beat them back to Selma. The brutal scene was captured on television, enraging many Americans and drawing civil rights and religious leaders of all faiths to Selma in protest.

The first march, which took place on March 7, 1965 is described as Bloody Sunday. Hundreds of civil rights marchers were attacked by state and local police rods and tear gas. The second march took place on March 9. Only the third march, which began on March 21 and lasted five days, made it to Montgomery. The marches drastically shifted public opinion about the Civil

Rights movement as a whole. The images of Alabama law enforcement officers beating the nonviolent protesters were shown all over the country and the world by the television networks and newspapers. The visuals of such brutality being carried out by the state of Alabama helped shift the image of the segregationist movement from one of a movement trying to preserve the social order of the South to a system of state endorsed terrorism against those non-whites.

The marches also had a powerful effect in Washington. After witnessing TV coverage of "Bloody Sunday," President Lyndon Johnson met with Alabama Governor to discuss with him the civil rights situation in his state. He tried to persuade the governor to stop the state harassment of the protesters. Two nights later, on March 15, 1965, Johnson presented a bill to a joint session of Congress. The bill itself later passed and became the Voting Rights Act.

The analysis

King gives this speech in an attempt to cognitively persuade his audience that the notion of segregation in his society must be resisted. He tries to practically convince his followers by sequencing his ideas, starting from the micro level of heinous actions, occurred against African-Americans in Selma, to a macro level of the concepts of segregation in the U.S. King applies such sequencing ideas to achieve the goals of conveying ideas effectively. That is clear from his audience's response to his words by saying, *Yes Sir, Speak Sir*. King also sequences his ideas and themes in a parallel order, which lends his remarks a strong sense of order, and helps persuade the audience. That is obvious in saying, *today I want to tell the city of Selma, today I want to say to the state of Alabama, today I want to say to the people of America and the notions of the word*, as he moves in the following order;

In the previous order, King employs a cognitive persuasive technique, which is response reinforcing. This strategy is based on strengthening already held convictions and making them more resistant to change. By refreshing the memories of his audience about the events that occurred from Selma city to a macro level, he activates the concept of reinforcing a specific idea for confronting oppression in his society.

Cognitively, King focuses on the strategy of objectification by simplifying his idea through the technique of using physical concepts such as, *money and churches*, and abstract ideas such as, *mores, southern minds, honest thinking*, which are mentioned in his utterance, *they segregated southern money from the poor whites, they segregated southern mores from the rich whites; they segregated southern churches from Christianity, and segregated southern minds from honest thinking*. On saying, *the negro, poor whites, rich whites, a society of justice, brotherhood, greed and poverty*, King places opposing words side by side, which enable him to crystallize points or concepts by comparing or contrasting to employ the response shaping as a persuasive technique, discussed in chapter one.

King activates the strategy of breaking down the barriers between the African Americans and whites on saying, *Yes, we are on the move and no move of racism can stop us*. King adeptly mentions the words to stress commonalities rather than differences. He focuses on the concepts of strong determination and willingness to overcome the racist issues and look forward for better, equal social life. He mentions the whites and their role that should be considered. In this way, King attempts to join himself firmly to the diverse audience as he draws attention to their shared American dream. King employs words that resonate as a way to shatter barriers and construct ties effectively. He, as a Christian preacher, often sprinkles his public remarks with words that evoke faith among other followers.

Rehearsal, as a cognitive strategy, is employed by King in his short term memory. By linking what happened in Selma with the general notion of segregation, King manages to activate the strategy of elaboration. He does this by linking new information of the disgraceful events in Selma with the previous stored information of segregation. Such mental operations which King attempts to employ in his speech are described as *encoding* process.

King also combines modality and speech acts on saying "*on our part, we must pay our profound respects to the white Americans,*" as he shows his social interaction with his audience by using the modal "must." He employs direct and indirect speech acts in the previous utterance. The direct one is a described as a directive, as he attempts to provide his advice to his audience, while the indirect one is expressive, since it implies an expression of thanking or appreciation. Here there is an overlap between the functions of a directive and that of an expressive.

King employs the social schemas based on previous experience. Such social schemas enable efficient categorization of information, and influence what we should pay attention to. By reminding the audience of burning the churches and the bombings, King attempts to activate the cognitive strategy of self-schemas by mentioning such general events. He attempts to appear as a persuasive person, so he employs quasilogical persuasion which is based on the logical structures of his argument. Johnstone (1989:145) affirms the role of quasilogical persuasion in discourse as saying:

> Persuaders in the quasilogical mode create the rhetorical impression that their arguments are logically inconvertible. The goal of quasilogical persuasion is to convince, to make it seem impossible for the audience using its powers of rationality not to accept the arguer's conclusion.

On the ideological level, Kings employs certain ideological techniques. On saying, *Today I want to tell the city of Selma, (Tell them, Doctor) today I want to say to the state of Alabama, (Yes, sir) today I want to say to the people of America and the nations of the world, that we are not about to turn around,* King employs the strategy of narrativization, which involves stories that shows the link between the past and the present. King refers to the history of his community to create a sense of belonging. By saying, *the southern aristocracy began immediately to engineer this development of a segregated society. (Right)*, King activates the ideological technique of "rationalization," which is based on using logic and rational logic. King also employs the strategy of "unification" on saying, *The confrontation of good and evil compressed in the tiny community of Selma (Speak, speak) generated the massive power*, as he attempts to unify and make all African Americans in his side. King uses this concept by using symbolic forms like, the confrontation of good and evil, as he uses symbolic ideas to strengthen his ideological style.

On the linguistic level, King uses metaphorical expressions to strengthen the power of his ideas, and push the listeners to search for implicit meanings. On saying, *the land of freedom*, King uses a concrete to abstract metaphor. On saying, *The wanton release,* King employs synaesthesia metaphor, as he uses senses to express his ideas..

When King says, *Negroes of the United States, following the people of India, have demonstrated that nonviolence is not sterile passivity, but a powerful moral force which makes for social transformation*, he activates an indirect speech act, which is expressive as he praises the struggle of African Americans. On saying, *the people of the world will have to discover a way to live together in peace, and thereby transform this pending cosmic elegy into a creative psalm of brotherhood,* King uses another indirect speech act, which is directive, because it implies an indirect advice to live in peace.

Table (2): Concordance of the pronoun "we"

Context	Word	Context
On our part	we	must pay our profound respects
the right to vote	we	are exposing the very origin
He said	we	have come over a way
Yes, sir	we	have come treading our paths
Till now	we	stand at last
the world, that	we	are not about to turn
Yes, sir	we	are on the move now
Yes, sir. Yes	we	are on the move
Yes, sir	we	are on the move no
Yes, sir	we	are on the move now
divert us	we	are on the move
discourage us	we	are on the move
Yes, sir	we	are moving to the land

The table above shows that the total frequency of "we" is 13, which is indicative in the discourse of unification and determination to get the rights of African Americans.

B) A push to move forward

Let us therefore continue our triumphant march (Uh huh) to the realization of the American dream. (Yes, sir) Let us march on segregated housing (Yes, sir) until every ghetto or social and economic depression dissolves, and Negroes and whites live side by side in decent, safe, and sanitary housing. (Yes, sir) Let us march on segregated schools (Let us march, Tell it) until every vestige of segregated and inferior education becomes a thing of the past, and Negroes and whites study side-by-side in the socially-healing context of the classroom.

Let us march on poverty (Let us march) until no American parent has to skip a meal so that their children may eat. (Yes, sir) March on poverty (Let us march) until no starved man walks the streets of our cities and towns (Yes, sir) in search of jobs that do not exist. (Yes, sir) Let us march on poverty (Let us march) until wrinkled stomachs in Mississippi are filled, (That's right) and the idle industries of Appalachia are realized and revitalized, and broken lives in sweltering ghettos are mended and remolded.

Let us march on ballot boxes, (Let's march) march on ballot boxes until race-baiters disappear from the political arena.Let us march on ballot boxes until the salient misdeeds of bloodthirsty mobs (Yes, sir) will be transformed into the calculated good deeds of orderly citizens. (Speak, Doctor)Let us march on ballot boxes (Let us march) until the Wallaces of our nation tremble away in silence. Let us march on ballot boxes (Let us march) until we send to our city councils (Yes, sir), state legislatures, (Yes, sir) and the United States Congress, (Yes, sir) men who will not fear to do justly, love mercy, and walk humbly with thy God.Let us march on ballot boxes (Let us march. March) until brotherhood becomes more than a meaningless word in an opening prayer, but the order of the day on every legislative agenda.

Let us march on ballot boxes (Yes) until all over Alabama God's children will be able to walk the earth in decency and honor.There is nothing wrong with marching in this sense. (Yes, sir) The Bible tells us that the mighty men of Joshua merely walked about the walled city of Jericho (Yes) and the barriers to freedom came tumbling down. (Yes, sir) I like that old Negro spiritual, (Yes, sir) "Joshua Fit the Battle of Jericho." In its simple, yet colorful, depiction (Yes, sir) of that great moment in biblical history, it tells us that:

Joshua fit the battle of Jericho, (Tell it)
Joshua fit the battle of Jericho, (Yes, sir)
And the walls come tumbling down. (Yes, sir. Tell it)
Up to the walls of Jericho they marched, spear in hand. (Yes, sir)
"Go blow them ramhorns," Joshua cried,
"'Cause the battle am in my hand." (Yes, sir)
These words I have given you just as they were given us by the unknown, long-dead, dark-skinned originator. (Yes, sir) Some now long-gone black bard bequeathed to posterity these words in ungrammatical form, (Yes, sir) yet with emphatic pertinence for all of us today. (Uh huh). The battle is in our hands. And we can answer with creative nonviolence the call to higher ground to which the new directions of our struggle summons us. (Yes, sir) The road ahead is not altogether a smooth one. (No) There are no broad highways that lead us easily and inevitably to quick solutions. But we must keep going.

My people, my people, listen. (Yes, sir) The battle is in our hands. (Yes, sir) The battle is in our hands in Mississippi and Alabama and all over the United States. (Yes, sir) I know there is a cry today in Alabama, (Uh huh) we see it in numerous editorials: "When will Martin Luther King, SCLC, SNCC, and all of these civil rights agitators and all of the white clergymen and labor leaders and students and others get out of our community and let Alabama return to normalcy?"

But I have a message that I would like to leave with Alabama this evening. (Tell it) That is exactly what we don't want, and we will not allow it to happen, (Yes, sir) for we know that it was normalcy in Marion (Yes, sir) that led to the brutal murder of Jimmy Lee Jackson. (Speak) It was normalcy in Birmingham (Yes) that led to the murder on Sunday morning of four beautiful, unoffending, innocent girls. It was normalcy on Highway 80 (Yes, sir) that led state troopers to use tear gas and horses and billy clubs against unarmed human beings who were simply marching for justice. (Speak, sir) It was normalcy by a cafe in Selma, Alabama, that led to the brutal beating of Reverend James Reeb.

It is normalcy all over our country (Yes, sir) which leaves the Negro perishing on a lonely island of poverty in the midst of vast ocean of material prosperity. It is normalcy all over Alabama (Yeah) that prevents the Negro from becoming a registered voter. (Yes) No, we will not allow Alabama (Go ahead) to return to normalcy. [Applause]. The only normalcy that we will settle for (Yes, sir) is the normalcy that recognizes the dignity and worth of all of God's children. The only normalcy that we will settle for is the normalcy that allows judgment to run down like waters, and righteousness like a mighty stream. (Yes, sir) The only normalcy that we will settle for is the normalcy of brotherhood, the normalcy of true peace, the normalcy of justice.

The analysis

It is clear from the previous part of King's speech his determination to apply the startegy of non-violence, which makes him distinctive amongst other political leaders of his time. King's religious beliefs play an important role in not using violent means to attain civil rights, and he was strongly influenced by the philosophy of Gandhi. King uses the first person plural pronoun in saying, *let us therefore continue our trimphant March*, and he repeats it to give his audience a sense of unity. King uses the same way of unifying his audience as Obama does in his presidential campaign 2008. Both employ the concepts of standardization and symbolization.

On the cognitive level, King builds a sense of dynamic images by repeating, *let us march on ballot boxes.* In the minds of his audience, the image of revoluting against social inequality becomes a moving, living thing. King deliberately uses this method since it helps to create a sense of forward momentum. King's way in using dynamic images illustrates that leaders who are seeking to convey vision can benefit from using words that create moving images. Imagery which becomes alive in the mind is likely to be remembered long after a speech is completed.

When King mentions the phrase, *the American dream,* he attempts to to use the cognitive persuaive strategy, which is response reinforcing, to strenghten his idea and deliver it strongly to his audience. This cognitive strategy is obvious by reminding his audience of the symbols America was and is still calling for. King deliberately uses such a phrase to show that all Americans have collective identity, and they should face together segregation. One obvious way King adopts in this speech to win the hearts and the minds of his audience is to know their background and understand the circumstances they face.

On the ideological level, King does not only show himself as leader who understands their social identity, but also as a leader who wants to convey his understanding to them. King's use of the phrases, *segregated housing, segregated schools, segregated and inferior education, poverty*, confirms his outstanding ability to connect his objectives with his audience's desires. The ideological strategy King adopts to win the hearts and minds of his audience is unification which is based on the use of details effectively. He does that by applying three principles: recognition, remebering, and responding.

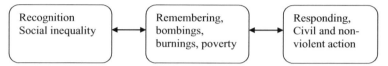

King shows his way of recognizing the social circumstances in which his society faces like racism, segregation and inequality. The second step is remembering the details of such circumstances. The third one is to push his audience to take an action like practising non-violent actions. Another strategy is to personalize his message. By repeating, *let us*, King attempts to personalize the message and create a greater sense of closeness, and to convince them about his goals.

King's Approach Within Unification Strategy

```
                    ┌─────────────────────┐
                    │ Unification Strategy │
                    └──────────┬──────────┘
                               │
                               ▼
                  Winning the Hearts and Minds
                               │
         ┌─────────────────────┼─────────────────────┐
         ▼                     ▼                     ▼
 Knowing the Audience   Using Details Effectively   Personalizng the Messages
```

Another strategy King attempts to apply is legitimation. He employs it three sub-ways rationalization, universlaization, and narrativization, (as discussed in chapter one, p. 31). On saying, *the Bible tells us that mighty men of Jehua merely walked about the walled city of Jericho and the barriers to freedom came tumbling down,* Kings attempts to convey his vision by linking his ideas to a religious reference. He does that to substantiate them as well as to make them more understandable and acceptable. King strenghtens his ability to use the rationalization by using such religious references to uphold his vision.

In addition, King employs narrativization in the above speech, through anecodotes as a powerful tool for convincing his audience. The startegy of anecdotes, within the ideological strategy of narrativization, allows him to use brief narration to go into greater depth and illustrate points in memorable ways. Such strategy demonstrates the ability to unite the audience across traditional societal dvisions. It conveys the speaker's points in a clear and simple way.

Obviously, King conveys his vision in a compelling manner by referring to history which makes his ideas more understandable. This way helps his followers relate his ideas to the shared history and cherished tradition. King's practice of giving ideas physicality plays a role in conveying vision effectively. The use of dynamic imagery represents another useful communication technique, in which effective leaders like King and Obama find ways to make pictures move in the mind. King masters the way of driving his messages home and achieveing the designated goals of his speech.

On the linguistic level, King delivers this speech, not only to inform, but also to influence, persuade, motivate and direct. The first way to drive his point home is prioritizing and focusing on themes. King puts aside low-priority issues and promotes the important issues, and shining a light on them by using metaphors. On saying, *full of hope and promise of the future,*" King employs synaesthesia metaphor as these words "hope, promise, and future" reflect feelings and senses. King uses this specific type of metaphor as it has a congitive function, since it is helps facilitate the memorizing process for the audience.

King also employs an abstract to concrete metaphor on saying, *the battle is in our hands*. King uses these metaphors as useful techniques for broadening the mental horizons of the audience by pushing them to think about the implicit meanings of the speaker's words. Metaphor expressions help King to emphasize certain points and pay attention to important issues.

This style of metaphor can function pragmatically as an indirect speech act, which is expressive, as he encourages his follwers about the victory they will get at the end of their struggle.

King also employs repetitive startegy called "anaphora." Anaphora is defined as the recurrence of the same words or phrases at the start of successive sentences. This is what King exactly does in this speech on saying ,*let us march on ballot boxes.* Such repetitive startegies help King to create a sense of common identity among the diverse members of the audience, and underscoring the principles they share and adding to a sense of unity.

Table (3): Concordance of the noun"battle"

Context	Word	Context
Joshua Fit the	battle	of Jericho.
Joshua fit the	battle	of Jericho
Joshua fit the	battle	of Jericho
Cause the	battle	am in my hand
the	battle	is in our hands.
the	battle	is in our hands.
the	battle	is in our hands in Mississippi

The above tabel shows that the total frequency of "battle" is 7, which is indicative in the discourse of motivation to get the rights of African Americans

3.2.3. Beyond Vietnam speech

April 4, 1967

A) Expanding the scope of awareness

Some of us who have already begun to break the silence of the night have found that the calling to speak is often a vocation of agony, but we must speak. We must speak with all the humility that is appropriate to our limited vision, but we must speak. And we must rejoice as well, for surely this is the first time in our nation's history that a significant number of its religious leaders have chosen to move beyond the prophesying of smooth patriotism to the high grounds of a firm dissent based upon the mandates of conscience and the reading of history. Perhaps a new spirit is rising among us. If it is, let us trace its movements, and pray that our own inner being may be sensitive to its guidance, for we are deeply in need of a new way beyond the darkness that seems so close around us.

Over the past two years, as I have moved to break the betrayal of my own silences and to speak from the burnings of my own heart, as I have called for radical departures from the destruction of Vietnam, many persons have questioned me about the wisdom of my path. At the heart of their concerns, this query has often loomed large and loud: "Why are you speaking about the war, Dr. King?" "Why are you joining the voices of dissent?" "Peace and civil rights don't mix," they say. "Aren't you hurting the cause of your people?" they ask. And when I hear them, though I often understand the source of their concern, I am nevertheless greatly saddened, for such questions mean that the inquirers have not really known me, my commitment, or my calling. Indeed, their questions suggest that they do not know the world in which they live. In the light of such tragic misunderstanding, I deem it of signal importance to try to state clearly, and I trust concisely, why I believe that the path from Dexter Avenue Baptist Church—the church in Montgomery, Alabama, where I began my pastorate—leads clearly to this sanctuary tonight.

Contextual orientation

Beyond Vietnam speech was Martin Luther King's formal public declaration of his opposition to US military action in Vietnam. As a Christian minister, King was opposed to the war inherently. As a scholar and believer of Gandhi's principals of nonviolence, he opposed violence as a way to resolve conflict. But in this speech he took it further. He solidified his opposition to the war, bringing the powers of his tremendously organized mind, and the weight of his moral authority to state his absolute resolve to actively oppose the U.S. military involvement in Vietnam. It was one year later on April 4, 1968 that he was shot on a balcony outside the Motel Lorraine in Memphis, Tennessee.

The Vietnam War continued between 1964 and 1975 on the ground in South Vietnam and bordering areas of Cambodia. Fighting on one side was a coalition of forces including the United States, the Republic of Vietnam, Australia, New Zealand, and South Korea. Fighting on the other side was a coalition of forces including the Democratic Republic of Vietnam (North Vietnam) and the National Liberation Front (NLF), a communist-led South

Vietnamese guerrilla movement. The Soviet Union provided military aid to the North Vietnamese and to the NLF, but was not one of the military combatants.

The war was part of a larger regional conflict involving the neighboring countries like Cambodia. In Vietnam, this conflict is known as the American War. On January 15, 1973 President Nixon ordered a suspension of offensive action in North Vietnam which was later followed by the unilateral withdrawal of U.S. troops from Vietnam. The Paris Peace Accords were later signed in 1973 which officially ended US involvement in the Vietnam conflict.

The analysis

Beyond Vietnam speech is obviously central for any understanding of King's position on the war issue, but it can be read in another way. Here King takes the best use of the situation for giving meaning to the civil rights movements. The speech also reveals some cognitive, ideological, and linguistic techniques. On the cognitive level, when King says, *to break the betrayal of my own silences and to speak from the burnings of my own heart*, he activates the technique of objectification, which aims to simplifying the ideas, and changing it into concrete image and understandable concept. When King says, to break the betrayal, he uses the ontologizing style which is based on using physical aspects to define his point. King used one physical aspect, break, with abstract concept, betrayal, to make his idea clear.

King activates the concept of social schema, on saying, *over the past two years*, as it shows the mental representations of the past experience stored in his memory. King applies event schemas, (explained in chapter one, p:70), to create cognitive generalizations about the event, derived from past experience, that organize and create the cognitive image of anyone. King also activates the role schema on saying, *as I have moved to break the betrayal of my own silences and to speak from the burnings of my own heart, as I have called for radical departures from the destruction of Vietnam, many persons have questioned me about the wisdom of my path.* By the previous words, King take the role of the wise leader who can make something positive in his society. His role can be achieved, based on his struggle against inequality in his society. This role can be also ascribed based upon the idea that by nature, King is an African American, who should defend the right of his community.

King's cognitive representations within the social schema about the issue of Vietnam war are the followings; the hopes of civil rights reformers and the social program of the great society have been shattered by the economic demands of the war. In addition, black and white boys can burn villages in Vietnam together, but they can not live in the same district in an American city. Moreover, it is impossible to speak against the use of violence in American towns without condemning the government's use of violence in southeast Asia. King feels that he has a personal responsibility as a Nobel peace prize recipient to oppose the war. He also has a responsibility as a minister who is committed to the teachings of Christianity to oppose the war.

On the ideological level, King employs the style of legitimization through the strategies of rationalization and universalization in his struggle against segregation. Rationalization which is based on using logic and facts is applied. on saying, *Perhaps a new spirit is rising among us. If it is, let us trace its movements.* He uses the logic concepts to convince his audience. He also uses another strategy which is universalization, which is based on universal ideas. On saying, *as I have called for radical departures from the destruction of Vietnam,* King applies a universal call at that time to finish the war in Vietnam. On saying, *but we must speak, And we must rejoice,* King activates the concept of unification by using the first person plural pronoun "we" to win the hearts and minds of his audience.

On the linguistic level, When King asks in his speech, *why are you joining the voices of dissent?* he uses a direct speech act, which is directive. Yet, he also uses another indirect speech act which is expressive, as he expresses his blame on his audience. When King describes what happens in Vietnam as, *destruction of Vietnam,* he uses a direct speech act, which is assertive, as he asserts the real situation in Vietnam. Generally, King uses the direct and indirect speech acts to attract his audience's attention that the sense of destruction exists within the American society. Vietnam is not the cause of destruction, but it is an outgrowth of inequality that resides in the U.S.

Metaphorically, King uses a animistic metaphor on saying, vocation *of agony,* in which he uses something that is not human, with a humanistic feature, which is "agony." King also employs another conceptual level of metaphor, which is orientational metaphor (discussed in chapter one:p 61) on saying, *beyond the darkness that seems so close around us.* In the previous utterance, Kings uses spatial concept, *so close around us,* and connect that with abstract concept, which is darkness. King activates a concrete to abstract concept by saying, *In the light of such tragic misunderstanding,* as he links the concrete concept "light" with an abstract. The main purpose of using such metaphor is to enforce his message, and push his audience to think deeply about various interpretations for his words.

Table (4): Concordance of the modal "must"

Context	Word	Context
agony, but	we	must speak
speak.	we	must speak
limited vision, but	we	must speak
speak. And	we	must rejoice
its guidance, for	we	are deeply in need

The above table shows that the approximate frequency of "we" is 5, which is indicative in the discourse of calling for strong actions to achieve a social change and supports his cognitive strategy of unity.

3.2.4. I have been to the mountaintop speech
April 3, 1968, Memphis, Tennessee

A) Showing a sense of courage

We aren't engaged in any negative protest and in any negative arguments with anybody. We are saying that we are determined to be men. We are determined to be people. We are saying -- We are saying that we are God's children. And that we are God's children, we don't have to live like we are forced to live. Now, what does all of this mean in this great period of history? It means that we've got to stay together. We've got to stay together and maintain unity. You know, whenever Pharaoh wanted to prolong the period of slavery in Egypt, he had a favorite, favorite formula for doing it. What was that? He kept the slaves fighting among themselves. But whenever the slaves get together, something happens in Pharaoh's court, and he cannot hold the slaves in slavery. When the slaves get together, that's the beginning of getting out of slavery. Now let us maintain unity.

Secondly, let us keep the issues where they are. The issue is injustice. The issue is the refusal of Memphis to be fair and honest in its dealings with its public servants, who happen to be sanitation workers. Now, we've got to keep attention on that. That's always the problem with a little violence. You know what happened the other day, and the press dealt only with the window-breaking. I read the articles. They very seldom got around to mentioning the fact that one thousand, three hundred sanitation workers are on strike, and that Memphis is not being fair to them, and that Mayor Loeb is in dire need of a doctor. They didn't get around to that. Now we're going to march again, and we've got to march again, in order to put the issue where it is supposed to be -- and force everybody to see that there are thirteen hundred of God's children here suffering, sometimes going hungry, going through dark and dreary nights wondering how this thing is going to come out.

And then I got into Memphis. And some began to say the threats, or talk about the threats that were out. What would happen to me from some of our sick white brothers? Well, I don't know what will happen now. We've got some difficult days ahead. But it really doesn't matter with me now, because I've been to the mountaintop. And I don't mind. Like anybody, I would like to live a long life. Longevity has its place. But I'm not concerned about that now. I just want to do God's will. And He's allowed me to go up to the mountain. And I've looked over. And I've seen the Promised Land. I may not get there with you. But I want you to know tonight, that we, as a people, will get to the promised land! And so I'm happy, tonight. I'm not worried about anything. I'm not fearing any man! Mine eyes have seen the glory of the coming of the Lord!!

Contextual orientation

"I've Been to the Mountaintop" is the common title of the last speech delivered by Martin Luther King. King spoke on 3 April 1968, in Memphis, Tennessee. The next day, King was assassinated. The speech primarily handles the Memphis Sanitation Strike. In his speech, King calls for unity, economic actions, boycotts, non-violent protests, and he supports a strike by garbage workers, giving a poignant vision of the victorious future of the civil rights struggles. In the manner of his speech, King cites the teachings of Jesus

Christ. Toward the end of the speech, King refers to threats against his life and he uses a language that seems to foreshadow his impending death.

Martin Luther King felt tired at the night when he delivered this speech, the last one of his life. The venue was a mass meeting held in a church in Memphis. King and his small entourage had led a march that day protesting low pay for black garbage collectors in Memphis. King felt he was too sick to preach. He asked his friend to speak instead and King would just have to say a few words. But King gave a long speech and his words energized the crowd and he spoke that night without any notes in his hand. King had warned in previous speeches that he might die before the struggle ended. It was not the first time he told listeners he had seen the promised land. King had been living with death threats for years.

No one in King's circle thought this was his final address. The next day was one of King's happiest. He stayed at the Lorraine Motel which was his habit to stay at this Motel when he visited Memphis. Surrounded by his brother, his staff and close friends of the movement, he laughed and joked all day until it was time to go to dinner at 6 PM. King stepped into the balcony of his room at the Motel, checking the weather to decide whether to bring a coat. As he leaned over the railing, talking with Jesse Jackson and others below, King was fatally shot in the Motel, which is currently known as the National Civil Rights Museum.

The analysis

Kings starts his speech by a cognitive concept of social schemas. He shows his mental representation of racism in deep rooted in society. King applies the event schema based on a specific event of what happened in Egypt by saying, *whenever Pharaoh wanted to prolong the period of slavery in Egypt*. King also applies another cognitive strategy, which is objectification. He activates this concept by simplifying his idea through a clear example of Egypt.

On saying the word, *pharaoh,* King employs the objectification strategy which is personification. He uses a specific person to convey his ideas. Another strategy is figuration, which is based on imagery concept. This is clear on saying, *And I've seen the Promised Land*, whereby he uses a imagery concept, *promised land*. Another cognitive strategy is ontologising, which is based on physical entities. This is clear on saying, *I've been to the mountaintop*, which shows physical concept "mountaintop" to increase the mental horizons of his audience about various meanings he wants to convey to them.

On the ideological level, King employs the strategy of *reification* which represents the historical state of affairs as if it was permanent. This is clear on mentioning, *whenever pharaoh wanted to prolong the period of slavery in Egypt*, whereby King focuses on the concept of historical truth. King also activates the strategy of *fragmentation* by mentioning two contrasting concepts, *fighting and unity, fair and violence*. King aims at making his audience conscious and very aware of unequal balance and distribution of power by contrasting the privileges and rights of the white race with those of the black race. King wants to convey a clear message that is; while the white race enjoys freedom and independence, the black race is denied them. While fragmentation strategy is used by the dominant group to increase physical and mental differences, King employs the contrasting concepts as a way to illuminate the difference in status between the two races with the intention of moving the conscience of his white audience.

King uses another ideological strategy, which is legitimation. He activates this strategy by shedding light on historical concept and he clarified that by using the strategy of narrativization. He uses that by involving stories that recount the past and treat the present as part of one concept. King shows that on saying, *whenever Pharaoh wanted to prolong the period of slavery in Egypt*. King uses another strategy which is rationalization, which is based on facts and logic concepts. This is clear on saying, *Now let us maintain unity*, whereby he affirms the concept of logic and unity. Therefore, by saying the word "let us" and repeating the person pronoun "we" frequently, he uses another strategy of unification, as he based his direction on logic symbols and standard way of unity.

On the linguistic level, King activates the direct and indirect speech acts. On saying, "*Now we're going to march again,*" King employs a direct speech act which is declarative, but also an indirect speech act which is commissive, as he vows to do more efforts to get the target. On saying, *When the slaves get together, that's the beginning of getting out of slavery,* King employs an indirect speech act, which is commissive, as it is an action that would happen in the future. On saying, *We've got to stay together,* King uses a direct speech act, which is directive, as King advises his followers. King activates the direct and indirect speech acts to reinforce the persistence for the struggle. King also uses the metaphors to strengthen his ideas. On saying, *the promised land,* King employs the abstract to concrete concept by connecting the promise with land. In the same utterance, King uses a another an ontologizing metaphor as it revolves around the abstract meaning.

Table(5) : Concordance of the noun "God"

Context	Word	Context
that we are	God'	children
we are	God	children
there are thirteen hundred of	God	children
I just want to do	God	God's will.

The above table shows that the approximate frequency of "God" is 4, which is indicative in the discourse of religious stance for pushing the audience to move forward.

3.3. Conclusion

The analysis of Martin Luther King's speeches within (pre and post 1964 era) shows that King diversify congintive, ideological, and linguistic devices to reach his goals of convincing his audience his beliefs. Among the tools that have been employed by King are metaphors, speech acts, and modality. King attempts to activate the mental aspects of his audience by refreshing their long and short term memories of the real concepts of America. He attempts to mix the social representations and religious concepts as part of his ideology. He applies different ideological strategies such as unfication and legitimation as a way to express his beliefs to make a social change.

Moreover, King attempts to balance between logic and emotion to strenghten his credibility among his audience. He employs the persusaive strategy of comparing different social events and evaluating them. Clearly,

King's discourse of post 1964 era has been tranformed. King handles a wide range of global-oriented issues like poverty and oppression in different countries to expand his macro view of social change. Finally, due to Gandhiism's influence on King's discourse, it is clear that King's invitation of peaceful social change was enough to be described as the American Gandhi. That influence is confirmed in his speeches by linking morality and spirituality with social change.

Chapter Four
Analysis of Obama's speeches (pre-presidency)

0. Introduction

This chapter provides a cognitive, ideological, and linguistic analysis of Obama's speeches within the period (January 2008 to August 2008), which marked his presidential campaign to get the office as the first African-American candidate in the U.S. history. The analysis follows the theoretical approach explained in chapter one, including the cognitive-linguistic devices, within the theory of critical discourse analysis. Analyzing political speeches necessitates an integrated approach that involves many disciplines to understand different aspects that may be combined with language use in political speeches.

As it is laid out in chapter one, the cognitive linguistic approach is the main approach in the analysis, including Thompson's (1990) ideological tools, and the cognitive tools of Pennington (2000). In addition, the analysis will show how the persuasive tactics, based upon credibility, emotions, and the logic, are influential in the audience's conceptual level. Modality and speech acts are employed in the analysis as linguistic devices. The selected data, to be analyzed in this chapter, consist of four speeches. These are:

1- Iowa caucus speech
2- The great need of the hour speech
3- International call for change speech
4- The American Promise speech

Each speech is analyzed on three levels; cognitive, ideological, and linguistic. The linguistic level is followed by a concordance to show the importance of frequent use of lexical items in comprehending the meaning.

4.1. The development of the African American discourse: Post-King's era and pre-Obama's era

The examination of the African-American discourse, post King's assassination, shows that there are explorations of the cognitive memories inhabited by African-Americans in their society. Based on Reed (1997), Morgan (2002), and African American's vision in the American society motivated them to act and produce certain kind of discourse that is significantly different from their own counterparts. African-American cognitive aspects are important avenue to understand how they face the tide of being deprived of their social rights and for being partially outside the parameters of the society.

In the 70s, both the black activists and citizens drew at large heavily on the social memories from the civil rights movement. They used their own social memories to develop and promote their discourses. These tendencies continued through the 80s and 90s, and the African-Americans use the social memory combined with language to focus on race as a tool for political organization and forging cooperative action. The direction of African-American organizational activity began at a high level and increased over the time. Throughout the three decades, African-Americans feature certain level of collective mobilization. The collective black mobilization impacts the politics, the rhetoric, and the character of Black life everywhere in the U.S.

The primary role of African-Americans in the 70s focused on providing jobs. According to Brown et al (2003:74), "By the 1970s, blacks were also making job gains in the private sector. Among black male workers, the proportion working as professionals or managers rose from 6.8 percent in 1960 to 17.4 percent by 1980." In the 70s with Black people holding significant nationwide offices, many African Americans are placed in powerful governmental positions. However, it is important to mention that the experiences, organizational and mobilizational capacity that African Americans got, made it possible for the election of a black candidate to be the 44th president of the United States. In addition, Obama's grassroots experiences in Chicago, his subsequent election to illionis senate, the U.S. senate, and ultimately to the white house were made possible by a deep and dynamic infrastructure created over decades.

African-Americans live in contradictions in the American society with all of its history, customs, culture and idiosyncrasies. Indeed, it is largely obvious because the Black people in the U.S. are a race-conscious people as they understand that the character of their existence has been explicitly determined by race. That affects how they conceive of themselves, how they feel about themselves, how they conceive of and feel about others. The African-Americans went through unprecedented change in the second half of the twentieth century. In 1940, African Americans were economically oppressed and exploited. Politically, their vast majority was denied the franchise.

By the early 1950s, the U.S. accounted for more than more than 50 percent of the world's wealth. Court decisions, executive actions and legislation had also contributed to substantive changes in the African-Americans' life as they had pressures from the international environment. During the 1960s, real changes began to appear on the stage and was revived by Martin Luther King and supported by the civil rights movement.

Following the 60s, despite the deficiency of the civil rights movement, African-Americans' gains persisted by using organizations, collective mobilization, activating the community and collective work that help them to gain their rights in the U.S. society. African Americans awareness of their political right has been embodied by the rise of Barack Obama in the nineties of the last century, until he became the first African American president of the U.S. Brown et al (2003).

4.2. Obama's biographical overview

According to *Dreams from My father* (2008), Barack Obama was born in Hawaii in 1961, the son of a Kenyan father, also named Barack, and a Kansas-born mother who met as students at the University of Hawaii. His parents divorced after his father left to pursue graduate work at Harvard when Obama was two years old. Father and son would meet only one more time before the elder Barack Obama died in a 1982 car accident after returning to Kenya. His mother remarried a native of Indonesia, where Obama lived between the ages of six and ten. Despite being young, his life in Indonesia made him aware of issues of poverty and inequality.

Obama later returned to Hawaii and attended a prestigious prep school, the Punahu Academy. As he describes in his autobiography *Dreams from My Father*, he struggled with his racial identity throughout his high school years. Living with a white mother and grandparents and attending a predominantly white school, he found it difficult to navigate between black and white worlds. He endured racial slurs, as he mentions that in his book *Dreams from my Father* (2008:49), from a basketball coach, among others, leading him to conclude:

> e were lw l i o t e w ite ' court b t e w ite ' rule . If t e ri ci l, or the coach, or a teacher wanted to spit in your face, he could, because he d t e ower d ou did 't. tever e decided to do, it was his decision to make, not yours, and because of t t fu d e t l ower e eld over ou distinction between good and bad whites held negligible e i . A d t e fi l iro : ould ou refu e t i defeat and lash out at your captors, they would have a name for that, too, a name that could cage you just as good. Paranoid. Militant. Violent. Nigger.

Compounding his alienation, his African American friends did not consider him to be completely one of them, charging that he had to learn how to be black from books. His confusion led him to experiment with illegal drugs during his teenage years. Later accounts by school contemporaries suggest that his alienation did not appear as outwardly declared as he reported it in his autobiography. In 1979 he left Hawaii to attend Occidental College in Los Angeles.

According to online version of Wikipedia, Obama continued to struggle with issues of identity, but became involved in political activity, protesting the u iver it ' i ve t e t i co ie doing business in the apartheid-era government of South Africa. His efforts led him to realize that he was an effective public speaker, even as he felt ambivalent about whether his words had much impact. After two years, he transferred to Columbia University in New York, where he majored in political science. During his time there, he became more academically focused, to the extent that some of his friends concluded that he was becoming a very different black person. Obama graduated from Columbia in 1983.

After an experience at a multinational consulting firm in New York, he moved to Chicago in 1985 to work as a community organizer for the Developing Communities Project, focusing on issues like jobs and public housing in the inner city. His decision to pursue community activism reflects his belief, inspired by the civil rights movement, that grassroots, bottom-up efforts are the key to social change. It is the concept of social change that Martin Luther King asked for in the fifties of the last century.

Ob ' i er io i treet-level community organizing taught him valuable, even sometimes frustrating, lessons about politics. In July 2004,

Obama wrote and delivered the keynote address at the 2004 Democratic National Convention in Boston, Massachusetts. Though it was not televised by commercial broadcast television networks, a combined 9.1 million viewers saw Obama's speech, which was a highlight of the convention and elevated his status within the Democratic Party. Obama was sworn in as a senator on January 4, 2005. He was the fifth African American Senator in U.S. history and the third to have been popularly elected. He was the only Senate member of the Congressional Black Caucus.

Obviously, Obama served as the junior United States Senator from Illinois from January 2005 until he resigned after his election to the presidency in November 2008. Obama's experience in Columbia and Harvard schools enable him to be the president of the Harvard Law Review. He was a community organizer in Chicago before earning his law degree. He worked as a civil rights attorney in Chicago and taught constitutional law at the University of Chicago Law School from 1992 to 2004. On February 10, 2007, Obama announced his candidacy for president of the United States in front of the Old State Capitol building in Springfield, Illinois.

The choice of the announcement site was viewed as symbolic because it was also where Abraham Lincoln delivered his historic "House Divided" speech in 1858. Throughout the campaign, Obama emphasized the issues of rapidly ending the Iraq War, increasing energy independence and providing universal health care. After a close campaign in the 2008 Democratic Party presidential primaries against Hillary Clinton, he won his party's nomination. In the 2008 general election, he defeated Republican nominee John McCain and was inaugurated as president of the United States on January 20, 2009.

O e c   t t Ob   d M rti Lut er i ' di cour e   re o e common grounds as they both have a dream and hope and both made their struggle against racism. They responded to their dream of overcoming racism with passion and added value to others. They also have faith in themselves and the courage to pursue their dream. This makes it necessary for their speeches to not only send messages to the audience, but also to have the ability to cognitively persuade them of their messages. This process of cognitive persuasion requires the use of some strategies in order to produce a persuasive discourse. In the following lines, the researcher presents a brief background of Obama's discourse.

4.3. The development of Obama's discourse

Ob ' e er e ce wit i t e ublic A eric co ciou e w ore characteristic of a cultural icon than a politician. In an era wherein politicians are regularly viewed as distant, and unconcerned with the average person, r c Ob ur ri i l e er ed w t ve de cribed "roc t r" of t e curre t A eric olitic l ce e (D uber, 2004; Leo old, 2004). Like those who rise to prominence in popular culture, Barack Obama became a household name, as it would seem, nearly overnight. As Monica Davey, a columnist for the *New York Times*, wrote in the months just prior to the 2004 De ocr tic N tio l Co ve tio (DNC), "Over i t, Mr. Ob , for er civil rights lawyer, has become a treasured commodity in the Democratic Party tio ll " (D ve , 2004). Ob erfor ce e ote DNC e er further solidified his place in subsequent political discussions.

As Clayton (2007:53) e l i , " ince the 2004 keynote address, Barack Obama has become the political superstar of t e De ocr tic P rt ." By many ccou t , Ob ' i cre i o ul rit i o ew t u ique, and connected in the memory of Americans as the first African American to witness such achievement. It was the first time people got in their minds the memories of Martin Luther King. Numerous political analysts have analyzed the various f ctor co tributi to Ob ' eed ri e to f e. I f ct, t ere re ever l obvious elements involved i Ob ' rowi o ul rit .

O e o ibilit for Ob 's growing popularity stems from his embodiment of broad and perhaps even divergent cultural and ideological sensibilities (Wilson, 2007). Part of the attention that people are giving Obama is due to his unique background, as the son of a white mother from Kansas and a black father from Kenya. As a boy lived with an Indonesian stepfather in Jakarta and later with his white grandparents in Hawaii, and who went to college in California, graduated from Harvard Law School, and lives in Chicago.

As the result of such divergent experiences, Obama is often perceived as an individual who challenges traditional social, political, and ideological boundaries. Obama continues to trade on such perceptions, positioning himself simultaneously in multiple worlds. For instance, Obama is influential, educated, and privileged, yet consistently identifies himself with poor, underprivileged, black communities. Additionally, Obama is running a cutting-edge Internet and multimedia campaign, all the while employing standard print media to produce texts like *The Audacity of Hope* which gain him a hearing among more traditional political constituencies (Tumulty, 2007).

Similarly, Obama remains strongly committed to progressive politics while publicly and passionately identifying himself as a religious Christian. Consistent with Obama non-traditional identity, he characterizes himself as one who is both well-versed in American political life and yet who can offer something that is new and different, something that is untainted by usual political practices. In all these ways, Obama brings a sort of shifting identity to contemporary presidential politics. And such an identity has undoubtedly contributed to Oba ' ublic i e d o ul rit .

I dditio to t e ort of i ue r i ed bove, Ob ' o ul rit bee considerably bolstered by his persistent employment of the theme of hope and the need for solidarity emergent from such concept. At this point, it is enough to note that Obama relies heavily upon the notion that his campaign represents something new, something different and hopeful. In his latest (2006: 25) book, *The Audacity of Hope*, Obama writes,

> A government that truly represents these Americ
> will require a different kind of politics. That politics
> will need to reflect our lives as they are actually lived.
> It wo 't be re c ed, re d to ull off t e elf.
> We will need to remind ourselves, despite all our
> differences, just how much we share: common hopes,
> commons dreams, a bond that will not break.

Consistent with this sort of sentiment, Obama regularly envisions a change in the way that American politics is performed and understood. Obama consistently calls for a different kind of politics, a call in which Martin Luther king spoke about before, a move beyond divisive partisan political disagreement, and a recognition of a common and hopeful American future. Obama is certainly focusing on an increased clamoring among Americans for social and political change (Lugo and Lugo, 2008). Obama capitalizes upon this call of change by consistently speaking about hopeful possibilities for the future of America. The result has been to create a general sense of hope and possibility within much of the American public.

4.4. Obama's speeches of pre-presidency era

The following analysis handles four speeches of president Obama before taking the office and other four speeches after taking the office.

4.4.1. Obama Iowa's speech
January 3, 2008, Iowa

Thank you, Iowa. You know, they said this day would never come. They said our sights were set too high. They said this country was too divided; too disillusioned to ever come together around a common purpose. But on this January night - at this defining moment in history - you have done what the cynics said we couldn't do. You have done what the state of New Hampshire can do in five days. You have done what America can do in this New Year, 2008. In lines that stretched around schools and churches; in small towns and big cities; you came together as Democrats, Republicans and Independents to stand up and say that we are one nation; we are one people;and our time for change has come. You said the time has come to move beyond the bitterness and pettiness and anger that's consumed Washington; to end the political strategy that's been all about division and instead make it about addition - to build a coalition for change that stretches through Red States and Blue States.

Because that's how we'll win in November, and that's how we'll finally meet the challenges that we face as a nation. We are choosing hope over fear. We're choosing unity over division, and sending a powerful message that change is coming to America. *You said the time has come to tell the lobbyists who think their money and their influence speak louder than our voices that they don't own this-government, we do; and we are here to take it back. The time has come for a President who will be honest about the choices and the challenges we face; who will listen to you and learn from you even when we disagree; who won't just tell you what you want to hear, but what you need to know. And in New Hampshire, if you give me the same chance that Iowa did tonight, I will be that president for America. Thank you.*

Contextual orientation

The Iowa caucus is commonly recognized as the first step in the United States Presidential nomination process for both the Democrats and the

Republicans. Barack Obama delivered this eloquent speech to thunderous ovation after he won the Iowa Democratic caucus on January 3, 2008, which was the first vote in the 2008 presidential primary race. His words in Iowa were strongly reminiscent of Barack Obama's Inspiring 2004 Democratic Convention Speech. His 2004 convention speech first brought Barack Obama to national attention. Barack Obama won the Democratic Iowa Caucus with more than the third of the vote. According to polls, most of the voters were women and Obama got most of the female vote.

Standing at a podium emblazoned with a banner that read "change," in front of a large crowd of supporters clearly pleased by his win, Obama spoke in a carefully measured language that impressed every one of the audience. The o t ot ble rt of Ob ' eec w ow lo it w . e o e for over an hour, without notes. He began by introducing his wife and two children, and moved on to introducing his organizers as well. Then he spoke alone, addressing the challenges facing the country, and his hope for the future. Much of the crowd, though, was still inspired by his message.

Throughout the speech, Obama never mentioned any of his Democratic opponents by name. Yet, the win by Obama, a black candidate, dealt a major blow to the campaigns of his opponents. As predicted, Obama appeared to have tapped into the support among first-time caucus-goers and younger voters. As for the Democratic victor, Obama is the first black presidential candidate to win the Iowa caucus and the most viable black candidate from any party with a chance to win the presidency in history. But even amid his historic victory, he stuck to his call for substantive political change and the power of unity over division.

The analysis

President Obama gives this speech to motivate people to vote for him and to persuade those who do not intend to vote that he is the right candidate to vote for. He uses an important slogan during his campaign, called "Change We Can Believe In." He also pays a great attention to the concept of hope. On the cognitive level, Obama employs the elements of power by using cognitive persuasion. On saying, *You know, they said this day would never come*, Obama uses response shaping by which he tries to shape his audience view about change. On saying, *they said this day would never come, They said our sights were set too high. They said this country was too divided*, Obama activates another cognitive stratgey of response reinforcing by confirming his basic idea through repeating the phrase, *they said*. He employs another congitive persuasive technique by saying, *But on this January night… you have done what the cynics said we couldn't do. You have done what the state of New Hampshire can do in five days. You have done what America can do in this New Year, 2008,* as he activates response changing. That is clear when Obama refers to the changes in which his audience can pursue.

Obviously, Obama uses the objectification strategy by simplifying his ideas and transforming them into concrete images in his audience minds. He employs a cognitive process of conceptual understanding in the short term memory (STM) and long term memory (LTM). By using the short term memory, which has a limited capacity, Obama uses the place where all incoming information from various senses is interpreted. Through his introduction, *they said this day would never come. They said our sights were set too high. They said this country was too divided; too disillusioned to ever come together around a common purpose,* Obama reminds his audience of what everyone has in his mind about the status of African Americans in the past. Thus, he focuses on the mental representations that people have over the African Americans.

That kind of STM which sometimes functions as a so-called working memory encompasses perception, understanding, thinking and is deliberately used by Obama to pave the way for the change he is looking for. On the other hand, by saying, *But on this January night, at this defining moment in history, you have done what the cynics said we couldn't do. You have done what the state of New Hampshire can do in five days. You have done what America can do in this New Year, 2008*, Obama uses what he has in his LTM of restored information after processing in STM. Thus, he reminds his audience about the racist ideologies and how he overcomes all of the obstacles to achieve change.

Racist Ideology

Obama employs an analytic cognitive way by focusing on the short and long term memories in order to achieve certain function;

A) To communicate with emotion which is a reasonable human desire and a goal of communication generally.

B) To urge the reader/listener to accept or cognitively believe what the addressors want to say.

C) To manifest the addressor's attitude and viewpoints about the subject matter that he tackles.

Obama employs two branches in his cognitive way, namely the textual function and the interpersonal function. In the textual functions, there are two sub branches; textual markers and interpretive markers. In the textual markers, he employs certain tools such as, reminders, which is clearly explained by repeating the utterance, *they said*. He also employs the logical connective "But" to join the previous concept he has in his memory about racial discrimination with new status for African Americans. Obama moves to interpersonal elements such as the certainly markers, *we will win, we will finally meet*, to express his full commitment to the truth value of his proposition.

On the ideological level, Obama uses a unification strategy in saying, *we are one nation, we are one people*, by using the positive words. It seems also that the level of generalization is high as he did not give more detailed or specific information about facts in his speech. On the other hand, to ensure his strategy, Obama uses the following utterances, *you have done, we will meet the challenges*, to show a kind of action and achievement the Americans make in support of the concept of change.

In addition, Obama employs another ideological strategy, which is legitimation by using the emotional and psychological aspects. He shows that by expressing his appreciation to his audience on saying, *We are choosing hope over fear. We're choosing unity over division*. Obama builds his credibility to his audience by making reference to such success as a kind of collective work. In other words, his ideological strategies are achieved through two methods, the image the speaker set of himself that he was not the only one who achieved that, and the content of speech. Obama relies on both as he sets a modest image of himself as a way of self-depreciation in order to be accepted by his audience.

On the other hand, on saying, *to build a coalition for change that stretches through Red States and Blue States,* Obama employs a specific ideological strategy that is, narrativization, which is clearly employed by reminding Americans of the forefathers of their country and their democratic transitory system. He applies powerful aspects of his language through *masking*, which Hung and Bradac (1993:143) define "as utterances that are written from the implicit perspective of the authority and are expressed in specialized linguistic forms." By employing the aspect of masking, Obama uses two different forms: truncation, or short sentences and generalization. In his utterance, *they said this country was too divided; too disillusioned to ever come together around a common purpose,* Obama uses very shortened forms of expression for two reasons:

1- To avoid any kind of redundant information.
2- To confirm his message about the right of all people to be equal.

On the linguistic level, Obama employs a variety of modals with different functions. On saying, *because that's how we'll win in November, and that's how we'll finally meet the challenges,* Obama uses a kind of root model to express his control over specific events in obligation and intention. His employed models are framed in a strongly-worded message to express cognitive persuasion. Therefore, persuasion and modality are used as tools in a sense that reveal the mental representation of the speakers who experience of racism and social inequality.

Obama is clearly activating the same strategy Martin Luther King used before which is employing a root modal to show power and a sense of emotional and logical persausion to their audience. Obama indicates his power of certainty as he presents to his audience a bunch of solutions that will serve the social, economic, and political situations. On saying, *who will be honest about the choices.... who will listen to you and learn from you even when we disagree; who won't just tell you what you want to hear*, he shows his way to get their presuasion of his candidacy. He employs three important steps;

1. Getting the attention of his audience
2. Stimulating desire for a different future
3. Reinforcing with reason

Obama employs a direct speech act on saying, *we are one nation; we are one people*, which is assertive, as he asserts a true idea about the unity of his nation. The uttrenace is also an indirect expressive speech act in which he expresses his praise to his people. Obama uses another direct speech act which is commissive on saying, *We are choosing hope over fear. We're choosing unity over division*, as he shows his vow to overcome fear and division by choosing hope and unity. On saying, *And in New Hampshire, if you give me the same chance that Iowa did tonight, I will be that president for America*, Obama employs another direct speech act, which is commissive, as he promises his audience to be the president if they give him a chance and vote for him, and an indirect speech act which is directive as he attempts to ask for an indirect request from his audience.

Table (1): Concordance of the pronoun"we"

Context	Word	Context
the cynics said	we	couldn't do
and say that we	we	are one nation
are one nation;	we	are one people
the challenges that	we	we face as a
	we	we are choosing hope
his government,	we	do and we
do and	we	are here to
And the challenges	we	face who will
You even when	we	disagree who won't

The above table (1) shows that the total frequency of "we" is 9, which is indicative in the discourse of unification and determination to get the rights of African Americans.

4.4.2. The great need of the hour speech
January 20, 2008. Atlanta, GA

As I was thinking about which ones we need to remember at this hour, my mind went back to the very beginning of the modern Civil Rights Era. Because before Memphis and the mountaintop; before the bridge in Selma and the march on Washington; before Birmingham and the beatings; the fire hoses and the loss of those four little girls; before there was King the icon and his magnificent dream, there was King the young preacher and a people who found themselves suffering under the yoke of oppression. And on the eve of the bus boycotts in Montgomery, at a time when many were still doubtful about the possibilities of change, a time when those in the black community mistrusted themselves, and at times mistrusted each other, King inspired with words not of anger, but of an urgency that still speaks to us today:"Unity is the great need of the hour" is what King said. Unity is how we shall overcome.

What Dr. King understood is that if just one person chose to walk instead of ride the bus, those walls of oppression would not be moved. But maybe if a few more walked, the foundation might start to shake. If a few more women were willing to do what Rosa Parks had done, maybe the cracks would start to show. If teenagers took freedom rides from North to South, maybe a few bricks would come loose. Maybe if white folks marched because they had come to understand that their freedom too was at stake in the impending battle, the wall would begin to sway. And if enough Americans were awakened to the injustice; if they joined together, North and South, rich and poor, Christian and Jew, then perhaps that wall would come tumbling down, and justice would flow like water, and righteousness like a mighty stream.Unity is the great need of the hour - the great need of this hour. Not because it sounds pleasant or because it makes us feel good, but because it's the only way we can overcome the essential deficit that exists in this country.

Contextual orientation

Speaking to hundreds of people at Atlanta's Ebenezer Baptist Church in the southeastern state of Georgia, where King launched the civil rights movement, Obama evoked the ongoing racial and ideological divide in America. Obama gave this speech at the historic church, where the Reverend King was ordained in 1948 and where he gave some of his most rousing sermons**.** Barack Obama pays tribute to the late African-American civil rights leader Martin Luther King, by focusing on community service, and his civil rights activities. Barack Obama was 2 years old when Dr. King talked about his dream. Barack Obama delivers such speech, loaded with history and promise**.** Obama was joined by civil rights leaders nationwide running service projects, ranging from cleaning up parks to assembling care packages for troops.

In general, the dream that both Obama and King talk about can be defined as having the opportunity and freedom that allows all citizens to achieve their goals in life through hard work and determination alone. Today, it generally refer to t e ide t t o e' prosperity de e d u o o e' ow bilitie d hard work, not on a rigid class structure, though the meaning of the phrase "the dream"   c   ed over A   eric '   i tor . For some, it is the opportunity to achieve more prosperity than they could in their countries of origin. For others, it is the opportunity for their children to grow up with an education and career opportunities. The concept of dream reflects the opportunity to be an individual without the constraints imposed by class, race, or ethnicity.

Ob   ow t t i ' le c i   ot o l   bout r ce, but e l o i religious leader whom many Americans view as a model of how faith and politics should connect. In addition, King has been a regular speaker in churches, particularly those with predominantly African American congregations. All of this means that Martin Luther King offers a potent moment for Obama to embrace faith and emphasize racial equality with public, high-profile events. That the candidate is a black man is perhaps an even more remarkable one.

The analysis

Obama starts his speech by linking his time with the era of the civil rights movements. He deliberately mentions that because he attempts to distinguish himself as a man of vision who has dared to pursue a dream of breaking historic barriers, redefining the divisions in the American society, and bringing about change. He believes that to convey his vision to his audience, it must be in an effective and compelling manner, and it should happen by enabling others to understand the vision and inspiring them ultimately to embrace it.

On the cognitive level, when Obama says, *there was King the icon and his magnificent dream, there was King the young preacher and a people who found themselves suffering under the yoke of oppression*, he activates the cognitive strategy of objectification by using symbolic words (icon, dream) to simplify his message. He achieves this style by using the concept of personification through mentioning the name "King." In his personification strategy, Obama activates the strong positive evaluation by employing the dynamic images in his speech. When Obama mentions the words, *walked, moved, marched*, he creates moving images, dynamic rather than static, in the mental representation of his audience, thus the image becomes a moving living thing. He probably uses such verbs to create a sense of momentum. Obama's success in employing such dynamic images illustrates that those who seek to convey vision excellently can benefit from using words that create moving entities.

Obama also employs such strategy by using figuration through focusing on abstract ideas like "*dream, hope.*" He uses a specific technique to show his power, that is; cognitive persuasion. First, he activates the concept of response shaping on saying, *Birmingham and the beatings; the fire hoses and the loss of those four little girls; before there was King the icon and his magnificent dream, there was King the young preacher and a people who found themselves suffering under the yoke of oppression*, as he attempts to shape his audience opinion by making his reference to history to convey his ideas so effectively and explain the principles of his vision which are: unity, responsive government, and change. On saying, *Unity is the great need of the hour*, he uses another cognitive persuasive stratgey which is response reinforcing, as he attempts to strenghten the core point of his message which is unity.

On the ideological level, Obama uses the legitimation strategy by using the historical concepts in narrativized way. On saying, *before Memphis and the mountaintop, before the bridge in Selma and the march on Washington; before Birmingham and the beatings*, he applies the narrativization strategy by using past anecdotes to increase a sense of belonging. This allows him to go into greater depth and illustrate points in memorable ways.

On saying, *North and South, rich and poor, Christian and Jew*, he applies the strategy of unification by using universal concepts like unifying north and south, rich and poor. King also uses symbolized idea on saying, *Unity is the great need of the hour*, as he refers to the necessity of being unified. On saying, *the only way we can overcome the essential deficit that exists in this country,* he activates a universal idea, that is; unity is the solution for America's problem. So, he applied the universalization strategy to win the hearts and minds of his audience.

On the linguistic level, Obama employs the direct speech acts, which is representative by saying, *unity is how we shall overcome*, as he tells the truth of his society. In the same utterance, he also uses an indirect speech act which is expressive, as he refers to a psychological state. he shows a sense of encouraging his audience; therefore he uses direct and indirect speech acts to convey his ideas to his followers. To make his strategy effective, he employs descriptive words to paint cognitive pictures with vivid words that call rich images to mind.

Obama applies the Fairclough's theory of intertextuality (Chapter one-P. 24.25). T e i ide of i terte tu lit i t t; "b ic ll t e ro ert te t have of being full of snatches of other texts, which may be explicitly de rc ted or er ed i ." F irclou (1992b: 5). Ob   ctiv te bot explicit (manifest) and impicit (interdiscursivity/constitutive) styles. Obama's reference to King in the utterance, *Unity is the great need of the hour" is what King said. Unity is how we shall overcome,* reflects the first style of inetrtextuality, as he explicitly mentions the words of King. He also uses the implicit part by saying, *civil right Memphis and the mountaintop, Selma, Washington; Birmingham and the beatings,* to refresh the memory of audience who are willing to make change and to give a chance to the black candidate "Obama." He also focuses on the use of symbolism in his speech by choosing words rich in meaning. Obama does this with great skill. The effectiveness of Obama's strategy of symbolism is that; he uses a word that is multi dimensional in the ideas and images it evokes.

In addition, Obama uses a simile strategy. When he says, *and justice would flow like water, and righteousness like a mighty stream,* he deliberately attempts to show how such words do have a positive value. In addition, such words elicit images of great achievement, great heroism and the quest for excellence in which his country is based on. This simile sets powerful imagery in his audience's mind. It sounds like Obama chooses his words carefully to provide greater impact to his audience. He also employs the technique of abstract to concrete metaphor on saying, *If teenagers took freedom rides from North to South, maybe a few bricks would come loose,* as he connects one abstract concept "freedom" with something concrete, which is "bricks."

On saying, *If a few more women were willing to do what Rosa Parks had done, maybe the cracks would start to show,* Obama combines a conceptual metpahor based on the abstract meaning of Rosa's Parks act, and the concrete meaning of cracks. When Obama mentions the sufferings of King, the historical action of Rosa Parks, the bus boycotts in Montgomery, he involves his use of enough details to support his argument. Obama uses the details to illustrate the depth of his knowledge about key issues.

Table (2): Concordance of the noun"King"

Context	Word	Context
before there was	King	the icon and
dream, there was	King	the young preacher
each other,	King	inspired with words
hour" is what King	King	said
	King	understood is that

The above table shows that the total frequency of "King" is 5, which is indicative in the discourse of memorization to get the rights of African Americans.

4.4.3. International call for change speech
July 24, 2008. Germany

This is the moment when we must defeat terror and dry up the well of extremism that supports it. This threat is real and we cannot shrink from our responsibility to combat it. If we could create NATO to face down the Soviet Union, we can join in a new and global partnership to dismantle the networks that have struck in Madrid and Amman; in London and Bali; in Washington and New York. If we could win a battle of ideas against the communists, we can stand with the vast majority of Muslims who reject the extremism that leads to hate instead of hope.

This is the moment when we must renew our resolve to rout the terrorists who threaten our security in Afghanistan, and the traffickers who sell drugs on your streets. No one welcomes war. I recognize the enormous difficulties in Afghanistan. But my country and yours have a stake in seeing that NATO's first mission beyond Europe's borders is a success. For the people of Afghanistan, and for our shared security, the work must be done. America cannot do this alone. The Afghan people need our troops and your troops; our support and your support to defeat the Taliban and al Qaeda, to develop their economy, and to help them rebuild their nation. We have too much at stake to turn back now.

This is the moment when we must renew the goal of a world without nuclear weapons. The two superpowers that faced each other across the wall of this city came too close too often to destroying all we have built and all that we love. With that wall gone, we need not stand idly by and watch the further spread of the deadly atom. It is time to secure all loose nuclear materials; to stop the spread of nuclear weapons; and to reduce the arsenals from another era. This is the moment to begin the work of seeking the peace of a world without nuclear weapons.

Contextual orientation

Barack Obama arrived in Berlin on July 24th and gave his speech at the monument in the heart of the German city that once symbolized Cold War division. In his speech, he spoke about the historic US-German partnership and about the importance of strengthening trans-Atlantic relations. Obama highlighted what he sees as common transatlantic goals in his pursuit for an international call of change. Obama was on the latest leg of an international trip intended to bolster his foreign policy credentials at home and set out his vision for a new era of transatlantic cooperation.

Obama started his speech saying he came to Berlin not as a U.S. Democratic presidential candidate, but as a citizen like any number of visitors. He probably said that because his speech was meant to take place at the Brandenburg gate, a symbol of Germany's Cold War division, as well as the site of Kennedy's speech. Ironically, the place, Obama chose for his speech, was relocated by the Nazis to its present site. Therefore, critics argued this location was not suitable for Obama, who delivers a message of global unity.

On the other hand, this monument is used for many different peaceful events. Questions remain, however, as to whether Obama was aware of the backdrop of the place where he gave his speech. Given that this location was built to celebrate military victories against Denmark, Austria and France, the location is very different from Obama's vision of Europe.

Berliners lined up to hear the speech more than five hours before it began. All day long, hundreds waited on the streets to catch a glimpse of the motorcade that shuttled Obama among meetings with German officials, starting with Chancellor Angela Merkel. The exact location of Obama's speech had become a matter of intense speculation in Berlin after his campaign team originally suggested an appearance at the Brandenburg Gate. Many, including German Chancellor Angela Merkel, questioned whether the site, where Presidents Ronald Reagan and Bill Clinton both spoke when they were in the White House, was appropriate for a candidate.

Barack Obama spoke to tens of thousands of Berliners chanting "Yes We Can" or "Obama." In his speech, Barack Obama highlighted the common challenges facing America and its allies, especially Europe. Obama needed to prove to Americans that he could defend U.S. interests abroad. While sharing pride for his country, Obama also discussed concerns shared with Europe, including: working for a successful NATO mission in Afghanistan, securing loose nuclear material, working with Russia, getting Iran to abandon its nuclear plan, securing a lasting peace between Israel and Palestine, bringing the Iraq war to a close, and addressing climate change problem.

The analysis

Obama gives this speech in Germany as he attempts to establish a common ground between the American people and the German people. Obama manages to break down barriers that could have served as insurmountable obstacles to other aspiring peoples. In his speech, Obama shows his ability to use communication to bring different peoples together despite their differences and to establish common ground. He deliberately employs certain tools to unite people, build friendship, and promote a sense of shared goals.

On the cognitive level, when Obama mentions the words, *NATO, Soviet Union*, in Berlin, he cognitively activates the mental representations that are stored in the German mind about their past experiences. Obama, to win the hearts and minds, understands the circumstances by which he delivers his speech. By activating the mental representations, he captures the mood and addresses the audience's key concerns, grievances, and desires.

As part of his power, Obama activates three cognitive persausive processes for conveying his meaning: shaping, changing, reinforcing. On saying, *This is the moment when we must defeat terror and dry up the well of extremism that supports it,* Obama uses the concept of defeating terror to shape his audience response about terror. Obama moves to change the audience attitude towards unity by saying, *If we could win a battle of ideas against the communists, we can stand with the vast majority of Muslims,* as he pushes them to overcome the religious differences to reach the target. By saying, *the work must be done*, Obama reinforces his idea about the completion of his mission.

By using the previous techniques, Obama succeeds in connecting the mental representations between the short and the long term memories. In the short term memory, it is the concept of war against terror, while in the long term memory, it is the ideological differences between the East and the West. Obama moves on to match the information in the short-term memory with the information in the long-term memory. On putting these issues in sequenctial ways, within simple sentences, he shows greater potency as a strong persuasive communicator in front of his audience.

On the ideological level, when Obama uses the first person plural pronoun "*we*" in the speech, he attempts to employ the ideological strategy of unification by dissolving differences between the two peoples and putting them in a collective unity that disregards racial, religious, social, or political differences. By employing the symbolization of unity which involves binding individuals together, he produces symbols of collective unity. He bears in his mind how to employ the details effectively. He understands that his audience needs three Rs, recognizing, remembering, responding. The audience wants an assurance that Obama recognizes the circumstances they face, remembers the details of those circumstances enough to reference them, and will be responsive to those issues.

On the linguistic level, Obama confirms his excellency in his communication to the audience by showing that he is aware of their circumstances, and he understands these chanlleges, and prepares to do something about them. When Obama says, *we can not shrink, we can join, we can stand with, we must renew, I recognize the enormous difficulties*, he attempts to personalize his message with skillfull use of pronouns "*we, I.*" When he personalizes his messages and refers to his own relevant experience, it helps to establish credibility and create his authority. Employing the pronoun "*we*" has a strong message that both the speaker and his audience are in the same team, on the same boat, facing the same fate.

He also combines three phrases in one sentence as a certain way to strenghthen his concepts. This triadic extension is clearly shown in his utterance, *to defeat the Taliban and al qaeda, to develop their ecnomy, and to help them rebuilding their notion*. Obama once again uses such strategy in saying, *it is time to secure all loose nuclear materials: to stop the spread of nuclear weapons: to reduce the arsenals from another area*. He deliberately uses these three combined pharses together to appear as a resaonable person in front of his audience and thereby to persuade them.

Obama's use of such triadic phrases with a sequenced order establishes both a strong sense of logic and underscoring a particular point of view. When he talks about the unity in confronting a danger, he knows how to create a strong sense of logic to his ideas and remarks. Obama key to create a strong sense of logic involves a sequencing ideas. He believes that the listener must be able to understand the flow of thoughts and find a logical and compelling sense, which help in achieving his goals.

Obama's strong conviction and determination to become the inspiring president of the U.S. and his calls for overcoming the obstacles is revealed through his use of modality. When Obama repeats the modal "*must*" in the utterances, *we must defeat terror, we must renew our resolve, we must renew the goal of a world*, he employs the root modal of obligation to show the necessity of taking a specific action and to present a level of certainty to his audience. Metaphorically, Obama employs a cognitive linguistic approach of using the abstract to concrete metaphor by saying, *and dry up the well of extremism that supports it*, as he uses the concrete word, "*well*" and combines it with the concept of "extremism."

Obama's technique in using contrasting words, *love, hate, build, destroy, terror, security*, helps in clarifying the meaning. One of the clear features of Obama's powerful oration is his outsatnding use of contrast words. He places opposing ideas side by side, which allows him to crystallize key points about the concepts. When contrasting the ideas, he employs the parallel structures which enable him to present clear concepts, and clarifying differences in ideas and contrasting different beliefs.

Obama activates the strategy of speech acts whether in a direct or indirect way. On saying, *we need not stand idly by and watch the further spread of the deadly atom*, Obama employs a direct speech act, which is directive, as he gives advice to his audience. On saying, *This is the moment when we must renew the goal of a world*, Obama activates a direct speech act, which is assertive, as he asserts the concept of renewing the goal. In the same utterance, he employs another indirect speech act, which is commssive, as he gives a vow to move forward to achieve the goal.

Obama's use of direct and indirect speech acts establishes a sense of momentum with an emphasis on the importance and urgency to future actions. By using resonating words, he evokes shared values, patriotic concepts, and valuable principles. Obama's cognitive, ideological, and linguistic techniques push him to finish his speech strongly. By explaining the shared history, shared destiny, and ending with high point, he succeeds in making his audience inspired, motivated, and focused on key issues.

Table (3): Concordance of the noun"must"

Context	Word	Context
moment when we	must	defeat terror and
moment when we	must	renew our resolve
security, the work	must	be done
moment when we	must	renew the goal

The above table shows that the total frequency of "must" is 4, which is indicative in the discourse of willingness and determination.

4.4.4. The American Promise Speech
Democratic National Convention
August 28, 2008
Denver, Colorado

We meet at one of those defining moments - a moment when our nation is at war, our economy is in turmoil, and the American promise has been threatened once more. These challenges are not all of government's making. But the failure to respond is a direct result of a broken politics in Washington and the failed policies of George W. Bush. America, we are better than these last eight years. We are a better country than this.This country is more decent than one where a woman in Ohio, on the brink of retirement, finds herself one illness away from disaster after a lifetime of hard work.This country is more generous than one where a man in Indiana has to pack up the equipment he's worked on for twenty years and watch it shipped off to China, and then chokes up as he explains how he felt like a failure when he went home to tell his family the news. We are more compassionate than a government that lets veterans sleep on our streets and families slide into poverty; that sits on its hands while a major American city drowns before our eyes.

Tonight, I say to the American people, to Democrats and Republicans and Independents across this great land - enough! This moment - this election - is our chance to keep, in the 21st century, the American promise alive. Because next week, in Minnesota, the same party that brought you two terms of George Bush and Dick Cheney will ask this country for a third. And we are here because we love this country too much to let the next four years look like the last eight. On November 4th, we must stand up and say: "Eight is enough."Now let there be no doubt. The Republican nominee, John McCain, has worn the uniform of our country with bravery and distinction, and for that we owe him our gratitude and respect. And next week, we'll also hear about those occasions when he's broken with his party as evidence that he can deliver the change that we need.

But the record's clear: John McCain has voted with George Bush ninety percent of the time. Senator McCain likes to talk about judgment, but really, what does it say about your judgment when you think George Bush has been right more than ninety percent of the time? I don't know about you, but I'm not ready to take a ten percent chance on change. These are my heroes. Theirs are the stories that shaped me. And it is on their behalf that I intend to win this election and keep our promise alive as President of the United States.

What is that promise? It's a promise that says each of us has the freedom to make of our own lives what we will, but that we also have the obligation to treat each other with dignity and respect. It's a promise that says the market should reward drive and innovation and generate growth, but that businesses should live up to their responsibilities to create American jobs, look out for American workers, and play by the rules of the road. Ours is a promise that says government cannot solve all our problems, but what it should do is that which we cannot do for ourselves - protect us from harm and provide every child a decent education; keep our water clean and our toys safe; invest in new schools and new roads and new science and technology.

Unlike John McCain, I will stop giving tax breaks to corporations that ship jobs overseas, and I will start giving them to companies that create good jobs right here in America. Now is the time to finally meet our moral obligation to *provide every child a world-class education, because it will take nothing less to compete in the global economy. Michelle and I are only here tonight because we were given a chance at an education. And I will not settle for an America where some kids don't have that chance. I'll invest in early childhood education. I'll recruit an army of new teachers, and pay them higher salaries and give them more support. And in exchange, I'll ask for higher standards and more accountability. And we will keep our promise to every young American - if you commit to serving your community or your country, we will make sure you can afford a college education.*

Now is the time to finally keep the promise of affordable, accessible health care for every single American. If you have health care, my plan will lower your premiums.. Now is the time to help families with paid sick days and better family leave, because nobody in America should have to choose between keeping their jobs and caring for a sick child or ailing parent. Now is the time to change our bankruptcy laws, and the time to protect Social Security for future generations. And now is the time to keep the promise of equal pay for an equal day's work, because I want my daughters to have exactly the same opportunities as your sons.

Contextual Orientation

Obama's speech in Denver, on August 28, 2008, was on the 45th anniversary of Martin Luther King's historic "I Have a Dream" address in Washington. Barack Obama, hoping to inject new energy into the Democratic convention, delivered this speech as the party's presidential nominee before an audience of 75,000 people. The Democratic Party officials claimed that they would open up the convention's pivotal moment to the public. The move was intended to symbolise Obama's promise of a transformational presidency, as well as the historic aspect of his candidacy as the first African-American to lead a major party into a US election. The United States 2008 Democratic National Convention is a quadrennial presidential nominating convention of the Democratic Party where it nominates its candidates for President and Vice President of the United States.

The convention was held in Denver, Colorado. Barrack Obama, the nominee for President, gave his acceptance speech in what the party called an "Open Convention." Obama officially received the nomination for President on presidency. He accepted his nomination the following night in a speech before a big crowd of people in attendance. The U.S. Senator Joe Biden of Delaware accepted the nomination for Vice President on the same night

Surrounded by an enormous, adoring crowd, Barack Obama promised a clean break from the broken politics in Washington and the failed policies of George W. Bush. He vowed to cut taxes for nearly all working-class families, end the war in Iraq and break America's dependence on Mideast oil within a decade. Fireworks lit the night sky as Obama accepted the cheers of his supporters. His wife, Michelle, and their daughters Malia and Sasha joined him, and the country music sounds filled the stadium. Campaigning as an advocate of a new kind of politics, he suggested at least some common ground was possible on abortion, gun control, and immigration.

The convention setting for giving this speech was different. Obama delivered his nominating acceptance speech before a crowd of unrivaled size with filled stadium. Obama was the first to deliver an outdoor convention acceptance speech since John F. Kennedy did so at the Los Angeles Coliseum in 1960. In his speech, Obama pledged to quit Bush's economic policy and replace it with his own designed to help hard-pressed families. Obama has called for raising taxes on upper-income Americans to help pay for expanded health care and other domestic programs.

The analysis

Obama starts his speech by describing the time in which an African American to be the nominee for the U.S. presidency as a defining moment. On saying, *We meet at one of those defining moments - a moment when our nation is at war, our economy is in turmoil, and the American promise has been threatened once more,* he activates the cognitive strategy of objectification, by using abstract concepts such as, *threats, challenges.* The cognitive style is figuration, which includes such abstract ideas. When he says, *These challenges are not all of government's making,* he applies the cognitive persuasive tactic, which is response shaping, in which he attempts to form an opinion about the challenges his country face. He moves to another cognitive strategy, which is response reinforcing, in which he tries to strengthen a specific idea in his audience minds.

On saying, *We are a better country than this*, he is clear that the country is not bad as some may expect. He links the events in the short memory, like war on Iraq, the fragile status of economy with the events in the long term memory like the notion of American dream. Intelligently enough, he mentions the phrase, *the American promise*, to link the ideal concepts of American promises and what is happening on the ground. He employs mental representations as a cognitive strategy of social knowledge based on previous experience.

He activates the social schemas by enabling efficient classification of information. His target is to win their persuasion as he is, even being black, the right candidate to lead his country. So, to apply such strategy, Obama creates a clear sense of logic based on sequencing ideas. He does that by classifying his ideas in parallel order, paragraph by paragraph, which lends his remarks a strong sense of conviction. He shows his ideas by talking about the war, the economy, and the dream. Therefore, on saying, *a moment when our nation is at war, our economy is in turmoil, and the American promise,* he moves from the international scene (war) to the domestic front (American promise).

On the ideological level, Obama stresses common values rather than differences. On saying, *this country is more generous than one where a woman in Ohio, this country is more generous than one where a man in Indiana* , Obama joins himself firmly to the diverse audience he is addressing by mentioning different stories to draw his addressees' attention to their shared American dream. Obama attempts to unite his audience, so he uses the concept of shared history of different sects in the American society. When he mentions various stories of a woman in Ohio, and a man in Indiana, he attempts to use the ideological strategy of unification by dissolving differences between individuals and putting them in a collective unity that overlooks racial, social, religious or political differences. On the other hand, on saying, *that brought you two terms of George Bush and Dick Cheney......, we must stand up and say: eight is enough,* Obama applies the ideological strategy of differentiation.

Obviously, he uses such strategy to show his audience what might be beneficial to their interests. In doing so, Obama activates two strategies; the first is the differentiation, which relies on differences between two ideological groups. This is clear on saying, *I say to the American people, two terms of George Bush and Dick Cheney will ask this country for a third, we must stand up and say eight is enough*, as he intends to create a sense of difference between himself and Bush and Cheney. The second method Obama employs within fragmentation strategy is the expurgation of the other. This method involves constructing an evil or threatening challenge which calls individuals to be united together to challenge and expurgate the threats of this challenge. That is clear on saying, *but the record is clear: John MccCain has voted with George Bush ninety percent.*

Obama applies another ideological strategy of legitimation by employing the method of rationalization through different elements. The first element is the way he shows his knowledge to his audience. That is clear on saying, *where a woman in Ohio, on the brink of retirement, finds herself one illness away from disaster after a lifetime of hard work. This country is more generous than one where a man in Indiana has to pack up the equipment he's worked on for twenty years and watch it shipped off to China*, by which Obama attempts to come closer to his followers by mentioning the stories of a man in Indiana, and a woman in Ohio. He explains their sufferings to appear as an effective leader, who not only knows their daily suffering, but also to help them in solving their problems.

Therefore, Obama uses language that captures the mood and addresses the audience's key concerns, grievances, and desires. He shows an outstanding ability to connect his audiences in his way. Another element Obama employs is how to use details effectively by recognizing their problems and by responding to them. He starts by recognizing the troubles Americans face in their daily life, and then he uses the concept of promise in his speech as a way of responding to their problems by repeating the word "promise" frequently.

On the linguistic level, Obama activates a specific way of personalizing his speech to win the hearts and minds of his audience by repeating the pronoun "*we*" The skillful use of "*we*" help transmit a clear message that both the speaker "Obama" and his addressees represent one part of the same team, facing the same fate, and confronting similar challenges. In showing his strong determination, Obama repeats the modal "will" more than five times by saying, *I will step giving tax breaks, I will start giving them to companies, I will eliminate capital gains, I will cut taxes, I will set a clear goal, we will finally end our dependence*, to affirm a degree of certainty in which he commits himself to do and to reveal his social interaction with his audience. He uses the modal "will" to express a direct speech act "promising" and at the same time, he employs that kind of root modals to reveal his power of certainty and ability. This modal auxiliary expresses power of certainty and its repetition is significant as it has a strong effect.

Metaphorically, Obama applies animistic metaphor of conveying his vision by employing the strategy of personification. On repeating the words, *it is a promise that says each of us*, Obama refers to the act of giving inanimate object such as "*promise*" to human characteristics "*to say something*." He attempts to link the abstract object with the concrete object in which he links the promise with tangible social change. Such strategy is effective to present ideas in a way that a listener will remember. By using such strategy, Obama applies "embodiment" which gives the imagery power in the minds of his audience.

One of the powerful functions of Obama's use of metaphor is to memorize and refresh his audience minds about his goals. On saying, *our promise live alive*, he moves from one sense "promise" to another sense which is "alive." Thus, he employs a synaesthesia metaphor. He uses that kind of metaphor to create new meanings and ideas, and to find a possible way to provide expressible thought. He also employs metaphors to facilitate the memorizing process, and to communicate his ideas through his speeches.

Table (4) Concordance of the modal "will"

Context	Word	Context
and Dick Cheney	will	ask this country
lives what we	will	but that we
John McCain, I	will	stop giving tax
overseas, and I	will	start giving them
because it	will	take nothing less
And I	will	will not settle for
And we will	will	keep our promise
your country, we	will	will make sure you
care, my plan will	will	lower your premiums

The above table shows that the total frequency of "will" is 9, which is indicative in the discourse of unification among his followers.

4.5. Conclusion

The analysis of Obama speeches, within the period of January 2008 to August 2008, shows that he employs different cognitive, ideological and linguistic tools to deliver his message strongly and be persuasive. Among the cognitive tools which are used by Obama; objectification, ontologising, figuration and personfication. Obama uses the cognitive tool of social schemas to evaluate and pay the attention of social representations of his society based on socio-cultural values. On the ideological level, he employs unification, legitimation, universalization. Obama looks for common grounds between him and his audience, and he succeeds in doing that by focusing on common values and history. Obama employs the persuasive tactics such as emotions, credibility, and logic.

On the linguistic level, the use of modality in Obama speeches is clear as a way to confirm his concepts of hope and change. In addition, the use of metaphor to convey his message in an indirect powerful way comes within the strategy of speech acts. In a nutshell, this indicates that those who resist racism in their society practice certain tactics of cognitive, ideological, and linguistic aspects to achieve their purpose. It also shows that such strategies can be used in the political discourse to achieve certain objectives based on the mental perception of the speaker and the audience.

Chapter Five
Analysis of Obama's speeches (post-presidency)

0. Introduction

This chapter provides a cognitive, ideological and linguistic analysis within the theory of critical discourse analysis (CDA) of Obama's speeches within the period (November 2008 to January 2010). Obama won the elections and officially became the first African-American president to the United State of America. The analysis applies the theoretical approach explained in chapter one. The cognitive linguistic approach is the main approach including Thompson's (1990) ideological tools, and the cognitive tools of Pennington (2000). The linguistic analysis covers speech acts, metaphor, and modality. The analysis will also focuses on the persuasive ways based upon the logic, emotions and credibility. The selecetd data, to be analyzed in this chapter, consist of four speeches. These are:

1- The victory speech
2- The inaugural speech
3- New begining speech
4- State of the union speech

5.1.1. Obama's victory speech
November 4th, 2008

If there is anyone out there who still doubts that America is a place where all things are possible; who still wonders if the dream of our founders is alive in our time; who still questions the power of our democracy, tonight is your answer. It's the answer told by lines that stretched around schools and churches in numbers this nation has never seen; by people who waited three hours and four hours, many for the very first time in their lives, because they believed that this time must be different; that their voice could be that difference. It's the answer spoken by young and old, rich and poor, Democrat and Republican, black, white, Latino, Asian, Native American, gay, straight, disabled and not disabled - Americans who sent a message to the world that we have never been a collection of Red States and Blue States: we are, and always will be, the United States of America.

It's the answer that led those who have been told for so long by so many to be cynical, and fearful, and doubtful of what we can achieve to put their hands on the arc of history and bend it once more toward the hope of a better day. It's been a long time coming, but tonight, because of what we did on this day, in this election, at this defining moment, change has come to America. I just received a very gracious call from Senator McCain. He fought long and hard in this campaign, and he's fought even longer and harder for the country he loves. He has endured sacrifices for America that most of us cannot begin to imagine, and we are better off for the service rendered by this brave and selfless leader. I congratulate him and Governor Palin for all they have achieved, and I look forward to working with them to renew this nation's promise in the months ahead.

The road ahead will be long. Our climb will be steep. We may not get there in one year or even one term, but America - I have never been more hopeful than I am tonight that we will get there. I promise you - we as a people will get there. There will be setbacks and false starts. There are many who won't agree with every decision or policy I make as President, and we know that government can't solve every problem. But I will always be honest with you about the challenges we face. I will listen to you, especially when we disagree. And above all, I will ask you join in the work of remaking this nation the only way it's been done in America for two-hundred and twenty-one years - block by block, brick by brick, calloused hand by calloused hand.

Contextual orientation

On November 4, 2008, Barack Obama was elected the 44th President of the United States, becoming the first African American to win the country's highest office. Joined by his wife, Michelle, and his two young daughters, Sasha and Malia, Obama addressed his fans and friends in Chicago's Grant Park, which 40 years earlier had been the scene of a violent confrontation between city police and demonstrators during the Democratic National Convention. In front of big number of crowds who descended upon the park to celebrate his election, a crowd whose diversity reflected Obama's appeal to cross racial, gender, or cultural differences.

The key issue that held Obama to win the elections was that; people yearn for change after eight years of Bush policy. Obama received nearly all of the

Black vote, a large majority of Latino and women voters, and a majority of Jewish voters. Obama won a landslide under the Electoral College system, securing huge number of the popular vote.

He won a majority of states, including red states won by the discredited President George Bush in 2004. The fact that a descendant of victims of colonialism and slavery could be elected reflects how the world has changed. Obama's win is considered as a historic as Blacks were denied citizenship and featured in the constitution as the legitimate property of slaveholders. It took a civil war in the 1860s to end slavery.

It took another 100 years to legally end segregation and gain the voting rights that have placed Obama in the White House. But the fact of Obama's win reveals that the younger generation born after the 1960s sees race more as an issue of diversity than divi io . It cert i l doe 't e that the U.S. is ending racism. It reflects that the rise of the Black middle class that Obama represents has become more integrated into the ruling political and economic power structures. Obama presidency will not change the fundamentals of US foreign and domestic policy. Tactics may change, but not objectives.

The explosion of joy that accompanied his victory is not related to what Obama will do or what policies he will defend. For African Americans, it is due to the hope that what can be achieved will no longer be related to skin colour. The result shows that even with institutional discrimination, which remains strong, changes have occurred that many thought impossible in the U.S. society.

The analysis

Obama starts his speech by using cognitive persuasive techniques. The first one is response shaping by saying, *If there is anyone out there who still doubts that America is a place where all things are possible*, which gives a sense that the speaker tries to shape his audience view that there is no doubt that America is a place for all possible things. Obama moves to another strategy, which is response changing on saying, *who still wonders if the dream of our founders is alive in our time, who still questions the power of our democracy, tonight is your answer*, as he tries to change the attitude of his audience by pushing them to have their own answers about the dream of America's founders. On saying, *It's the answer spoken by young and old, rich and poor, Democrat and Republican, black, white, Latino, Asian, Native American, disabled and not disabled,* Obama uses the opposite concepts together to strenghten his view and his message. Thus, he applies the response reinforcing strategy.

Crucial in the phases of speech comprehension is the role of memory, with its two main branches, the short term memory and the long-term memory. When Obama mentions the word *"doubts,"* he shows that in his long term memory, there is certain knowledge that there are still some people in his society who still doubt that America is a place of where things are possible. Obama's long term memory is conceived as the container of his permanent knowledge and skills. Besides, it includes his knowledge of the language, social and political aspects. On saying, *doubts*, Obama stored information in his mental representation shows that some people may have doubts about the American dream.

He activates the idea of objectification by using personification, which is based on persons to explain various concepts. On saying, *Senator McCain. He fought long and hard in this campaign, and he's fought even longer and harder for the country he loves*, Obama relies heavily on personifications by mentioning his opponent's name "McCain" as a hero of America to evoke patriotic feelings that are effective in persuading his audience. The use of personification holds a strong expressive force for any speaker. Since the presidency of Barrack Obama was dominated by a common sense of optimism for change and hope, it is not surprising that he frequently employs personsification when making positive evaluations.

Strong positive evaluation shows the positive features of a specific topic in the speech. The use of personifications frequently clarifies the major themes of his speeches. Obviously, Obama has a strong preference for personifications that is clear by saying, *the dreams of our founders, the power of our democracy*. Obama personifies the concept of dreams as a property that is created and possessed by the founders of the U.S. to give a cognitive sense that the root of dreams comes originally from his country. This is because the idea of dreams, which Obama uses to affect his audience, has a powerful emotional effect for many Americans.

On the ideological level, Obama builds the strategy of unification by involving his audience in his argument. When he uses the pronoun "our" in the utterance, *our founders, our time, our deomocracy*, he shows a sense of credibility by using personalized message. Personalizing the message and referring to his relevant experience help Obama convey his point clearly, and to establish his authority. Obama chooses such pronouns "our, you," to figure out that both the speaker and the audience are part of the same team. To appear persuasive, Obama makes a combined references to "I" in the utterances "*I just received a very gracious call from senator Mccain, I congratulate him, I look forward to* ," wit refere ce to t e "*your*," in the utterance "*your answer*" to create a greater sense of closeness to his audience.

Obama also appears very rational when he creates a chain of reasoning which seeks to defend his argument. He links between the "*doubts*" and the "*dream*" in if conditional structure firstly to show that he is very convinced that the dreams can not be achieved with the existence of doubts. Secondly, to cognitively activate certain types of schema. Obama shows the self-schemas by using the generalizations in the long-term memory that it was impossible for any African-American to be the president of the U.S.

He also uses the ideological strategy of universalization in which certain concepts represent global values by saying, *it is the answer spoken by young and old, rich and poor, democrat and republican*. Obama involves references to the traditions of his society by saying, *the dream of our founders is alive in out time,* in order to strengthen a sense of belonging. To appear as the right person to get the presidency, he employs the positive self-presentation by firstly using the promises in saying, *I will always be honest with you, I will listen to you, I will also join you in the work*. Secondly, he employs positive self-presentation by the historical facts on saying, *young and old, Rich and poor, democrat and republican, a collection of Red states and Blue states.*

On the linguistic level, Obama uses modality as it reveals a relative power status between the participants in the speech situation. In addition, modals have a significant role in exposing the ideology of the speaker and his degree of commitment to truth. On saying, *the road ahead will be long, our climb will be steep, we as a people will get there,* Obama employs "will" to reveal his power of certainty and ability. First, the use of "*will*" embodies a specific level of inference in the utterance, *the road ahead will belong*, as it shows that Obama is certain that this is the road to restore the image of America as a land of dreams. He is also certain that there will be setbacks and the starting point would not be an easy track.

He shows a strong belief that many people would not agree with every decision or every policy. Then, he attempts to be quite close to his audience by listening to them, especially when there is any disagreement. He acknowledges and addresses their prevailing moods and what they may expectedly face by saying, *there will be set backs and false starts. There are many who won't agree with every decision or policy I make as president and we know that the government can not solve.* He attempts to be close by addressing the concerns that both Obama and his audience share.

When he mentions the details of John Mccain and his activities during the campaign, he attempts to appear as a candidate who has credibility that has to be achieved since listeners tend to accept the message if they accept the speaker. Such credibility is established by the sender of the message, and is directly related to his character and his attitude towards what he is saying. That means the speaker, who is trying to convey a particular message, will not be accepted by his audience unless he is first accepted personally by them.

As Obama moves on to his personal life and his family on saying, *Michelle Obama, Sasha and Malia. I know my grandmother is watching,* he manages to build credibility by compiling together his personal experiences as a son of black father and white mother, his competence and fluency, and his strong verbal power. He adds his personal image to help in creating a positive perception as a charismatic public speaker. It is not only the credibility that Obama attempts to build, but he also stands for logic and reason as they appeal for the minds of the audience and have a great persuasive role. Obama also attempts to affect the audience emotionally. When Obama uses the emotion, it motivates the listeners to accept his argument as it appeals to their emotional and psychological motives.

Obama employs the speech acts strategy. On saying, *The road ahead will be long. Our climb will be steep,* he uses a direct speech act, which is assertive, as he confirms a reality. Yet, in the same utterance, he employs an indirect speech act, which is directive, as he tries to give an implicit advice to his audience. On saying, *I promise you,* Obama uses another direct speech act, which is commssive, as he delivers a direct promise. Obama uses another indirect speech act by saying, *But I will always be honest with you about the challenges we face. I will listen to you, especially when we disagree,* as he gives an indirect promise. Therefore, he uses a commissive speech act.

In addition, Obama uses metaphorical expressions to express his view strongly. On saying, *dream of our founders is alive,* Obama connects one inanimistic feature, which is "dream," with animistic element, related to human being, which is "alive." Therefore he employs animistic metaphor. Obama uses another type of metaphor, which is abstract to concrete metaphor. On saying, *change has come to America,* Obama connects the abstract concept of "change" with concrete entity, which is "America" in order to broaden the mental horizons of his audience. Obama uses metaphorical expressions to provoke the curiosity of his listeners and therefore, pushing them to search for different implicit meanings.

Table (1): Concordance of the word "America"

Context	Word	Context
still doubts that	America	is a place
United States of	America	
has come to	America	
sacrifices for	America	that most of
one term, but	America	I have never
been done in	America	for two-hundred

The above table shows that the total frequency of "America" is 6, which is indicative in the discourse of unifying his audience to get the rights of African Americans

5.1.2. Obama's inaugural speech
January 20th, 2009

I stand here today humbled by the task before us, grateful for the trust you have bestowed, mindful of the sacrifices borne by our ancestors. I thank President Bush for his service to our nation, as well as the generosity and cooperation he has shown throughout this transition. Forty-four Americans have now taken the presidential oath. The words have been spoken during rising tides of prosperity and the still waters of peace. Yet, every so often, the oath is taken amidst gathering clouds and raging storms. At these moments, America has carried on not simply because of the skill or vision of those in high office, but because

We the People have remained faithful to the ideals of our forebearers, and true to our founding documents. So it has been. So it must be with this generation of Americans.On this day, we gather because we have chosen hope over fear, unity of purpose over conflict and discord. On this day, we come to proclaim an end to the petty grievances and false promises, the recriminations and worn-out dogmas, that for far too long have strangled our politics.

We remain a young nation, but in the words of Scripture, the time has come to set aside childish things. The time has come to reaffirm our enduring spirit; to choose our better history; to carry forward that precious gift, that noble idea, passed on from generation to generation: the God-given promise that all are equal, all are free, and all deserve a chance to pursue their full measure of happiness. In reaffirming the greatness of our nation, we understand that greatness is never a given. It must be earned. Our journey has never been one of shortcuts or settling for less. It has not been the path for the fainthearted -- for those who prefer leisure over work, or seek only the pleasures of riches and fame.

Rather, it has been the risk-takers, the doers, the makers of things -- some celebrated, but more often men and women obscure in their labor -- who have carried us up the long, rugged path toward prosperity and freedom. For us, they packed up their few worldly possessions and traveled across oceans in search of a new life. For us, they toiled in sweatshops and settled the West; endured the lash of the whip and plowed the hard earth. For us, they fought and died, in places like Concord and Gettysburg; Normandy and Khe Sahn.Time and again, these men and women struggled and sacrificed and worked till their hands were raw so that we might live a better life. They saw America as bigger than the sum of our individual ambitions; greater than all the differences of birth or wealth or faction.

This is the journey we continue today. We remain the most prosperous, powerful nation on Earth. Our workers are no less productive than when this crisis began. Our minds are no less inventive, our goods and services no less needed than they were last week or last month or last year. Our capacity remains undiminished. But our time of standing pat, of protecting narrow *interests and putting off unpleasant decisions -- that time has surely passed. Starting today, we must pick ourselves up, dust ourselves off, and begin again the work of remaking America.*

Contextual orientation

The presidential inauguration of Barack Obama was held in Washington, DC on January 20, 2009. A week of festivities included the Inaugural Address, Inaugural Parade and numerous inaugural concerts, balls and galas honoring the new President of the United States. The official theme for the inauguration was " e ewi   A eric '   Pro i e,"   vi io   t t u der cored t e   ew administration's commitment to restoring opportunity and possibility for all and re-e t bli i   A eric '   t di   be co of o e rou d t e world.

Overall, the event ran smoothly. However, some areas were so congested that people could not move. Thousands of people who had tickets to the swearing-in ceremony could not get there in time. The cost of the 2009 inauguration was an estimated of more than fifty million dollars, higher than any prior inauguration. The biggest expenditures were for law enforcement, communication, transportation and emergency services. With larger crowds, more security and services were needed than ever before. In an effort to make this inaugural celebration open and accessible to all Americans, the event was planned to include a wide variety of ordinary citizens.

However, the event had limited space and many individuals were disappointed with their inability to obtain tickets.   r c Ob   ' i u ur l address touches on the topics of fear and uncertainty as well as on service, unification, and optimism for the future. In front a record-setting crowd estimated at roughly two million attendees, Obama begins his speech humbly, with history in mind, thanking the American people for their trust and offering his thanks to George W. Bush for his service to the nation. Obama then quickly transitioned into discussing the major issues that have been at the fore-front of   A eric '   i d : co flict   bro d, t e eco o   t o e, job ,   e lt care, and education.

Ob   oi t to A eric '   collective f ilure to   e   rd c oice . Yet he continued on to say that Americans will meet the challenges ahead and that they have, *chosen hope over fear, unity of purpose over conflict and discord.* He appealed to hard work, noting that greatness must be earned and that power must be prudently, cautiously, and respectfully employed. He honored the Americans that have gone before, and those who offered their labor and even their lives to build the nation. When he had successfully addressed these domestic endeavors, he reminded Americans that the time has come to think more globally and to build stronger ties with the rest of the world. Obama also offers friendship and sets a positive example.

The analysis

President Barrack Obama makes history as he swears in as his country's first African-American president and delivers such speech that is remembered as a new era of leadership and communication. On the cognitive level, Obama employs various types of social schemas based on what his predecessor "Bush" has done internationally and domestically on the political, economic and even cultural level. Obama activates mental representation of social knowledge by the following steps. Categorizing the information by clarifying his points in sequence, establishing common grounds, speaking to the audience concerns, knowing what to emphasize and what to ignore. By activating these social schemas, he makes his influence for what is remembered through the historical battles "Gettsburg, Normandy," which refreshes the memory of his audience with the U.S.

He activates the cognitive persuasive tactic, which is response shaping. On saying, *We the People have remained faithful to the ideals of our forebearers*, he attempts to apply response shaping style by stating that his audience attitude is that Americans remain loyal to the American traditions and symbols. By saying, *We remain a young nation, but in the words of Scripture, the time has come to set aside childish things*, Obama applies the strategy of response changing by mentioning that Americans must stand up to the challenge they face. Obama moves on to the startegy pf response reinforcing. On saying, *This is the journey we continue today. We remain the most prosperous, powerful nation on Earth,* He affirms the concept that America will remain the most powerful nation on earth, which helps in strengthening the ideas his audience hold.

On the ideological level, Obama's inaugural address is an attempt to link the inaugural speech with the social process and to decipher covert ideology of the speech. Obama starts his speech by saying, *my fellow citizens*, to appear closer to his audience. The previous utterance indicates Obama applies the unification strategy which he repeatedly speaks about throughout his campaign. He attempts, by applying such strategy, to shift the audience from placing blame and complaint to taking charge and solving the problem. Within the strategy of unification, Obama applies some methods of winning the hearts and minds of his audience. The first one is ethos, in which Obama attempts to create his credibility by showing the audience the various options like, *hope over fear, unity of purpose over conflict and discord*.

Some of the factors which contribute to establishing speaker's credibility are the power of his words like, *greatness of America, Gettsburg, hope*, which reflect Obama's awareness of the main issues most of his audience are aware of. Achieving credibility on the part of Obama was challenging task, yet he manages to build credibility by compiling his personal experiences, his competence and wisdom, his strong verbal power, and his logical and well-formed arguments. Moreover, his own personal image and appearance add a positive perception of him as a charismatic leader. The second method is that; Obama employs the pathos to sway the audience's emotions. He appeals to his audience's different motives to achieve his goal. These motives are; affiliative, achievement and power.

When Obama says, *we have chosen hope over fear, unity of purpose over conflict*, he appeals to their affiliative motives based on loyalty and patriotism towards their country with the hope to make a change in his audience's minds. On saying the utterance, *we remain the most prosperous, powerful nation on earth, our workers are no less inventive*, Obama employs the achievement motives based on the track record of his country, the success, prestige and creativity. Obama also employs the power motives by showing authority on saying, *in reaffirming the greatness of our nation*, as he uses the positive presentation through the historical facts of his country, the promise he would pursue once he is elected, and his way of sequencing his ideas.

He applies another ideological stratgey, which is, rationalization. On saying, *we understand that greatness is never a given. It must be earned,* Obama uses logic and facts, which helps him be persuasive in front of his audience. Obama uses another strategy, which is narrativization, by saying, *For us, they fought and died, in places like Concord and Gettysburg; Normandy and Khe Sahn.Time and again, these men and women struggled and.* Here he uses narrative style to be closer to his listeners. He also uses another strategy of universalization by saying, *On this day, we gather because we have chosen hope over fear, unity of purpose over conflict and discord.* In this utterance, Obama uses universal concepts of hope and purpose.

On the linguistic level, Obama employs speech acts theory to strenghten the power of his message. On saying, *I thank President Bush for his service to our nation*, Obama applies direct speech act, which is expressive, as he expresses his thanks to president Bush. Obama shows a real fact by saying, *have remained faithful to the ideals of our forebearers, and true to our founding documents.* So he uses a direct speech act, which is assertive, as he tries to confirm a fact in his society. In the same utterance, Obama employs another indirect speech act, which is expressive, as he expresses his praising. Obama uses another direct speech act by saying, *On this day, we come to proclaim an end to the petty grievances and false promises*, in which he, as a president who holds the authority and power to make some decsions, declares the end of false promise. So, he employs a declarative speech act in a direct way.

Table (3): Concordance of the word "nation"

Context	Word	Context
service to our	nation	as well as
remain a young	nation	but in the
greatness of our	nation	we understand that
powerful nation	nation	on earth

Table (3) shows that the total frequency of "nation" is 4, which is indicative in the discourse of unification.

5.1.3. Obama's new beginning speech in Cairo, Egypt
June 4th, 2009

Good afternoon. I am honored to be in the timeless city of Cairo and to be hosted by two remarkable institutions. For over a thousand years, al-Azhar has, had stood as a beacon of Islamic learning. And for over a century, Cairo University has been a source of Egypt's advancement. Together, you represent the harmony between tradition and progress. I'm grateful for your hospitality and the hospitality of the people of Egypt. And I'm also proud to carry with me the good will of the American people and a greeting of peace from Muslim communities in my country: Assalamu Alaikum. We meet at a time of great tension between the United States and Muslims around the world, tension rooted in historical forces that go beyond any current policy debate. The relationship between Islam and the West includes centuries of coexistence and cooperation but also conflict and religious wars.

I've come here to Cairo to seek a new beginning between the United States and Muslims around the world, one based on mutual interest and mutual respect, and one based upon the truth that America and Islam are not exclusive and need not be in competition. Instead, they overlap and share common principles, principles of justice and progress, tolerance and the dignity of all human beings. I do so recognizing that change cannot happen overnight. I know there's been a lot of publicity about this speech, but no single speech can eradicate years of mistrust nor can I answer in the time that I have this afternoon all the complex questions that brought us to this point.

But I am convinced that in order to move forward, we must say openly to each other the things we hold in our hearts and that too often are said only behind closed doors. There must be a sustained effort to listen to each other, to learn from each other, to respect one another, and to seek common ground. As the holy Quran tells us: "Be conscious of God and speak always the truth." That is what I will try to do today, to speak the truth as best I can. Humbled by the task before us and firm in my belief that the interests we share as human beings are far more powerful than the forces that drive us apart. Now, part of this conviction is rooted in my own experience. I'm a Christian. But my father came from a Kenyan family that includes generations of Muslims. As a boy, I spent several years in Indonesia and heard the call of the azaan at the break of dawn and at the fall of dusk.

As a young man, I worked in Chicago communities where many found dignity and peace in their Muslim faith. As a student of history, I also know civilization's debt to Islam. It was Islam at places like al-Azhar that carried the light of learning through so many centuries, paving the way for Europe's Renaissance and Enlightenment. It was innovation in Muslim communities... It was innovation in Muslim communities that developed the order of algebra, our magnetic compass and tools of navigation, our mastery of pens and printing, our understanding of how disease spreads and how it can be healed. Islamic culture has given us majestic arches and soaring spires, timeless poetry and cherished music, elegant calligraphy and places of peaceful contemplation. And throughout history, Islam has demonstrated through words and deeds the possibilities of religious tolerance and racial equality.

I also know that Islam has always been a part of America's story. The first nation to recognize my country was Morocco. In signing the Treaty of Tripoli in 1796, our second president, John Adams, wrote: "The United States has in itself no character of enmity against the laws, religion or tranquility of Muslims." And since our founding, American Muslims have enriched the United States. They have fought in our wars. They have served in our government. They have stood for civil rights. They have started businesses. They have taught at our universities. They've excelled in our sports arenas. They've won Nobel Prizes, built our tallest building and lit the Olympic torch.

And when the first Muslim American was recently elected to Congress, he took the oath to defend our Constitution using the same holy Quran that one of our founding fathers, Thomas Jefferson, kept in his personal library. So I have known Islam on three continents before coming to the region where it was first revealed. That experience guides my conviction that partnership between America and Islam must be based on what Islam is, not what it isn't. And I consider it part of my responsibility as president of the United States to fight against negative stereotypes of Islam wherever they appear.

Contextual orientation

Barrack Obama delivered a speech entitled "A New Beginning" on June 4, 2009, from the Major Reception Hall at Cairo University in Cairo, Egypt. The speech honors a promise Obama made during his presidential campaign to give a major address to Muslims from a Muslim capital during his first few months as president. Experts indicated that Egypt was chosen because it is a country that in many ways represents the heart of the Arab world. Egypt is considered a key player in the Middle East peace process as well as a major recipient of American military and economic aid. The speech would attempt to mend the United States' relation with the Muslim world, which was severely damaged during the presidency of George W. Bush

A day before delivering his speech in Cairo, Obama met with King Abdullah of Saudi Arabia t t e i ' r c out ide Riyadh on his way to Cairo. They discussed the issues of peace and economies. Obama stayed overnight at the ranch. While there, the president continued to prepare his speech to be given at Cairo University the next day. On 4 June, before delivering the speech, Obama held talks with Egyptian President Hosni Mubarak at Koubbeh Palace. They discussed how they can move forward in a constructive way that brings about peace and prosperity for all people in the region. President Obama later visited the Sultan Hassan Mosque, before going to Cairo University to deliver his speech.

The president opened his speech seeking a common ground between Muslims and the United States. He quoted from the Quran, *Be conscious of God and always speak the truth*. Obama described Muslim contributions to Western civilization, citing the founding of algebra, the development of navigational tools, and the influence of Islamic architecture. He described his own personal experiences with Islam, including having Muslim family members, growing up in Indonesia, a majority-Muslim country and hearing the call of the azaan, and working in Chicago communities where many found dignity and peace in their Muslim faith.

He also listed several of the United States' connections to Islam, including Morocco being the first country to recognize the United States, American Muslim sportsmen (such as Muhammad Ali and Kareem Abdul Jabbar) and civil rights leaders (such as Malcolm X), the Nobel Prize winner Ahmed Zewail, the election of Keith Ellison as the U.S.'s first Muslim congressman, and the presence of over 1,200 mosques in the U.S. On economic development, Obama described several new funds, scholarship programs and partnerships to support education, technological development and better health care in Muslim-majority countries.

The analysis

President Obama's speech in Cairo is described as remarkable and he adopts new ways of speaking about Muslims in a way that may help in redefining the Islamic relations. On the cognitive level, he uses response shaping about Muslims. He uses the Muslim greeting words, *Assalamu Alaikum,* to shape his audience attitudes about the speaker's knowledge of Islam. Obama, then, moves to response changing by his attempt to change his audience view about America. On saying, *I've come here to Cairo to seek a new beginning between the United States and Muslims around the world,* he wants to convey a message that there will be a new beginning between America and the Muslim world. In addition, he applies the third cognitive tactic, that is; response reinforcing. He activates this strategy by saying, *I do so recognizing that change cannot happen overnight,* by which he confirms the idea that there is a change, and such change will not happen immediately.

Obama uses a cognitive strategy called implicit personality theory (discussed in chapter one, p. 68-69). Based on this theory, Obama activates the recency effect style, which has the greatest influence on the impression formed. The audience may have their impression about Obama, yet when he says, *Assalamu Alaikum,* he confirms this impression that he is aware of Islamic traditions. Part of Obama cognitive strategy is to use his charisma to convey his enthusiasm and passion effectively. That is what he does on saying, *to listen to each other, to learn from each other, to respect one another and to seek common ground,* as he appears passionate to the things he talks about, cares deeply about the subjects and is eager to share experience.

Another way that gets Obama very effective to earn trust of the audience is his success in creating strong first impression. Obama does that by starting his speech with "*Assalamu Alaikum,*" as he understands that a first impression is a critically defining moment. When he starts with such statement to create an impression that he is aware of the Islamic culture, and he is ready to be involved with Muslims in cultural understanding that create a new beginning strategy between the U.S. and Muslim world.

On the ideological level, Obama activates a variety of terms that supports his strategy of unification. When Obama says, *Muslim communities, Muslims around the world,* he offers his country's hand of friendship to Islam to face together a number of conflicts dividing the Western and Islamic cultures. Obama quoted certain verses from the Quran as he expounds on Islam's glories and rights. On saying, *As the holy Quran tells us: "Be conscious of God and speak always the truth." That is what I will try to do today,* Obama uses the standardization way to confirm the strategy of unification by quoting the verses of Quran.

On the other hand, Obama employs the strategy of symbolism to assert his message. The symbols he uses, like verses from Quran, represent Islam and his familiarity with it is very powerful. He deliberately employs symbolism to convey to his audience and to the world that he knows more about Islam and its beliefs. That is clearly shown through his use of the Arabic words "*Assalamo alaikum*" translated as "peace be upon you."

Obama employs words that are resonant and tie them effectively to his tendency. By mentioning what John Adams wrote, *the United States has in self no character of enmity against the laws, religion or tranquility of Muslims,* and by mentioning some verses of Quran, Obama's use of such language establishes a high level of awareness. The verses are familiar to many ears and resonate in many hearts and that helps to build bridges. Obama, in this part of his speech, breaks down barriers and establishes common ground among diverse sets of people.

Obama uses another ideological strategy, which is narrativization, by saying, *I'm a Christian. But my father came from a Kenyan family that includes generations of Muslims. As a boy, I spent several years in Indonesia and heard the call of the azaan at the break of dawn and at the fall of dusk,* as he tries to use his personal story in a narrated way to personalize his message and to enable him to make great strides in winning hearts and minds. He applies another ideological strategy, which is rationalization, by saying, *I also know that Islam has always been a part of America's story. The first nation to recognize my country was Morocco,* as he uses logic and facts to be persuasive in front of his audience.

On the linguistic level, Obama employs specific metaphorical expressions. On saying, *a beacon of Islamic learning,* he activates a concrete to abstract metaphor, as he uses something concrete "beacon" with something abstract "learning." On the same way, Obama uses the same metaphorical expression on saying, *but no single speech can eradicate years of mistrust,* by connecting something concrete "eradicate" with something abstract "mistrust." Obama employs another metaphorical expression on saying, *civilization's debt to Islam,* as he uses concrete element, which is civilization, to something abstract, which is debt.

Obama also uses speech acts whether in a direct way, or indirect way. On saying, *For over a thousand years, al-Azhar has, had stood as a beacon of Islamic learning,* Obama employs a direct speech act, which is assertive, as he asserts a real fact. The same utterance another has also indirect speech act, which is expressive, as he expresses his praise to Al Azhar's role. On saying, *I'm grateful for your hospitality and the hospitality of the people of Egypt,* Obama uses a direct speech act, which is expressive as he expresses his thanks to the people of Egypt. He wants to provoke the curiosity of his audience by saying, *but no single speech can eradicate years of mistrust.* In the previous utterance, Obama employs a direct speech act "assertive" by asserting certain concepts in the minds of his audience. By using the speech act strategy, Obama breaks down barriers and establishes common ground among diverse sets of people.

Table (2): Concordance of the word "Islam"

Context	Word	Context
Relationship between	Islam	and the West
that America and	Islam	are not exclusive
civilization'sdebt to.	Islam	
It was	Islam	at places
history,	Islam	has demonstrated
that	Islam	has always
So I have known	Islam	on three continent
America and Islam	Islam	must be
based on what	Islam	is, not
stereotypes of	Islam	Wherever they appear.

Table (2) shows that the total frequency of "Islam" is 10 which is indicative in Obama's discourse of tolerance and understanding to achieve his purpose of reaching out to the Muslim world.

5.1.4. State of the union speech
January 27th, 2010

This week, I'll be addressing a meeting of the House Republicans. I'd like to begin monthly meetings with both Democratic and Republican leadership. I know you can't wait. (Laughter.) Throughout our history, no issue has united this country more than our security. Sadly, some of the unity we felt after 9/11 has dissipated. We can argue all we want about who's to blame for this, but I'm not interested in re-litigating the past. I know that all of us love this country. All of us are committed to its defense. So let's put aside the schoolyard taunts about who's tough. Let's reject the false choice between protecting our people and upholding our values. Let's leave behind the fear and division, and do what it takes to defend our nation and forge a more hopeful future -- for America and for the world. (Applause.)

That's the work we began last year. Since the day I took office, we've renewed our focus on the terrorists who threaten our nation. We've made substantial investments in our homeland security and disrupted plots that threatened to take American lives. We are filling unacceptable gaps revealed by the failed Christmas attack, with better airline security and swifter action on our intelligence. We've prohibited torture and strengthened partnerships from the Pacific to South Asia to the Arabian Peninsula. And in the last year, hundreds of al Qaeda's fighters and affiliates, including many senior leaders, have been captured or killed -- far more than in 2008.

And in Afghanistan, we're increasing our troops and training Afghan security forces so they can begin to take the lead in July of 2011, and our troops can begin to come home. (Applause.) As we take the fight to al Qaeda, we are responsibly leaving Iraq to its people. As a candidate, I promised that I would end this war, and that is what I am doing as President. We will have all of our combat troops out of Iraq by the end of this August. (Applause.) We will support the Iraqi government -- we will support the Iraqi government as they hold elections, and we will continue to partner with the Iraqi people to promote regional peace and prosperity. But make no mistake: This war is ending, and all of our troops are coming home. (Applause.)

Tonight, all of our men and women in uniform -- in Iraq, in Afghanistan, and around the world -- they have to know that we -- that they have our respect, our gratitude, our full support. And just as they must have the resources they need in war, we all have a responsibility to support them when they come home. (Applause.) I campaigned on the promise of change -- change we can believe in, the slogan went. And right now, I know there are many Americans who aren't sure if they still believe we can change -- or that I can deliver it. But remember this -- I never suggested that change would be easy, or that I could do it alone. Democracy in a nation of 300 million people can be noisy and messy and complicated. And when you try to do big things and make big changes, it stirs passions and controversy. That's just how it is.

But I also know this: If people had made that decision 50 years ago, or 100 years ago, or 200 years ago, we wouldn't be here tonight. The only reason we are here is because generations of Americans were unafraid to do what was hard; to do what was needed even when success was uncertain; to do what it took to keep the dream of this nation alive for their children and their grandchildren.

Our administration has had some political setbacks this year, and some of them were deserved. But I wake up every day knowing that they are nothing compared to the setbacks that families all across this country have faced this year. And what keeps me going -- what keeps me fighting -- is that despite all these setbacks, that spirit of determination and optimism, that fundamental decency that has always been at the core of the American people, that lives on. It lives on in the struggling small business owner who wrote to me of his company, "None of us," he said, "...are willing to consider, even slightly, that we might fail." It lives on in the woman who said that even though she and her neighbors have felt the pain of recession, "We are strong. We are resilient. We are American."

It lives on in the 8-year-old boy in Louisiana, who just sent me his allowance and asked if I would give it to the people of Haiti. And it lives on in all the Americans who've dropped everything to go someplace they've never been and pull people they've never known from the rubble, prompting chants of "U.S.A.! U.S.A.! U.S.A!" when another life was saved. The spirit that has sustained this nation for more than two centuries lives on in you, its people. We have finished a difficult year. We have come through a difficult decade. But a new year has come. A new decade stretches before us. We don't quit. I don't quit. (Applause.)

Let's seize this moment -- to start anew, to carry the dream forward, and to strengthen our union once more. (Applause.)

Contextual Orientation

The 2010 State of the Union Address was given by United States President Barack Obama on January 27, 2010, to a joint session of Congress. The speech was delivered in the United States House of Representatives, the United States Capitol. As always, the presiding officers of the Senate and the House of Representatives, Vice President Joe Biden and House Speaker Nancy Pelosi sat behind the president. Among the topics that Obama covered in his speech were proposals for job creation and federal deficit reduction.

In his speech, Obama mixed defiance with compromise and provided details of new jobs and plans to the American people. He defended early and expensive actions to save the economy, but acknowledged that he had underestimated public anger over the economy despite the official end of recession. Obama's state of the union address, a 71-minute speech, is ranked as the sixth longest in presidential history. From the start of the speech to its ends, the common track was an appeal to the country's shared values.

Obama spoke a lot about jobs but he also repeated his attacks on the banks and certain people in Wall Street, which was on behalf of the ordinary working American. While the focus was on domestic issues, the president also touched on American foreign policy and on combating terrorism as well as on Iraq. Obama's State of the Union address focused heavily on the economy and the domestic political agenda. Speaking on the international issues, the war in Afghanistan, which involves a hundred thousand American troops, took barely a paragraph of his speech.

There was no mention of victory over the enemy, just a reiteration of the re ide t' led e to be i wit dr w l i Jul 2011. Needle to ay there was nothing in the speech about the importance of international alliances, and little mentioning of the sacrifices made by America's allies alongside the United States on the battlefields of Afghanistan. Obviously, in Obama's speech, the global war against al-Qaeda was hardly mentioned, and there were no measures outlined to enhance US security at a time of mounting threats from the terrorists. The Iranian nuclear threat, likely to be the biggest foreign policy issue of Obama administration, was given just two lines in the speech.

The analysis

When Obama delivers his speech, Americans expect him to lay out his strategy of change and his vision of unifying his country. To achieve his vision, Obama understands that it is necessary to communicate with his audience in an effective and compelling manner, and inspiring them to embrace his own vision. On the cognitive level, Obama deliberately applies the cognitive tactic of response shaping. On saying, *I'd like to begin monthly meetings with both Democratic and Republican leadership,* he uses such words to shape the opinion of his audience that he wants to form a unified front to face the challenges. He, then, moves on to the strategy of response reinforcing by saying, *We are strong. We are resilient. We are American,* in which he affirms the concept of making America strong. Therefore, he manages to move from the level of shaping his audience opinion to reinforcing their opinion.

On the ideological level, Obama understands that his country faces an economic serious situation, so he employs the strategy of dissimulation by refreshing the memory of Americans of unity to overcome all obstacles. he stresses common dreams and values of hope and unity. On saying, *it lives on the struggling small business owner who wrote to me,* Obama uses anecdotes of different backgrounds to go into greater depth and illustrate points in a memorable way. One observable point in Obama's speech is his way of employing details effectively.

He employs the rationalization principle based on his realization of the circumstances of the American forces in Iraq, Afghanistan, the economic recession, and the daily sufferings of Americans. He deliberately tends to explain such issues in a convincing way. So, he activates the unification strategy based upon the logic, emotion, and his credibility. He establishes credibility by several means in this speech such as; employing the details and stories of normal citizens, personalizing few points by employing the pronoun "we" and the pronoun "*I*" in saying, *I promised that I would end this war,* and by saying, *we have finished a difficult a difficult year, we have come through a difficult decade.*

He focuses on the emotions to achieve his goal. On saying, *let's seize this moment, to start a new, to carry the dream forward,* Obama attempts to employ ideological mental representation of social knowledge based on previous experience. He realizes that Americans would face tough times, so he mentions the word "*dream*" to activate the long-term memory of his audience by connecting the current events with the concept of the dream..

On the linguistic level, Obama shows his certainty by employing the modal "will" in the following utterances, *we will reword, we will have, we will support*. That kind of modality can be described as relational modality, in which the speaker "Obama" expresses his authority of doing some acts in the future with a sense of determination. Therefore, he shows a sense of authority in relation to others. He also resorts to "will" to express certainty as in the utterance, *we will have a responsibility to support them,* as he is certain that his audience will agree with him that it is the honorable duty to support the troops in war. In brief, the modals used by Obama reveal his certainty as well as his power relation, and help him convey his ideas in a powerful and convincing way.

Speech acts theory is another key Obama uses to make his message strong. He attempts to be in a positive self presentation by focusing on indirect speech acts by saying, *we do not quit, I do not quit*. This indirect speech act is commissive as he conveys a clear promise or vowing to his audience. Obama uses another direct speech act by saying, *We will support the Iraqi government*, as he asserts the American support to the Iraqi government. So, he uses an assertive direct speech act. In the same utterance, he also employs an indirect speech act, which is commissive, as he gives another promise to his audience.

Table (4): Concordance of the word"let's"

Context	Word	Context
so	let's	put aside the
who's tough.	let's	reject the false
our values.	let's	leave behind
I don't quit.	let's	let's seize this moment

The above table shows that the total frequency of "let's" is 4, which is indicative in the discourse of invitation to move forward for any kind of change.

5.2. Conclusion

The analysis of Barack Obama's speeches in the period of pre and post presidency reveals the followings;

First, Obama succeeds in breaking down the barriers between him and his audience and by establishing common grounds among diverse sets of people. Obama shows that he can transcend traditional divisions of race, ethnicity, age, gender and religion. He shows his skills in establishing a sense of shared goal by his reference to common history and values.

Second, Obama shows his power in using the ideological strategies to challenge and confront the existing ideologies in his white-dominant society. These strategies include unification, legitimation, rationalization, universalization, and narrativization. In unification, he employs the strategy of standardization and symbolization of unity. He establishes such strategy based on disregarding racial, social, religious or political differences. In legitimation, he employs three sub strategies; rationalization, universalization, and narrativization. Rationalization is based on reasoning. Universalization is based on universal concepts. The third strategy "narrativizaton" is based upon reference to the traditions and history of the society to create a sense of belonging.

Third, Obama's use of modality reveals his ideology of power as it expresses his attitude towards his message and his audience. Obama shows that he is able to convey his view by manipulating different modals and using them in various contexts. He does that by employing power modals which appear in the climaxes of his speech to voice a sense of hope, change and power. It also reveals a sense of certainty, determination, and a high degree of obligation to encourage his hearer, and convince them to support him.

Fourth, Obama uses the persuasive tactics, such as credibility, emotions and the logic to achieve his purpose. He bases his arguments on the same logic that governs his audience's thinking. His aim is to transform the conception held by white audience from the negative to the positive side, and to get their support in helping the first African-American take the U.S. presidency. He also employs the strategies of sequencing his ideas, addressing non-rhetorical questions, addressing objections, comparing and contrasting to make his language very persuasive.

Fifth, Obama employs different cognitive tools such as social schemas, objectification. He combines them with ideological tools like unification in order to show the cognitive function of discourse, which is to organize the social representations of a society. This approach leads to a distribution made between the factual beliefs in discourse "true or false knowledge" and evaluate beliefs "opinions, attitudes" which are based on the application of socio-cultural values.

Finally, the use of metaphor and speech acts, as linguistic tools, do not only have a cognitive effect, but they also enable the speaker and the listener to implicate the intended meaning indirectly. Motivated by the desire to deliver a message in a powerful way that can not be achieved by a literal expression, Obama resorts to an indirect way of conveying his message through the use of metaphor. Moreover, Obama's use of metaphor emphasizes meaning by requiring a deep thinking to get the intended meaning. In addition, it is a technique of persuasion since its comprehension requires the involvement in a reasoning process.

Summary and Conclusion

This study was designed to reveal the cognitive, ideological, and linguistic strategies, used by Martin Luther King and President Barrack Obama in their speeches. The database was divided into two parts. The first part represented selected forms of King's speeches before and after winning the Nobel prize. In analyzing these speeches, they were further classified into two main sections. The first examined four of his speeches before being awarded the Nobel prize in 1964, while the second examined other four speeches after winning the Nobel prize in 1964 until his assassination in 1968. These speeches were selected as representative samples to undergo cognitive, ideological, and linguistic analyses.

The second part of the analysis tackled Obama's speeches before and after presidency. These were also divided into two sections. The first covered his speeches from January 2008 to August 2008 (pre-presidency). The second handled his speeches within the period of November 2008 to January 2010 (post-presidency).

The speeches were analyzed within the framework of critical discourse l i (CDA) de cribed b V Dij ' rticle "Critic l Di cour e A l i " (2001). it i t t fr ework, the selected data were analyzed in terms of the cognitive, ideological, and linguistic levels employed to produce a cognitive persuasive discourse focusing on the strategies of mental representation in the selected speeches. However, other related tools, such as persuasive techniques, were also used for their relevance to the analysis of the data. In so doing, this study revealed the followings:

First, King and Obama employed major cognitive linguistic techniques in their speeches such as; metaphors, modality, personification with positive evaluation and negative evaluation. They also employed other cognitive tools like rehearsal, elaboration, encoding and retrieval. King delivered his speeches with biblical quotations, religious references and other positive features related to the ideological background of African-Americans.

In addition, both leaders used various ideological strategies like, legitimation, dissimulation, unification, fragmentation, reification. King used his language as an instrument to express his ideological beliefs, and as a tool by which he manipulated and influenced the minds of his audience to make social change. On the other hand, Obama's discourse, during his presidential campaign and even after taking office in January 2009, was an idealistic discourse, based on idealistic values and principles.

King combined the idealistic ideas with religious modes, which could be traced back to his religious heritage. This heritage was rooted in both the African American church and the White church. The combination of these traditions allowed King to reach African American and white audiences with the same message. Thus, King's rhetorical style was grounded primarily in the traditions of the African-American churches

Second, King and Obama showed themselves as persuasive speakers, not only using the three traditional elements of persuasion (ethos, pathos and logos), but they also employed the quasilogical persuasion technique which was based on the logical structure of their speeches. They also used presentational persuasion which was based on making the argument strongly persistent in the audience's consciousness by using repitition, paraphrasing, and metaphors. They also employed the third persuasive technique of analogical persuasion, based on comparsion and evaluation.

Third, Obama followed King's approach in establishing common ground with his audience. Obama, like King, looked for any kind of change. So, he placed himself in the course of history, affirming in most of his speeches that he dreamed the same as most Americans. Both pursued such strategy of speaking to audience concerns, and winning their hearts and minds. They demonstrated their ability of activating such strategy by strenghtening the influence of their words, and giving details and personalizing their messages. Such strategy enabled both leaders to be closer to their audience. Therefore, by using symbolic words, vivd language and personalized ideas, both were able to drive their points home by repeating their references of hope and change.

Fourth, one important aspect of convincing their audience was that; King and Obama shared a specific charisma that pushed both to play a role in earning trust, and in energizing and motivating their audience. They also succeeded in breaking down barriers by stressing common dreams and values, paying attention to shared history, and transcending traditional divisions of race, ethnicity, age, gender, religion and region. King and Obama made the best use of the three strategies; recognition, remembering, and responding. By using recognition, they showed their realization of the circumstances they are facing. Both focused on cognitive strategy of rememberance as a way of refreshing their audience minds of the principles and values of their country. They also activated the stragey of responsiveness by being aware about the surrounding issues they face in their society.

Fifth, the concordance of King and Obama's speeches showed that there were high frequency words, which was indicative and had a great importance in the process of persuasion. The high frequency words included the first person pronoun "we" and "I." In this way, it was clear that both Obama and King attempted to personalize their messages with skillful use of pronouns "we" and "I" They did that since they tried to transit a message that the speaker and the audience were part of the same team, and to create a greater sense of closeness.

Sixth, another important aspect that both leaders shared in their discourse is reference to history. Both employed such strategy to make their ideas more understandable in their speeches. They also focused on the technique of personification to refer to the act of inanimate objects or ideas as human characteristics, such as emotions and actions. They also attempted to tie emotions to concrete images as part of physicality or embodiment process, which played a role in conveying vision effectively, and made the ideas more memorable. This was because embodiment created dynamic images in the audience' minds. It also helped to make their notions moving and living, and it created a sense of forward momentum.

Seventh, among the important ideological tools both Obama and King applied in their sppeches was "rationalization," where by Obama and King used symbolic words to create a sense of reasoning which were used for defining their concepts and thereby to persuade their audience. Another strategy used by both leaders was called "universalization" by which they tried to establish unified principles that all people agreed on. King deduced from the general set of moral laws found in biblical sources, and then illustrated these laws from the American political culture with references to American prominent leaders like Lincoln and Jefferson.

Eighth, King's insistence on the moral values of personality provided him with many ways to be used in several aspects of the civil rights movement discourse. King's argument enabled him to attack segregation not only morally but also in a religious sense. He used the ethical religious examples by telling his audience of the biblical stories of Jesus acts and then placed them before his audience as an example of how a truly religious righteous life should be lived. King used such strategy as an incitement to act and as a confirmation that the ways of the struggle had righteous forms.

Ninth, Gandhiism became an integral part of King's rhetoric and the civil rights struggle and that confirmed the idea of describing King as the American Gandhi. Gandhiism became synonymous with non-violence strategy which was applied by King. In addition, Gandhiism helped King to depict himself as a non-violence leader and to make non-violence tactics function in different situations. King linked the non-violence strategy of the civil rights movement with Gandhi and his philosophy to show that his tactic was a universal method of goodness with a number of concepts like morality, spirituality, redemption and beloved community. These ideals were manifested in his speeches and they represented what a social struggle could lead to if it was allied with a religious power.

Tenth, King applied the concept of emotions and he tried to make his speeches met the goals and illustrated his views. He used the emotion by mentioning different concepts like love, hatred, fear, and also motivation or desires which gave rise to emotions. Both emotions and motives helped King to be persuasive by building his ideas on three principles: happiness, holiness, and love. King also used other psychological elements which were; identification, suggestion, and attention. King started his speeches by identifying his own argument, suggesting different visions and paying attention to specific elements.

Eleventh, King made a certain level of transformation in his discourse post 1964. Rather than handling the local-oriented issues like racism and segregation in his society, he developed his rhetoric to include many international issues. These issues included his opposition to the vietnam war, his endeavors to link his efforts with Gandhiism, his struggle against colonialism in Africa and the cold war. Such concepts offered King the opportunity to use them as a means of creating new meanings in his discourse.

Twelfth, the study showed that there was a connection between language and racism. This came in the form of A) lexicon; selection of words that may be more or less negative about certain groups. B) Metaphorical devices, like metaphors to focus attention on positive and negative concepts. C) Indirect speech acts, to convey specific ideas in the optimal way and make it to the point. D) Interaction, by disagreeing, interrupting others and non-responding questions, among other forms of direct interactional discrimination.

Both Obama and King employed metaphorical expressions to stimulate the inventive power of their audience, not to retent their ideas. These metaphorical expressions conveyed thoughts and meaning that were difficult to the audience in non-metaphorical language, or precisely because there was no literal utterance that expressed exactly what the speaker meant.

In addition, both leaders used metaphors as an effeicient tool of cognitive memorizing strategy. This was because metaphors helped overcome the human problems of limited active memory, and enabled the speakers to convey large chunks of information through few words. Therefore, metpahors were cognitive tool that facilitated the memorizing ability by providing vivd and concrete images, transferring exoerience from well-known to less know contexts, and expressing the meanings of human experience that could not be expressed otherwise.

Both Obama and King applied cognitive strategy of social schemas, which was simply based upon mental representation of social events, created by previous experiences. Both derived many sub types of social schemas, like person schemas, which was based on expectations about other people. Role schema, which was based on behaviours expected in a social situation. Within role schemas, there were the ascribed and achieved roles.

Finally, Obama and King's speeches defined what history is. Both affirmed the fact that history and historical change were closely associated. They also used the sense of history's rationality which was included both in their guarantees that achieving success in the struggle and expecting changes in the American society can be very possible. King and Obama's skillful maneuvering of linguistic techniques helped them in achieving their goals and in controlling the minds of their White and Black audience. Clearly, King succeeded to reverse power relation set by the dominant White race and gradually achieve his goals.

Bibliography

Aitchison, J. (1999). *Linguistics*. UK: Bookpoint Ltd.

Allam, N. (2002). *"A Linguistics Study of Political Discourse During the Gulf War."* Unpublished Ph.D Thesis, Ain Sham University.

American Heritage Dictionary 2nd *ed,* (1991). Boston. Houghton Mifflin Company.

Andersen, R. (1988). *The Power and the Word*. London: Paladin Grafton Books- Collins Publishing Group.

Assmundson, M. (2008). *Persuading the Public, A Linguistic Analysis of Barack Obama's Speech on "Super Tuesday" 2008*. Sweden. Högskolan Dalarna.

Bach, K. (1999). "The Myth of Conventional Implicature," in *Linguistics and Philosophy* 22, 327:366.

Baradat, L. (1979). *Political Ideologies*. New Jersey: Prentice Hall, Inc.

Barker, C. and Galasinski, D. (2001). *Cultural Studies and Discourse Analysis*. London: Sage.

Baron, R. A. and Byrne, D. (2000). *Social Psychology*. Boston: Allyn and Bacon.

Beard, A. (2000). *The language of Politics*. London: Routledge.

Bell, A. and Garrett, P. (1998). *Approaches to Media Discourse*. Oxford: Blackwell Publishers.

Belsey, C. (1980). *Critical Practice*. London: Hethuen.

Berko, W., and Wolvin, D. (1989*). Communicating: A Social and Career Focus* (4th ed). Boston: Houghton Mifflin Company.

Bjork, E. and Bjork, R. (1996). *Handbook of Perception and Cognition*. London: Academic Press.

Black, M. (1962). "Metaphor," in *Models and Metaphors: Studies in Language and Philosophy*. NY: Cornell University Press.

Black, M. (1979). "More about Metaphor," in A. Ortony, *Metaphor and Linguistic Theory* (P 19-43). New York: Cambridge University Press.

Blackledge, A. (1984). *Discourse and Power in A Multilingual World*. Philadephia, John Benjamins Publishing Cmpany.

Blaxter, L., Hughes, C. and Tight, M. (1996). *How to Research*. Open University Press: Buckingham.

Bloomfield, L. (1961). *Language*. New York: Holt, Rincehart and Winston.

Bloomaert, J. and Bulcaen, C. (1997). *Political Linguisics*. Amsterdam: John Benjamins Publishing Company.

Bloor, T. and Bloor, M. (1995). *The Functional Analysis of English: A Hallidayan Approach*. London & New York: Arnold.

Blum-Kulka, S. (1997). "Discourse Pragmatics," in *Discourse as Social Interaction*, Teun V. Dijk. London: Sage Publications pp.38-63.

Bower, G. and Cirilo, R. (1985). "Cognitive Psychology and Text Processing." In Van Dijk's *Handbook of Discourse Analysis*, Volume 1. London: Academic Press.

Brock, B. L., Huglen, M. E., Klumpp, J. F., and Howell, S. (2005). *Making Sense of Political Ideology: The Power of Language in Democracy*. New York: Rowman & Littlefield Publishers, Inc.

Brown, G. and Yule, G. (1983). *Discourse Analysis*. Cambridge. Cambridge University Press.

Brown, M., Carnoy, M., Currie, E., Duster, T., Oppenheimher, D., Shultz, M., and Wellman, D. (2003). *White Washing Race. The Myth of Color-blind Society*. Berkely: University of California.

Cameron, D. (2001). *Working with Spoken Discourse*. London: Sage.

Campbell, W. G. and Ballou, S. V. (1978). *Form and Style*. Houghton Mifflin Company: Boston.

Carnap, R. (1943). *Introduction to Semantics and Formalization of Logic*. Massachusetts, Harvard University Press.

Carter, R. (1997). *Investigating English Discourse*. London: Routledge.

Casey, E. (2004). "Public Memory in Place and Time," in Kendall Phillips, *Framing Public Memory*. University of Alabama Press.

Celce-Murcia, M. and Larsen-Freeman, D. (1983). *The Grammar Book*. Massachussetts: Newbury House Publishers Inc.

Charteris-Black, J. (2004). *Corpus Approaches to Critical Metaphor Analysis*. London: Palgrave Macmillan.

Chierchia, G. and McConnel-Ginet, S. (1990). *Meaning and Grammar*. Cambridge, MA: MIT press.

Chilton, P. (1996). *Security Metaphors: Cold War Discourse from Containment to Common House*. New York: Peter Lang.

Chilton, P. and Schaffner, C. (2002). *Politics as Text and Talk: Analytic Approaches to Political Discourse*. Philadelphia:. John Benjamins Publishing Company.

Chomsky, N. (1988). *Language and Politics*. New York: Black Kose Books.

Chouliaraki, L. and Fairclough, N. (1999). *Rethinking Critical Discourse Analysis*. Edinburgh University Press.

Clark, E. (1973). "What's in a word? On the Child's Acquisition of Semantics in his First Language." In T. Moore (ed), *Cognitive Development and the Acquisition of Language*. New York: Academic Press, (P 65-110).

Clayton, D. (2007). "The Audacity of Hope," in *The Jounal of Black Studies*. Sage.

Cook, G. (1989). *Discourse*. Oxford: Oxford University Press.

Coultard, M. (1977). *An Introduction to Discourse Analysis*. England: Longman.

Coulthard, C. R. C. and Coulthard, M. (1996). *Text and Practices: Readings in Critical Discourse Analysis*. London: Routledge.

Cruse, A. (2000). *Meaning in Language*. Oxford: Oxford University Press.

Crystal, D. and Davy, D. (1969). *Investigating English Style*. London: Longman.

Cummings, L. (2005). *Pragmatics: a multidisciplinary perspective*. Edinburgh: Edinburgh University Press.

Cutting, J. (2002). *Pragmatics and discourse*. London: Routledge.

Dallmayer, F. R. (1984). *Language and Politics*. Indiana: University of Notre Dame Press.

Dauber, J. (2004). "A Star is born," in *The Christian Science Monitor*, retrieved 6 – 03-2009.

Davies, A. and Elder, C. (2004). *The Handbook of Applied Linguistics*. Malden, MA: Blackwell Pub.

Davis, H. and Walton, P. (1983). *Language, Image, Media*. Oxford: Basil Blackwell Publisher Limited.

Davey, M. (2004). "As quickly as overnight, a Democratic star is born," in *The New York Times*: p. 20. Retrieved 13- 09-2012.

Deese, J. (1974). "Mind and Metaphor: Acommentary." In *New Literary History*, 6 (1), 195-236.

Dunne, M. D. (2003). *Democracy in Contemporary Egyptian Political Discourse*. Philadelphia: John Benjamins Publishing Company.

Dupuis, M. and Boeckelman, K.(2008). *Barack Obama, the New Face of American Politics*. Connecticut: Praeger.

Edmondson, W. (1981). *Spoken Discourse*. New York: Longman Inc.

Essed, D. (2002). "Everyday Racism," in P. Essed & D.T. Goldberg (Eds), *Race Critical Theories* (pp 174-194). Blackwell Publishers.

Evans, V. (2007). *Cognitive Linguistics, The Encyclopedia of Pragmatics*, ed. By Louis Cummings. London: Routledge.

Evans, V. and Green, M. (2006). *Cognitive Linguistics, Introduction*. Edinburgh: Edinburgh University Press.

Fairclough, N. (1989). *Language and Power*. New York: Longman.

Fairclough, N. (1992a). *Critical Language Awareness*. London: Longman.

Fairclough, N. (1992b). *Discourse and Social Change*. Cambridge: Polity Press.

Fairclough, N. (1995a). *Critical Discourse Analysis: The Critical Study of Language*. New York: Longman.

Fairclough, N. (1995b). *Media Discourse*. London: Edward Arnold.

Fairclough, N. and Wodak, R. (1997). "Critical Discourse Analysis". In T.Van Dijk, *Discourse As a Social Change*. London: Sage.

Falk, J. S. (1978). *Linguistics and Language: A Survey of Basic Concepts and Implications*. New York: John Wiley & Sons, Inc.

Finch, G. (2003). *How to Study Linguistics*. New York: Palgrave Macmillan.

Finegan, E. (1994). *Language: its Structure and Use*. Orlando: Harcourt Brace College Publishers.

Fillmore, C. (1975). "An Alternative to checklist Theories of Meaning". *Proceedings of the First Annual Meetings of the Berkeley Linguistics Society*, P 123 – 131.

Firth, J.R. (1950). *Paper in Linguistics*. London: Oxford University Press.

Fishbein, M. & Ajzen, I. (1975). *Belief, Attitude, Intention and Behaviour: An Introduction to Theory and Research*. Massachusetts: Addison-Wesley.

Fiske, S. T. and Taylor, S. E. (1991). *Social Cognition*. New York: McGraw-Hill.

Foucault, M. (1977). *Discipline and Punish*. London: Lane.

Foucault, M. (1980). *The Archeology of Knowledge*. New York: Pantheon Books.

Fowler, R, (1991). *Language in the news: Discourse and Ideology in the Press*. London: Routledge.

Fowler, R. (1996). "On Critical Linguistics," in Carmen Rosa Caldas Coulthard & Malcom Coulthard (Eds), *Texts and Practices: Readings in Critical Discourse Analysis*. London: Routledge.

Fowler, R. (1999). *Language in the News: Discourse and Ideology in the Press*. London: Routledge.

Fowler, R. and Kress, G. (1979). "Critical Linguistics" in Fowler et al., *Language and Control* (pp.185:213). London: Routledge.

Fox, R. and Fox, J. (2004). *Organizational Discourse: A Language – Ideology- Power Perspective*. London: Praeger.

Fromkin, V., Rodman, R. and Hyams, N. (2003). *An Introduction to Language*. Massachusetts: Heine.

Gazdar, G. (1979). *Pragmatics*. New York: Academic Press.

Gee, P.J. (2000). *An Introduction to Discourse Analysis*. London: Routledge.

Geis, M. (1987). *The Language of Politics*. New York: Springer-Verlag New York Inc.

Geis, M. (1995). *Speech acts and conversational interaction*. NY: Cambridge University Press.

Ghadessy, M. (1999). *Text and Context in Functional Linguistics*. Philadelphia: John Benjamins Publishing Company.

Gibald, J. and Achtert, W. S. (1980). *MLA Handbook for Writers of Researches Papers, Theses and Dissertations*. Modern Language Association: New York.

Goatly, A. (1997). *The Language of Metaphors*. London: Routledge.

Gramsci, C. (1971). Selections from the prison notebooks. London: Lawrence Wishart.

Graesser, A., Gernsbacher, M., and Goldman, S. (1997)." Cognition," in *Discourse as Structure and Process*. (p. 292-319). London: Sage Publications Ltd.

Green, G. M. (1996). *Pragmatics and Natural Language Understanding*. New Jersey: Lawrence Erlbaum Associates Publishers.

Grishman, R. (1994). *Computational Linguistics, An Introduction*. Cambridge: Cambridge University Press.

Gronbeck, B. E. (1990). *Principles and Types of Speech Communication*. New York: Scott & Foresman.

Grundy, P. (1995). *Doing Pragmatics*. London: Arnold.

Halliday, M.A.K. (1985). *An Introduction to Functional Grammar.* London: Arnold.

Hamp, E. P., Housholder, F. W., and Austerlitz, R. (1966). *Readings in Linguistics.* Chicago: The University of Chicago Press.

Hassan, F. (2003). *Ideology and Power in Some American Newspaper Texts: A Pragma-Syntactic Analysis.* Unpublished M.A Thesis, Ain Shams University

Hatch, E. and Brown, C. (1995). *Vocabulary, Semantics and Language Education.* Cambridge: Cambridge University Press.

Hermeren, L. (1978). *On Modality in English: A Study of the Semantics of the Models.* Sweden: Printab Lund.

Heywood, A. (1992). *Political Ideologies, an Introduction.* New York, St Martin's Press.

Hodge, R. & Kress, G. (1993). *Language as Ideology.* London: Routledge.

Hoey, M. (1983). *On the Surface of Discourse.* London: George Allen&Unwin.

Hoffman, J. and Graham, P. (2006). *Introduction to Political Ideologies.* London: Pearson Education Limited.

Hoover, K. (1987). *Ideology and Political Life.* California: Brooks/Cole Publishing Company.

Huang, Y. (2007). *Pragmatics.* New York: Oxford, University Press Inc.

Hudson, G. (2000). *Essential Introductory Linguistics.* Massachaussetts: Blackwell Publishers Inc.

Hung NG, S. and Bradac, J. J. (1993). *Power in Language: Verbal Communication and Social Influence.* London: Sage Publications.

Jaszczolt, K.M. (2002). *Semantics and Pragmatics.* Great Britain: Pearson Education.

Jeffries, L. (1998). *Meaning in English.* London: Macmillan Press Ltd.

Johnson, M. (1987). *The Body in the Mind: The Bodiliy Basis of Meaning, Imagination and Reason.* Chicago: Chicago University Press.

Johnson, M. (1992). "Philosophical Implications of Cognitive Semantics," in *Cognitive Linguistics*, 3 (4), 345-366.

Johnstone, B. (2002). *Discourse Analysis.* Massachusetts: Blackwell.

Joseph, J. (2006). *Language and Politics*. Great Britain: Edinburgh University Press.

Kennedy, G. (1998). *An Introduction to Corpus Linguistics*. London: Longman.

King, M, L, Jr., (1958). *Stride toward Freedom: The Montgomery Story*. New York, Harper & Row.

King, M. L, Jr., (1963). *Why We Can't Wait*. New York, Harper & Row.

King, M. L, Jr., (1963). *Where Do We Go from Here: Chaos or Community?* New York, Harper & Row.

King, M. L, Jr., (1968). *The Trumpet of Conscience*. New York, Harper & Row.

Klinge, A. and Muller, H. (2005). *Modality, Studies in Form and Function*. London: Equinox.

Kress, G. and Hodge, R. (1979). *Language as Ideology*. London: Routledge.

Lakoff, G. (1990). "The Invariance Hypothesis: Is Abstract Reason Based on Image-Schema?" *in Cognitive Linguistics*, 1, 1, 39-74.

Lakoff, G. (1991). "Metaphor and War: The Metaphor System Used to Justify war in the-Gulf."Http://Lists.Village.Virginia.edu/sixties/html_docs/texts/scholarly/Lakoff_Gulf_metaphor_2.htm.

Lakoff, G. and Thompson, H. (1975). " Introduction to Cognitive Grammar," *Proceedings of the 1st Annual Meeting of the Berkeley Linguistic Society*. (P 295-313).

Lakoff, G. & Johnson, M. (1980). *Metaphors We Live By*. Chicago: Chicago University Press.

Lakoff, G. & Johnson, M. (1999). *Philosophy in The Flash: The Mind and its Challenge for Western Thought*. New York: Basic Books.

Lakoff, G., & Turner, M. (1989). *More Than Reason: A Field Guide to Poetic Metaphor*. Chicago: Chicago University Press.

Lakoff, R. T. (1990). *Talking Power: The Politics of Language in our Lives*. New York: Basic Books, Inc.

Langacker, R. W. (1967). *Language and its Structure: Some Fundamental Linguistic Concepts*. New York: Harcourt, Brace&World Inc

Leanne, S. (2009). *Say It Like Obama*. New York: McGraw-Hill Companies, Inc.

Leech, G. N. (1974). *A Linguistic Guide to English Poetry*. London: Longman.

Leech, G. N. (1983). *Principles of Pragmatics*. New York: Longman.

Leopold, T. (2008). "The day American met Barrack Obama," in CNN. Retrieved 07-03-2009.

Levinson, S. C. (1983). *Pragmatics*. Cambridge: Cambridge University Press.

Lugo, C and Lugo, M. (2008). "Black as Brown: The 2008 Obama Primary Campaign and The US Browning of Terror. *Journal of African American Studies June 2009, Volume 13, Issue 2, pp 110-120*.

Lukes, S. (1986). *Power*. New York: New York University Press.

Mac Carmac, E. R. (1985). *A Cognitive Theory of Metaphor*. Massachusetts: MIT.

McCombs, M., & Shaw, D. L. (1972)."The Agenda-Setting Function of Mass Media". *Public Opinion Quarterly*, 36: 176-187.

McCuen, J. R. and Winkler, A. C. (1995*). From Idea to Essay*. Massachussetts: A Simon & Schuster Company:

Macdonell, D. (1986). *Theories of Discourse, an Introduction*. Oxford: Basil Blackwell.

Mandler, J. (1992)."How to Build a Baby II, Conceptual Primitives," in *Psychological Review*, 99, 567-604.

Mandler, J. (2004). *The Foundations of Mind: Origins of Conceptual Thought*. Oxford: Oxford University Press.

Markus, H. (1977). "Self-Schemata and Processing Information about the Self," in *Journal of Personality and Social Psychology*, 35, 63-78.

Martin, J. R. and Rose, D. (2003). *Working with Discourse*. London: Continuum.

Mazid, B. (1999). *Ideology and Control in Some Speech and Newspaper Genres: A Politicolinguistic Approach to Discourse Analysis*. Unpublished Ph.D Thesis, Ain Shams University.

Merriam Webster's Collegiate Dictionary. (1999). Tenth Edition. Merriam Webster Incorporated.

Mey, J. L. (2001). *Pragmatics: An Introduction*. Oxford: Blackwell.

Miles, R. (1993). *Racism*. London: Routledge.

Miller, E. (1979). Metaphor and Political Knowledge. *The American Political Science Review*, 73 (1), 155-170.

Miller, S. (1998). *Understanding & Creating Editorial Cartoons*. Wisconsin: Knowledge Unlimited Inc.

Mills, S. (1997). *Discourse*. London: Routledge.

Morgan, M. (2002). *Langauge, Discourse, and Power in African American culture.* London: Cambridge University Press.

Moscovici, S. (1981). "On Social Representations," in J. P. Frargas, *Social Cognition: perspectives on Everyday Understanding.* London: Academic Press.

Moscovici, S. (1984). "The Phenomenon of Social Representations," in R. M. Farr and S. Moscovici, *Social Representations.* Cambridge: Cambridge University Press.

Moscovici, S. and Hewstone, M. (1983). "Social Representations and Social Explanations: From the "Naïve" to the "Amateur" Scientist," in M. Hewstone (ed,), *Attrition Theory: Social and Functional Extensions*, Oxford: Blackwell.

Obama, B. (2004). *Dreams from my Father.* New York: Three Rivers Press.

Obama, B. (2006). *The Audacity of Hope.* New York: Crown Publishers.

O'Halloran, K. (2003). *Critical Discourse Analysis and Language Cognition.* Edinburgh: Edinburgh University Press.

Ortony, A. (1979). *Metaphor and Thought.* Cambridge: Cambridge University Press.

Oshima, A. and Hogue, A. (1991). *Writing Academic English.* California: Addison Wesley Publishing Company.

Palmer, F. R. (1979). *Modality and the English Models.* London: Longman.

Palmer, F. (1981). *Semantics.* Cambridge: Cambridge University Press.

Palmer, F. (1984). *Grammar.* England: Penguin Books.

Palmer, F. (1986). *Mood and Moality.* Cambridge: Cambridge University Press.

Pan, Z. and Kosciki, G. M. (1993). "Framing Analysis: An Approach to News Discourse," in *Political Communication*, Vol: 110, 61.

Pardo, M. L. (2001). "Linguistic Persuasion As an Essential Factor in Current Democracy: Critical Analysis of the Globalization Discourse in Argentina at The Turn and at The End of the Century." Discourse & Society, 12 (1), 91-118. London: Sage Publication.

Pennycook, A. (2001). *Critical Applied Linguistics: A Critical Introduction.* New Jersey: Lawrence Erlbaum Associates.

Pennington, D. (2000). *Social Cognition.* London: Routledge.

Perkins, M. R. (1983). *Modal Expressions in English*. New Jersey: Ablex Publishing Corporation.

Perloff, M. R. (2002). *The Dynamics of Persuasion*. New Jersey: Lawrence Erlbaum Associates.

Phillips, L. and Jorgensen, M. (2002). *Discourse Analysis as Theory and Method*. London: Sage Publications.

Pinto, D. (2004). "Indoctrinating the Youth of Post-War Spain: A Discourse Analysis of a Fascist Civics Textbook," in *Discourse & Society*, 15 (5), 649-667. London: Sage Publications.

Price, S. (2007). *Discourse Power Address: The Politics of Public Communication*. England: Ashgate Publishing Limited.

Purvis, T. and Hunt, A. (1993). "Discourse, ideology, discourse, ideology, discourse, ideology......," *British Journal of Sociology*, Vol.44: No 3: 473-499.

Recanati, F. (1987). *Meaning and Force*. Cambridge: Cambridge University Press.

Recanati, F. (2004). *Literal meaning*. Cambridge, Cambridge University Press.

Reed, A. (1997) *W.E.B Du Bois and American Political thought*. London: Oxford University Press.

Reisigl, M. & Wodak, R. (2001). *Discourse and Discrmination: Rhetorics of Racism and anti Semitism*. London: Routledge.

Richards, I. A. (1936). *The Philosophy of Rhetoric*. New York: Oxford University Press.

Rose, G. (2001). *Visual Methodologies*. Thousands Oaks, California: Sage Publication.

Ross, D. W. (1952). *The Works of Aristottle*. Oxford: Clarendon Press.

Royster, D. (2003). *Race and Invisible Hand*. Berkely: University of California.

Saeed, J. I. (2003). *Semantics*. Oxford: Blackwell.

Salkie, R. (1995). *Text and Discourse Analysis*. London: Routledge.

Saussure, L. D. and Schulz, P. (2005). *Manipulation and Ideologies in the Twentieth Century: Discourse, Language, Mind*. Amsterdam: John Benjamins Publishing Company.

Sbisa, M. (1999). "Presupposition, Implicature and Context in Text Understanding." *Lecture Notes in Computer Science*. Issue 1688, pages 324-338.

Schaffner, C. (1997). *Analysing Political Speeches*. Philadelphia: Multilingual Matters Ltd.

Schaffner, C. and Holmes, H. K. (1996). *Discourse and Ideologies*. Great Britain: Short Run Press.

Schiefflin, B. B., Woodlard, A. K., and Kroskrity, V. P. (1998). *Language Ideologies: Practice and Theory*. New York: Oxford Universiy Press.

Schiffrin, D. (1987). *Discourse Markers*. Cambridge: Cambridge University Press.

Schiffrin, D. (1994). *Approaches to Discourse*. Massachussetts: Blackwell Publishers Inc.

Schiffrin, D., Tannen, D., and Hamilton, H. E. (2003). *The Handbook of Discourse Analysis*. Oxford: Blackwell Publishing.

Searle, J.R. (1969). *Speech Acts: an Essay in the philosophy of Language*. Cambridge: Cambridge University Press.

Seuren, P. A. M. (1985). *Discourse Semantics*. Oxford: Basil Blackwell Ltd.

Shabana, I. (2006). *A Pragmatic Study of Aspects of Political Discourse in Press Headlines*. Unpublished Ph.D Thesis, Al Azhar University.

Sherif, M. (1967). "Introduction," in C.W. Sherif & M. Sherif (Eds.), *Attitudes, Ego-Involvement and Change* (p 1-5). New York: Wiley.

Simons, W. H. (2001). *Persuasion in Society*. London: Sage Publications.

Stark, F. M. (1996). *Communicative Interaction, Power and the State: A Method*. Toronto: University of Toronto Press.

Swanson, D. R. (1978). "Toward A Psychology of metaphor." *Critical Inquiry*, 5 (1), 163-166.

Tannen, D. (1982). *Analyzing Discourse: Text and Talk*. Washington, D.C. Georgetown University Press.

Tannen, D. (1989). *Talking Voices: Repetition, Dialogue and Imagery in Conversational Discourse*. Cambridge: Cambridge University Press.

Tawfik, E. (2005). "*Power Language in Selected Speeches by Frederick Douglass*." Unpublished M.A Thesis, Ain Shams University.

Teo, P. (2000). "Racism in the News: A Critical Discourse Analysis of New Reporting in Two Australian Newspapers," *Discourse & Society*. London. Sage Publications.

Thomas, J. (1995). *Meaning in Interaction: an Introduction to Pragmatics*. London: Longman.

Thompson, G. (1996). *Introducing Functional Grammar*. New York: Arnold.

Thompson, J. (1984). *Studies in the Theory of Ideology*. Cambridge: Polity Press.

Thompson, J. (1990). *Ideology and Modern Culture*. California: Stanford University Press.

Thompson, N. (2003). *Communication and Language*. New York: Macmillan.

Thornborrow, J. (2002). *Power Talk: Language and Interaction in Institutional Discourse*. London Pearson Education Limited.

Todd, L. (1993). *An Introduction to Linguistics*. Essex: Longman Group U.K Limited.

Toomey, S. T., and Korzenny, F. (1989). *Language Communication and Culture*. California: Sage.

Troutman, D., Smitherman, G., Tooney, S., and Van Dijk, T. (1997). "Discourse, Ethnicity, Culture and Racism" in Van Dijk, *Discourse as Social Interaction*. (p 144-180). London: Sage Publications Ltd.

Tumulty, K. (2007). "Obama's Viral Marketing Campaign" In Time Magazine: P.41. New York. Retrieved 5-07-2007.

Turner, M. & Fauconnier, G. (1998). "Conceptual Integration," *Cognitive Science*, 22 (2), 133-187. From http://Markturner. Org/cin.web/cic.html.

Tyler, A., and Evans, V. (2003). *The Semantics of English Prepositions: Spatial Scenes, Embodied Meaning, and Cognition*. Cambridge: Cambridge University Press.

Ullmann, S. (1957). *The Principles of Semantics*. Oxford: Basil Blackwell.

Ullmann, S. (1978). "Semantic Universals," in Greenberge, *Universals of Language*. MIT Press (P 217-262).

Van Dijk, T. A. (1983). Processes of Prejudice and the roots of racism, A Socio-Cognitive Approach. Working paper no. 3, Department of General Literary Studies, Section of Discourse Studies, University of Amsterdam.

Van Dijk, T. A. (1984). *Prejudice in Discourse*. Amsterdam: Benjamins.

Van Dijk, T. A. (1985). *Discourse and Communication*. New York: Walter de Gruyter.

Van Dijk, T. A. (1988). *News as Discourse*. New Jersey: Lawrence Erlbaum Association, Inc.

Van Dijk, T. A. (1991). *Racism in the Press*. London: Routledge.

Van Dijk, T. A. (1993a). "Discourse and Cognition in Society," in D. Crowley & D. Mitchell, *Communication Theory Today.* (pp. 107-126) Oxford: Pergamon.

Van Dijk, T. A. (1993b). *Elite Dicsourse and Racism.* London and New York: Sage Publication.

Van Dijk, T. A. (1993c). *Racism and the Press.* London: Routledge.

Van Dijk, T. A. (1995a)."Discourse Analysis as Ideology Analysis," in C. Schaffner & A Wenden, *Language and Peace.* (pp. 17-33) Aldershot: Dartmouth Publishing.

Van Dijk, T. A. (1995b)."Ideological Discourse Analysis," in Eija Venlola and Anna Solin, Special Issue *Interdisciplinary Approaches to Discourse Analysis.* (p.135-161). English Dept, University of Helsinki.

Van Dijk, T. A. (1995c). "Discourse Semantics and Ideology," in *Discourse & Society*, 6: 243-289.

Van Dijk, T. A. (1996). "Discourse, Power and Access," in Carmen Rosa Caldas Coulthard & Malcom Coulthard (Eds), *Texts and Practices*: *Readings in Critical Discourse Analysis.* London: Routledge.

Van Dijk, T. A. (1997). *Discourse as social Interaction.* London: Sage.

Van Dijk, T. A. (1998a). *Ideology: A Multidisciplinary Approach.* London: Sage Publications Ltd.

Van Dijk, T. A. (1998b). "Opinions and Ideologies in the Press," in Bell, Allan and Peter Garrett (Eds). *Approaches to Media Discourse.* Oxford: Blackwell.

Van Dijk, T. A. (1998c). *News Analysis: Case Studies of International and National News in the Press.* Hillsdale, N.J.: Lawrence Erlbaum Associates.

Van Dijk, T. A. (2001). "Critical Discourse Analysis," in Deborah Schiffrin, Deborah Tannen, and Heidi E. Hamilton, *Handbook of Discourse Analysis.* Cambridge: Cambridge University Press.

Van Dijk, T.A. (2002). "Political Discourse and Political Cognition," in P. Chilton and C. Schaffner, *Politics as Text and Talk*, (p. 203-237) Philadelphia: John Benjamins Publishing Co.

Van Dijk, T.A. (2004). "Ideology and Discourse Analysis," in *Ideology Symposium*. Oxford: U.K.

Van Dijk, T.A. (2005). *Racism and Discourse in Spain and Latin America.* Philadelphia: John Benhamins Publishing Company.

Van Dijk, T.A. (2006). "Ideology and Discourse Analysis," in *Journal of Political Ideologies,* 11(2), 115-140. London: Routledge.

Verschueren, J. (1999). *Understanding Pragmatics.* London: Arnold.

Wardhaugh, R. (1977). *Introduction to Linguistics.* New York: Mc Graw- Hill, Inc.

Webster's New World Dictionary of the American Language. (1966). New York: World Publishing Co.

Weizman, E. (1983). *Pragmatics and the Philosophy of Mind: Thought in Language.* Amsterdam: John Benjamins.

Wetherell, M. and Potter, J. (1992). *Mapping the Language of Racism. Discourse and the Legitimation of Exploitation.* New York: Harrester Wheatsheef.

Widdowson, H.G. (2004). *Text, Context, Pretext: Critical Issues in Discourse Analysis.* Oxford. Backwell Publishing Ltd.

Williams, R. (1976). *Key Words: A Vocabulary of Culture and Society.* London: Fontana/Croom Helm.

Wilson, J. (1990). *Politically Speaking.* Oxford: Basil Blackwell Ltd.

Wilson, J. (2007). *Barack Obama: This Improbable Quest.* Colorado: Paradigm Publishers.

Winter, S. & Gardenfors, P. (1995). "Linguistic Modality as Expressions of Social Power," in *Nordic Journal of Linguistics* 18 (2): 137-166.

Wodak, R. (1989). *Language, Power and Ideology.* Amsterdam/Philadelphia: John Benjamins Publishing Company.

Wodak, R. (1995). "Critical Linguistics and Critical Discourse Analysis," in Jef Verschuren, Jan Olaostmam, and Jan Blommaert., *Handbook of Pragmatics.* Amsterdam/ Philadelphia: John Benjamins Publishing Company.

Wodak, R. (1996). *Orders of Discourse.* New York: Longman.

Wodak, R. (2006). "Mediation between Discourse and Society: Assessing Cognitive Approaches in CDA," in *Discourse Studies,* Vol8 (1): 179-190.

Wodak, R. and Chilton, P. (2005). *A New Agenda in Criical Discourse Analysis: Theory, Methodology and Interdisciplinarity.* Philadelphia: John Benjamins Publishing Company.

Wodak, R. & Ludwing, Ch. (1999). "Challenges in a Changing World: Jesus in *Critical Discourse Analysis*," Vienna: Passagenverlag.

Wodak, R. & Reisigel, M. (2003). "Discourse and Racism," in Deborah Schiffrin, Deborah Tannen, and Heidi E. Hamilton. The *Handbook of Discourse Analysis*. Oxford: Blackwell.

Wrong, D. (1995). *Power, its Forms, Bases, and Uses*. London: Transaction Publishers.

Yule, G. (1996). *Pragmatics*. Oxford: Oxford University Press.

yes
i want morebooks!

Buy your books fast and straightforward online - at one of world's fastest growing online book stores! Environmentally sound due to Print-on-Demand technologies.

Buy your books online at
www.get-morebooks.com

Kaufen Sie Ihre Bücher schnell und unkompliziert online – auf einer der am schnellsten wachsenden Buchhandelsplattformen weltweit! Dank Print-On-Demand umwelt- und ressourcenschonend produziert.

Bücher schneller online kaufen
www.morebooks.de

 VDM Verlagsservicegesellschaft mbH
Heinrich-Böcking-Str. 6-8   Telefon: +49 681 3720 174   info@vdm-vsg.de
D - 66121 Saarbrücken   Telefax: +49 681 3720 1749   www.vdm-vsg.de

Druck: KN Digital Printforce GmbH · Schockenriedstraße 37 · 70565 Stuttgart